BARRON'S

Strategies and Practice
for the PSAT/
NMSQT

2nd Edition

Brian W. Stewart, M.Ed.

BWS Education Consulting

BARRON'S

Dedication

Dedicated to my wife Caitlin, my son Andrew, and my daughter Eloise—without your love and support, this book would not have been possible. I would like to especially thank my Mom, my Dad, Andy, Hannah, Mitchell, Alaina, Mercedez, and Andrew for their invaluable help with this undertaking. I am grateful to everyone at Barron's, especially Pete Mavrikis.

Thanks so much to all of my students over the years—I have learned far more from you than you have learned from me.

About the Author

Brian W. Stewart is the founder and President of BWS Education Consulting, Inc., a boutique tutoring and test preparation company based in Columbus, Ohio. He has worked with thousands of students to help them improve their test scores and earn admission to selective schools. Brian is a graduate of Princeton University (A.B.) and The Ohio State University (M.Ed.). You can connect with Brian at *www.bwseducationconsulting.com.*

© Copyright 2017, 2015 by Barron's Educational Series, Inc.

All inquiries should be addressed to:
Barron's Educational Series, Inc.
250 Wireless Boulevard
Hauppauge, New York 11788
www.barronseduc.com

ISBN: 978-1-4380-0888-2

Library of Congress Control Number: 2016962754

Printed in the United States of America
9 8 7 6 5 4 3 2 1

10% POST-CONSUMER WASTE

Paper contains a minimum of 10% post-consumer waste (PCW). Paper used in this book was derived from certified, sustainable forestlands.

CONTENTS

Introduction 1

   FAQs About the PSAT and National Merit Scholarship Qualifying Test 1

1 Reading 5

   14 PSAT Reading Strategies 5

   Putting It All Together: Applying the Reading Strategies 8

   Practice Passages with Explanations 13

2 Writing and Language 49

   Review of Key Grammar Concepts 49

   12 PSAT Writing and Language Strategies 63

   Putting It All Together: Applying Grammar Concepts and Strategies 66

   Practice Passages with Explanations 68

3 Math 87

   The Math Concepts You Must Know 87

   18 PSAT Math Strategies 109

   Putting It All Together with Example Problems 112

   Heart of Algebra Practice 116

   Problem Solving and Data Analysis Practice 124

   Passport to Advanced Math Practice 133

   Additional Topics in Math Practice 141

PRACTICE TESTS

Practice Test 1 149

   Evidence-Based Reading and Writing 149

      Reading Test 149

      Writing and Language Test 161

   Math 171

      Math Test (No Calculator) 171

      Math Test (With Calculator) 176

   Answer Key/Scoring Guide 186

   Answer Explanations 188

Practice Test 2...**209**

   Evidence-Based Reading and Writing...209

      Reading Test...209

      Writing and Language Test..221

   Math...231

      Math Test (No Calculator)..231

      Math Test (With Calculator)...236

   Answer Key/Scoring Guide...244

   Answer Explanations..246

Introduction

FAQs ABOUT THE PSAT AND NATIONAL MERIT SCHOLARSHIP QUALIFYING TEST

What is the PSAT?

The PSAT is a preliminary SAT that is used both for assessing student academic progress and for determining eligibility for the National Merit Scholarship competition. Some major features of the PSAT are listed below:

- 2 hours and 45 minutes in length
- 2 major sections
  - Evidence-based reading and writing
  - Math
- The 2 sections can each have scores between 160 (minimum) and 760 (maximum), for a total possible PSAT score between 320 and 1520.
- Administered in mid-October, typically during the school day

> The most important PSAT strategy is to *really focus on fully understanding the questions*. The test is more about your thought process than about how much you know. So if you think through what the questions are asking and set them up well, you will do fine.

What is the Format of the PSAT?

The sections come in the following order:

1. Reading Test: 60 minutes, 47 questions, 5 passages
2. Writing and Language Test: 35 minutes, 44 questions, 4 passages
3. Math Test—No Calculator: 25 minutes, 17 questions (13 multiple choice, 4 grid-in)
4. Math Test—Calculator Permitted: 45 minutes, 31 questions (27 multiple choice, 4 grid-in)

What is a National Merit Scholarship?

It is a prestigious scholarship administered by the National Merit Scholarship Corporation. The National Merit Scholarship recognizes students based on their academic merit and uses PSAT scores as the principle eligibility factor. To be considered, choose to opt in to the Student Search Service when you take the PSAT. The scholarships vary. Some are single-payment $2,500 scholarships. Others are college-sponsored scholarships that provide a full ride for tuition, room, and board plus a stipend for all four years of school. Out of the 1.5 million high school juniors who take the PSAT, about 50,000 receive some sort of National Merit recognition, such as being named a Commended Scholar or a Semi-Finalist. For African-American students who choose to be considered, there is also the possibility of being named a National Achievement Scholar. Only about 7,500 students nationwide receive a National Merit Scholarship. To be a National Merit Scholar, you must typically perform in the top ½ of 1 percent of students. To learn more about the National Merit program, go to *www.nationalmerit.org*.

How is the PSAT Different from the SAT?

The PSAT and SAT are far more similar than they are different. They both have the same types of math, writing, and reading questions. Preparing for the PSAT will definitely help you prepare for the SAT, just as preparing for a half-marathon will help you prepare for a full marathon. The PSAT is different from the SAT in these important ways:

- The PSAT is shorter than the SAT.
- The PSAT is primarily for the National Merit Scholarship contest, while the SAT is primarily for college admissions.
- The PSAT does NOT have an essay, while the SAT has an optional in-depth essay.
- The PSAT is administered once a year, and the SAT is administered several times a year.

What Should I do Before the PSAT?

If the PSAT were a test you could cram for, it would make sense to stay up late studying the night before. Since it is more of a critical-thinking test, you need to be as relaxed and as well-rested as possible to do your best. Before the PSAT, make sure you do the following:

- Go to bed at a reasonable hour starting a week before the test. If you wait until the night before the test to get a good night's sleep, you may not be rested enough come test day. After all, calming down and relaxing the night before a major assessment can be extremely difficult.
- Know the test directions—you do not want to waste time reading the directions on each section. At a minimum, know that you SHOULD INCLUDE AN ANSWER for every question since there is no guessing penalty.
- Become comfortable with timing. Do at least some practice with timing so you will not work too quickly or slowly on test day.

What Should I Bring to the PSAT?

- A scientific or graphing calculator; see *www.collegeboard.org/psat-nmsqt/approved-calculators* for a list of acceptable calculators.
- Several sharpened number 2 pencils.
- A watch to monitor your pacing (bring one that does not make noise).
- If you are taking the test at a school different from your own, bring a photo ID.
- Have a professional-sounding e-mail address you can use to receive information from colleges, and enter it on your answer document.
- Do NOT bring snacks, drinks, or a cell phone into the room. You will have a break, so you may want to have a small snack at that time.

How Can I Manage my Test Anxiety on the PSAT?

With only one shot to perform well on the PSAT for National Merit consideration, taking the PSAT can be a very stressful process. Being nervous is completely normal. Here are a few things to keep in mind if you find anxiety interfering with your ability to perform at your best:

- When it comes to college admissions, how you perform on the actual SAT and/or ACT will be much more important than your PSAT performance. You will have many opportunities to take the SAT and/or ACT.
- Colleges will receive your scores only if you opt-in to the informational services.

- Mentally rehearse *ahead of time* to think about how you can best respond to the pressure of the PSAT. Are you someone who tends to rush through tests? Instead, are you someone who tends to get stuck on questions? Knowing your tendencies will help you recognize if your thought process is off track, enabling you to make adjustments on test day.
- Realize that if the PSAT does not go well even after quite a bit of preparation, you will have built skills that will help you on both the SAT and ACT since those two tests have very similar questions to much of what you will find on the PSAT.
- One of the best things you can do to alleviate your fears on test day is to take the actual SAT in October before taking the PSAT. Since the SAT is extremely similiar to the PSAT, doing this gives you a great opportunity to work out any issues with pacing and test anxiety.

> The PSAT will be scored on a curve. So if the test seems more difficult or easier than you thought it would be, do not worry. Everyone is taking the same test, and the curve will reflect how people did.

How Can I Use This Book to Prepare?

IF YOU HAVE ONE DAY

- Read the strategies from the Reading, Writing, and Math chapters.
- Look over a full practice PSAT, and try a few questions.
- Be sure you understand the directions and time restrictions for the sections.

IF YOU HAVE ONE WEEK

- Read the "Review of Key Grammar Concepts," "The Math Concepts You Must Know," and the reading, math, and writing strategies.
- Take one full-length practice PSAT with time restrictions.

IF YOU HAVE ONE MONTH

- Do everything in this book: content review, strategies, practice problems, and practice tests.

If you wish to do even more long-term preparation, one of the best things you can do is build your literacy skills. At a minimum, install an e-reading app on your phone so you can easily spend a few minutes a day reading a book, no matter where you are. If you want to go all out, seek out the types of reading that you find most difficult and read more material from those genres so that your weaknesses turn into strengths. Reading books will help your reading comprehension, your ability to pick up the meaning of vocabulary in context, and your feel for English grammar. In addition to this book, check out *Barron's New PSAT/NMSQT*, *Barron's PSAT/NMSQT 1520*, and *KhanAcademy.org* for additional practice and review.

Reading

The PSAT Reading Test is scored along with the Writing and Language Test to give you your total "Evidence-Based Reading and Writing" score. It is a single section with the following features:

- 60 minutes long
- 47 questions
- 5 passages total: 1 literature passage, 2 history/social science passages, 2 science passages
- One of the passages will be comprised of two smaller passages that you will need to compare/contrast in the questions
- 1–2 graphs accompanying the reading that you will need to analyze
- The questions for a given passage generally go in order of where the material is found in the passage (e.g., question 1 is about lines 1–5, question 2 is about lines 6–9, etc.)
- The questions are in a random order of difficulty

This chapter contains:

- 14 key strategies for success on the PSAT Reading Test
- "Putting It All Together" strategies with a sample passage
- A variety of practice passages and questions to show you the full range of what you will encounter on test day

14 PSAT READING STRATEGIES

1. Take Your Time

The PSAT Reading Test has only about 3,000 words in the various reading passages and 47 questions. However, it gives you a full 60 minutes to finish. In comparison, the ACT Reading has about the same number of words of reading and 7 fewer questions but gives you only 35 minutes to finish. Most test takers will find that the PSAT Reading Test is quite manageable to complete. You will likely do your best if you use the full amount of time to read the passages well and think through the questions carefully. There is no prize for finishing the section early. If you do have difficulty finishing the PSAT Reading Test, you can pick your battles by focusing on just those passages and questions that come to you most easily and by guessing on the questions you do not have time to attempt. Remember—there is no guessing penalty.

> You do not need to speed read on the PSAT. If you can read about as quickly as you can talk—for most people around 150 words per minute—you will have enough time to finish the test.

2. Read the Passages Before Answering the Questions

Most students find reading through the passages before answering the questions to be very useful. Why? Most of the questions require students to understand the meaning of the passages in a deeper way—this sort of understanding is easiest to attain by actually reading the passages well. If the PSAT Reading Test involved mostly text recall questions, looking at the questions first would make sense. Since the test mainly has questions involving inference, function, suggestion, tone, and purpose, though, you should put your energy into developing a strong initial understanding of what is written.

3. Focus on the Overall Meaning of the Passage(s) as You Read

You should be able to restate the "gist" of what you have read—do not worry about memorizing details from the passage. You can change your focus depending on the passage type in order to maximize your comprehension:

- **LITERATURE**—Read the first paragraph or two a bit more carefully, and read the remainder of the passage normally. This can help you fully understand the characters and setting before you move into the rest of the story.
- **NONFICTION**—Read the first paragraph, first sentences of each paragraph, and last paragraph a bit more carefully, and read the rest normally. Nonfiction is typically more structured than fiction. So reading certain portions very carefully will typically give you critical information, such as the thesis of the essay and general topics of each paragraph.
- **PASSAGE 1 AND PASSAGE 2**—Read these with a focus on the overall meaning, but pay close attention to the *overall relationship* between the two passages. Why? Several questions will involve comparing the similarities and differences between the two reading selections.

Before each passage is a very brief summary that will give you some information about what you are about to read. Be sure to read this before reading the actual passage, as it will help you preview the general meaning of what follows. If any of the topics is unfamiliar or the passage language seems too lofty, do not be alarmed. If you carefully read the passages, you will have the information necessary to answer the questions well. The writers of the PSAT do not expect you to be a master of all potential topics and potential writing styles.

4. Do Not Hesitate to Skip and Come Back to Questions

The first questions after a passage will typically be about the overall meaning of the passage. If you have not fully grasped the overall meaning, come back to the general questions after answering more specific questions. If you find yourself stuck on a question, come back to it so that you can allow your subconscious mind to process the possibilities. Once you come back to the question with fresh eyes, you will often surprise yourself at how easily you can answer it.

5. Cover the Answers as You Read the Questions

On factual recall tests, checking out the answer choices before you have formulated an answer can help you narrow down which choice is correct. With the critical thinking questions on the PSAT, in contrast, you will often find yourself misled by persuasive but ultimately incorrect answer choices. Take control of the questions. Do not let them control you.

6. Underline and Circle Key Words as You Read

Reading a question carelessly will likely cause you to choose a wrong answer. Instead of quickly reading through a question and then rereading it because you are unsure of what it is asking, read the question carefully just one time. Underline and circle the most important words as you do so. This will ensure that you do not miss wording critical to understanding what the question is asking, such as "not," "primary," "infer," "suggest," and so on. You are able to write on the PSAT test booklet, so do it!

7. Create Your Own General Answer by Considering the Context

The primary reading skill tested on the PSAT is your ability to paraphrase (put in your own words) what you read. After reading the question but prior to looking at the answer choices, create a broad idea of what the answer could be. Whenever possible, take a look at the context related to the question so that you have all the relevant information available.

8. Do Not Hesitate to Refer Back to the Passage

Most tests you take are closed book—the PSAT Reading Test, though, is open book. If you had an open book test in school, you would surely use your textbook and notes to help you answer the questions. With so many PSAT questions giving line references and key words, referring back to the passage whenever necessary just makes sense.

9. Use Evidence-Based Questions to Help You Answer the Questions That Come Right Before

There will be several evidence-based questions on the PSAT Reading Test that ask you to find textual evidence that best supports the answer to the previous question. If you are stuck on a question that is followed by an evidence-based question, check out the lines mentioned in the choices of the evidence-based question to help you formulate an answer. The information you need will be found in the lines cited in one of those choices.

10. A Single Flaw Makes an Answer 100% Wrong

A single word can contaminate an answer, making it completely wrong. When you narrow the choices down to two options, do not just look for the best answer—look for the flawless answer. Try to debate the correctness or incorrectness of each answer choice quickly. Remember that one choice is definitely correct and that three choices are definitely wrong. The College Board has put a great deal of effort into creating the questions and answer choices you will see on the PSAT. So, you can safely assume they will be of the very highest quality.

11. Focus on Meaning, Not on Matching

On typical school tests, you often match the choices with facts you recall from the assigned reading or from the in-class lecture. On the PSAT, though, the fact that an answer has wording similar to that in the passage text is no guarantee that the answer choice is correct. There is nothing wrong with picking an answer because it includes wording that is in the passage. Just do not pick an answer *only because* it has matching wording. Be certain the overall meaning of an answer choice gives the correct idea.

12. Determine Word Definitions Based on Context Clues

Although memorizing vocabulary will help you prepare for the test, you should especially sharpen your skills in picking up on the meanings of words based on their context. Even if you know the definitions of a particular word, you will need to determine which definition is most applicable in the particular situation. Build on this skill by making a habit of trying to pick up on definitions as you read.

13. Just Because You Do Not Know a Word's Meaning Does Not Mean It Is Wrong

One of the most frequent mistakes students make on vocabulary-in-context questions is going with a word that "sort of works" simply because they know the meaning of the word. If you narrow the question down to two words, one of which you know and does not quite fit, and the other of which you do not know, *go with the word you do not know since it has the potential* to be 100% correct.

14. When in Doubt, Give the PSAT the Benefit of the Doubt

While many strategies from other tests you have taken will sometimes be applicable on the PSAT—process of elimination, plugging in answers, educated guessing—you should not worry about whether the questions have multiple correct answers. The PSAT is an extraordinarily well-constructed assessment, with the College Board devoting a tremendous amount of time and money crafting each test. As a result, do not waste your time and energy looking for flaws in the PSAT. Instead, give the PSAT Reading Test the benefit of the doubt on seemingly ambiguous questions; each question will, in fact, have one correct answer. Focus on how you can improve your reading comprehension and critical thinking skills, not on silly tricks or gimmicks that only work on poorly written tests.

PUTTING IT ALL TOGETHER: APPLYING THE READING STRATEGIES

What follows is a nonfiction passage. When reading it, focus on paraphrasing the general meaning of the passage. Do not worry about memorizing details because you can go back to the passage as often as you like. Since the passage is nonfiction, pay particular attention to the first paragraph, the topic sentences, and the last paragraph to maximize your overall understanding, while still reading everything else in the passage well.

Questions 1–9 are based on the following passage and supplementary material.

This passage is from "Arcology," taken from a journal article written in 2013.

As "low-impact" or "green" architecture grows steadily *en vogue* into the 21st century, it will become rapidly apparent that reclaimed building materials and energy-efficient designs alone cannot offset the backlash of the deleterious customs modern cities have endorsed at
Line least since the start of the Industrial Revolution. Only a profound and comprehensive rein-
(5) vention of our homes and communities will carry our societies onward into the coming ages.

Fortunately, a handful of premonitory architects and civil engineers have already been grappling with this predicament for nearly 100 years. Frank Lloyd Wright—the esteemed leader of the Prairie School—proposed his solution to chaotic suburban development and impractical land use in the form of Broadacre City: a preplanned community in which each

(10) resident would possess one acre of land arranged in such a way as to provide easy access to an extensive and efficient network of roads and public transportation. Broadacre—which never evolved beyond the design phase—could hardly be described as "green" by today's standards, but it constitutes one of the first endeavors of the modern era to integrate fully the residential and the commercial, the consumer and the consumed, on an efficacious, city-wide scale.

(15) "Arcology," a portmanteau of "architecture" and "ecology," is the term coined by architect Paolo Soleri to describe the largely theoretical self-contained cities he's been designing since the late 1950's. Like Broadacre, one goal of an arcological structure is to maximize the efficiency of land use in a community. For Soleri, this means combating "suburban sprawl" by balancing urban expansion in three dimensions. But by incorporating significant agricul-
(20) tural and industrial components alongside commercial facilities and residences, arcology takes civic efficiency a step further than Broadacre. According to Soleri, a true arcological city would be both economically and ecologically self-sufficient. It would contain all the resources necessary for power and food production, for climate control, and for air and water treatment. But perhaps even more radically, it would eliminate the need for private transpor-
(25) tation through a combination of high-population density housing and carefully calculated infrastructural design.

Although Soleri has designed hundreds of buildings, to date, his only large-scale arcological project to be realized—Arcosanti in central Arizona, a town intended to sustain up to 5,000 residents—today houses just 150 individuals. But while the American public's response to Soleri's
(30) bold innovations is, by and large, resistant, certain facets of arcology have already permeated more conventional cities. Comprehensive pedestrian skyways like those in downtown Calgary, Minneapolis, and the Las Vegas strip are derived from arcological notions of multi-dimensional public transit, and Co-op City in the Bronx, New York, reflects arcological influences in its high-density residential construction and self-contained resources, which include public
(35) schools, shopping centers, religious centers, medical facilities, a fire station and a power plant.

Community projects that embrace the revolutionary precepts of arcology have always struggled for funding, and all too often are abandoned by their investors prior to completion. But over the past ten years the world has seen a steady groundswell of interest in "green" arcological structures, with ambitious and novel projects cropping up from Tokyo to Moscow. In
(40) 2006, the United Arab Emirates initiated the construction of Masdar City, which will incorporate a fully sustainable "zero-waste and zero-carbon" ecology with a projected metropolitan community of 50,000 inhabitants—all on just six square kilometers of land.

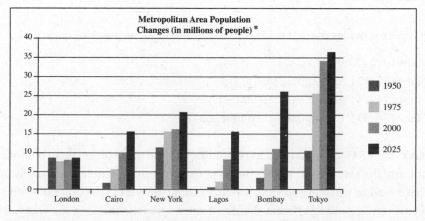

*Source: United Nations, World Urbanization Prospects: The 2007 Revision.
http://www.prb.org/Publications/Lesson-Plans/HumanPopulation/Urbanization.aspx

What should be your overall understanding of the passage? Your understanding should be something like this:

- Arcology is a movement to make cities more sustainable and self-sufficient.
- Architects like Wright and Soleri have designed many arcological developments, but few have actually been implemented in real life.
- Even though not many arcological cities have been created, the movement has inspired the construction of arcological components, like skyways. Also, there may be more actual arcological cities in the future.

Now look at the questions one by one. With each question, be sure to take these steps:

- Cover the answer choices.
- Underline/circle key words as you carefully read the question.
- Create your own general answer using context.
- Critically analyze the choices, focusing on the overall meaning needed and eliminating choices that contain even a single flaw.

1. The author's overall point of view on the need for arcology is best described as

   (A) tepid appreciation.
   (B) mild skepticism.
   (C) strong advocacy.
   (D) outright rejection.

Solution: **(C)** Try to formulate your own answer before looking at the choices. The author states his thesis at the end of the first paragraph, saying in lines 4–5 that "only a profound and comprehensive reinvention of our homes and communities will carry our societies onward into the coming ages." When put another way, the author believes that society will be in serious trouble unless significant changes are made to how cities are structured. So the answer needs to express that the author has taken a firm stance that arcology, which would support such changes, is needed. This stance is most like "strong advocacy" in choice (C). Choice (A) is not correct because "tepid" means mild or lukewarm, and the author has a much stronger belief in favor of arcology. Choice (B) is incorrect because the author is not skeptical, i.e., questioning, about the need for arcology—he believes that it must happen. Choice (D) is certainly not right because the author accepts, not rejects, the need for arcology.

2. Which choice provides the best evidence for the answer to the previous question?

   (A) Lines 4–5 ("Only . . . ages.")
   (B) Lines 15–17 ("Arcology . . . 1950's.")
   (C) Lines 21–24 ("According . . . treatment.")
   (D) Lines 36–37 ("Community . . . completion.")

Solution: **(A)** The PSAT contains question types like this one that expect you to demonstrate your understanding of the evidence. That way, the PSAT can ascertain whether you actually understand what you have read or whether you were just lucky when answering the other question correctly. The correct answer is choice (A) because this selection gives the thesis of the essay. It expresses that the author believes society must change how it constructs cities in order to prevent a decline in society. Choice (B) is not correct because it simply defines arcology. Choice (C) is incorrect because it simply explains what an arcological city would be like. Choice (D) is not correct because it states that arcology has had difficulty earning widespread public support.

3. The example of Broadacre City primarily serves as an example of

(A) the first successfully implemented arcological urban development.
(B) an early proposed solution to suburban sprawl.
(C) the architectural masterpiece of world-renowned designer Frank Lloyd Wright.
(D) a significant instance of cutting-edge environmental technology.

Solution: **(B)** Be sure you focus on what the question is asking—you need to determine the primary function of the example of Broadacre City. Lines 8–9 best provide this information. They state that Frank Lloyd Wright "proposed his solution to chaotic suburban development and impractical land use in the form of Broadacre City." So Broadacre City is given as an example of how a famous architect proposed a solution to suburban sprawl, which is the overexpansion of urban development. Choices (A) and (C) are both incorrect because Broadacre City was not actually built. Choice (D) is not correct because line 12 states that Broadacre "could hardly be described as 'green' by today's standards."

4. As used in line 15, "portmanteau" most nearly means

(A) innovation.
(B) transition.
(C) environment.
(D) combination.

Solution: **(D)** Line 15 defines arcology as "a portmanteau of 'architecture' and 'ecology.'" You can reasonably infer that this comes from the prefix "arc-" in "architecture," and the suffix "-ology" in "ecology," which combine to give us the word "arcology." Given how the word "arcology" is used elsewhere in the passage, the word should clearly be a combination of architectural elements and ecological elements since it is focused on designing cities in an environmentally sustainable way. Although "innovation," "transition," and "environment" are related to architectural and ecological ideas, they do not capture the overall meaning of the term.

5. The passage suggests that Paolo Soleri would have what view about the economic activity of major cities?

(A) Both imports and exports should be maximized.
(B) Both imports and exports should be minimized.
(C) Imports should be maximized while exports minimized.
(D) Imports should be minimized while exports maximized.

Solution: **(B)** Imports are goods that are brought into a city, and exports are goods sold from a city. According to lines 21–24, Soleri believes that "a true arcological city would be both economically and ecologically self-sufficient. It would contain all the resources necessary for power and food production, for climate control, and for air and water treatment." If a city is to contain all its necessities within its borders, it will not need to import or export anything. So choice (B) is the correct option.

6. Which choice provides the best evidence for the answer to the previous question?

    (A) Lines 18–19 ("For Soleri . . . dimensions.")
    (B) Lines 19–21 ("But by . . . Broadacre.")
    (C) Lines 21–24 ("According . . . treatment.")
    (D) Lines 24–26 ("But perhaps . . . design.")

Solution: **(C)** These lines focus on the economic nature of arcological cities. They state that arcological cities would be self-sufficient, which would remove any need for the importing or exporting of goods. Choice (A) is incorrect because it focuses on the spatial aspects of cities. Choice (B) is not right because it highlights issues of civic efficiency. Choice (D) is incorrect because it focuses on transportation.

7. It can be reasonably inferred from the passage that the overall attitude of the American public toward arcology is

    (A) generally skeptical.
    (B) positively enthusiastic.
    (C) bitterly cynical.
    (D) largely neutral.

Solution: **(A)** This is best seen in lines 29–31, which state, "the American public's response to Soleri's bold innovations is, by and large, resistant, certain facets of arcology have already permeated more conventional cities." In other words, Americans are generally skeptical of arcology. Although they have been open to its implementation in some situations, they have not embraced it completely. Choice (B) is not correct because if the American public was positively enthusiastic about arcology, you would expect to see much more implementation of arcology than has happened. Choice (C) is incorrect because being "cynical" means to have extremely negative views toward something, which is not the case here. Choice (D) is wrong because there is "resistance" in general to arcology, which is more negative than being just "neutral."

8. As used in line 36, "precepts" most nearly means

    (A) warrants.
    (B) buildings.
    (C) politics.
    (D) principles.

Solution: **(D)** Lines 36–37 state, "Community projects that embrace the revolutionary precepts of arcology have always struggled for funding, and all too often are abandoned by their investors prior to completion." The word "principles" makes the most sense here. The passage describes arcology as a general philosophy of design that has certain key ideas, or principles, about methods of sustainable development. Choice (A) is wrong because arcology was not inspired by government documents. Choice (B) is incorrect because arcology is an entire philosophy of design, not just a type of structure. Choice (C) is not correct because arcology is more of a design philosophy than a political one.

9. Assume that the urban areas in the chart have achieved the maximum of their geographic expansion. The author of the passage would think that which of the following cities (assuming that they continue on their current trajectories of growth) will be most likely in the year 2125 to have the greatest need to implement arcological principles?

    (A) London
    (B) New York
    (C) Bombay
    (D) Tokyo

Solution: **(C)** Be prepared to answer a few graph analysis questions on the PSAT. The closest things to these on a current major standardized test are the ACT Science Reasoning questions. The PSAT Reading Test will ask you to use graphical information to come to a conclusion that incorporates information from the reading passage. To attack this question, focus on what it is asking—you need to determine which city would most need arcology in 2125. Arcology focuses on sustainable development in response to the growth of urban areas. So the author would most likely believe that a city that was experiencing the most significant growth in population would probably be in most need of more sustainable design principles. London is barely growing at all, and New York and Tokyo are growing at relatively slow rates. Bombay, however, is on a steep growth curve. If Bombay's growth continues at its current rate, it will be the largest of these cities by 2125, making it the one the author would most likely believe to be in need of arcological principles.

PRACTICE PASSAGES WITH EXPLANATIONS

This passage is from literature. Pay close attention to the introduction so that you fully understand the setting and characters, and read the rest of the passage at a normal pace. With fiction passages, picking up more subtle meanings is important—be sure to monitor your comprehension as you read.

Questions 1–10 are based on the following passage.

This passage is from "The Boardwalk at Rehoboth Beach," written in 2012.

When I was younger, much younger—almost in another life—I spent every other summer at Rehoboth Beach. The day of departure had something of the quiet, methodical frenzy that I suspect surrounds the evacuation en masse of infantry. All morning we marched in and
Line out of the house, hauling tin coolers and huge, blue Samsonite suitcases, piling them like
(5) bulwarks in the driveway, while my Father—his body half-buried in the back of a County Squire station wagon—hollered out his orders for what should be loaded next. Being second to youngest, my place was invariably in the last row of the wagon, walled in on all three sides by the inevitable impedimenta of annual beachgoers—rope sandals, snorkels, the bright, polychrome canopies of sun umbrellas—all of it still somehow shedding fine, gray streams
(10) of sand with every nudge. While pressing my nose to the glass for a farewell glimpse of our vacated home, my Mother put the car in gear, and I smacked my forehead on the window as it lurched forward. Between the bobbing heads of five siblings I could see my Father's blue Chevy Bel Air, bearing my three older brothers and whatever luggage refused to fit into the meticulously overloaded wagon, leading us, like a harbinger, six hundred miles east to the
(15) Atlantic Ocean.

The beach itself at Rehoboth was neither exceptional nor squalid. It was entirely ordinary, of middling breadth, and middling color, made up of more mud than sand, and of more jagged shells and bottle caps than one typically prefers. In early and late summer the water was really too cold to stay in longer than half an hour or so, and in hue it remained a murky green

(20) all year. But Rehoboth Beach was special, perhaps even magical, because it was, in its entire length, rimmed by a magnificent boardwalk. At Rehoboth Beach, save for breakfast and supper, my siblings and I were autonomous, and from the age of about eight onward I spent hours wandering alone among the lush, interminable spectacles and seminude crowds of the boardwalk.

(25) Being both pale and somewhat plain, the people were, I suppose, predominately rust belt Midwesterners like myself, there at the shore to terminate their brief annual vacations. But they seemed so different, so transformed in manner and appearance by the proximity of the sea, that I often imagined the beach populated by denizens of an exotic, epicurean culture, and when I stepped upon the boardwalk, I saw myself entering one of the strange and

(30) majestic bazaars so tantalizingly pervasive of my serial adventure novels. I snaked between vendors of blown glass, odd, multifarious souvenirs constructed of driftwood and jetsam, and heaps of beachwear proclaimed by the hand-painted signs that accompanied them as the latest fashion on the French Riviera. Running my palm along a rack of wooden popguns, I imagined myself a soldier of the Foreign Legion, on leave in Lisbon, Yalta or Algiers. In the

(35) distance I could see the pier, indomitable, bisecting the boardwalk at a right angle and jutting far out over the water.

The vendor appraised my interest, "We have some very nice beads here as well—genuine sea glass."

"No, thank you," I answered, and pressed onward. Overhead, between the fluttering, var-

(40) iegated canopies, I saw no fewer than two dozen kites hanging in the sky, and everywhere the smells of the ocean comingled with those of chili dogs, cola, and Dolle's saltwater taffy.

Around sunset, with the breeze still sweeping in from the Atlantic, it turned a little chilly; women pulled lace and cotton dresses over their bikinis, and the men strode back from the shore wearing blue and white blazers above their sandy, dampened swimming trunks.

(45) I shivered and crossed my arms. The children on the boardwalk were becoming scarce, and I more conspicuously unattended. But this was by far my favorite time at Rehoboth. As more orange rays of sunlight fell behind the houses to the west and were extinguished, the boardwalk grew more vibrant, more fantastic. All around bulbs of blue, red, orange and green incandescent light flashed to life. Voices became more boisterous as people sought

(50) to speak over the sprightly marching tunes that blasted from the horns of carnival rides, which always seemed much louder in the evening air. I had walked quite far, I realized—the ferris wheel was far behind me; I could see it writing huge, luminous O's in the darkening distance. Childless couples were leaving the restaurants, some of them staggering a little as they opened the door onto the boardwalk. In the dim alcoves there grew a vague but thrill-

(55) ing sense of danger.

I wanted to walk out to the very edge of the pier; it was only another several hundred yards, I thought. I wanted to stand there, and look for far off lights on the ocean where ships were traversing the deep, dark water. I felt a large hand grasp my bare shoulder.

"Lost, missy? Need someone to call your folks?"

(60) "No. I know my way around," I shuddered. Slowly, begrudgingly, I turned away from the place where the pier issued from the shore, and started back along the boardwalk. One day my body would learn contentment, steeling it against the ill-defined threats of wanderlust.

But my mind would remain an endless boardwalk, from which I might ascend any one of the infinite ocean piers, and go anywhere, anywhere at all.

1. The narrator can best be described as a/an

   (A) nervous explorer.
   (B) adventurous misanthrope.
   (C) imaginative observer.
   (D) rebellious pedestrian.

2. The passage is primarily organized

   (A) by cause and effect.
   (B) chronologically.
   (C) in gradually increasing order of importance.
   (D) from microcosm to macrocosm.

3. The boardwalk is most appealing to the narrator as a result of

   (A) the widespread use of kites by its users.
   (B) the happy memories she has of time she spent there with family.
   (C) the opportunities it gives for independent scholarly research.
   (D) the freedom it gives her to explore independently.

4. Which choice provides the best evidence for the answer to the previous question?

   (A) lines 20–21 ("But Rehoboth . . . boardwalk.")
   (B) lines 45–46 ("The children . . . Rehoboth.")
   (C) lines 51–53 ("I had . . . distance.")
   (D) lines 60–61 ("No . . . boardwalk.")

5. As used in line 8, "impedimenta" most nearly means

   (A) clutter.
   (B) hardships.
   (C) expenses.
   (D) drudgery.

6. It can be inferred that which of the narrator's four siblings is most likely to be in the same row that she occupies in the car?

   (A) The youngest one
   (B) The middle child
   (C) The next to the oldest
   (D) The oldest

7. Which choice provides the best evidence for the answer to the previous question?

    (A) Lines 2–3 ("The day . . . infantry.")

    (B) Lines 6–8 ("Being second . . . beachgoers.")

    (C) Lines 21–24 ("At Rehoboth . . . boardwalk.")

    (D) Lines 58–59 ("I felt . . . folks?")

8. As used in line 21, "save" most nearly means

    (A) preserved.

    (B) except.

    (C) ameliorate.

    (D) digest.

9. In the eyes of the narrator, the relationship of the beach to the boardwalk is most analogous to

    (A) a forest floor in the mountains occasionally populated by wildlife.

    (B) a clear, blue sky that is polluted with the smoke from human activity.

    (C) an amusement park that incorporates the latest computer technology.

    (D) a commonplace platter that is topped with a spectacular dessert.

10. The passage suggests that the person who grasps her "bare shoulder" (line 58) is likely motivated by

    (A) avarice.

    (B) power.

    (C) vigilance.

    (D) fear.

Solutions

ANSWER KEY

1. **C**	4. **B**	7. **B**	10. **C**
2. **B**	5. **A**	8. **B**	
3. **D**	6. **A**	9. **D**	

ANSWERS EXPLAINED

1. **(C)** The narrator is recounting her experiences as a young child, enjoying the unusual freedom of exploring a boardwalk. As she observes various things on the boardwalk, she imagines herself to be a soldier or like someone from an adventure novel. So she can best be described as an imaginative observer. Choice (A) is not correct because the narrator does not demonstrate a consistent level of anxiety; rather, she finds the looming danger thrilling. Choice (B) is incorrect. A misanthrope is someone who does not like people, and the narrator is enjoying the interactions with and observations of people. Choice (D) is not correct because the narrator is far more than a mere pedestrian, i.e., someone who is walking along.

2. **(B)** The passage starts with a recounting of the narrator's car trip, followed by a step-by-step retelling of her adventures exploring the boardwalk. Therefore, the structure is best described as chronological. Although certain factors have surely caused the narrator's behavior, the passage does not focus on connecting the causes and effects of her behavior. Instead, it focuses on her general impressions, making choice (A) incorrect. One event does not seem to have more significance than another as the passage progresses. Instead, a number of interesting personal impressions are provided throughout, making choice (C) incorrect. Choice (D) is not right because such an organization would go from a small-picture to a big-picture perspective. However, the first-person perspective remains fairly consistent throughout.

3. **(D)** Immediately after introducing the boardwalk in lines 21–24, the narrator states that she was able to spend "hours wandering alone" on the boardwalk. Additionally, the narrator discusses in lines 45–46 that she enjoyed being unattended. So the narrator clearly enjoys how the boardwalk gives her the freedom to explore independently. Choice (A) mentions something too specific and irrelevant to the narrator's overall opinion of the boardwalk. She does not seem to spend much time with her family on the boardwalk, wandering along it alone instead, making choice (B) incorrect. The narrator is a young child having fun, not a researcher, making choice (C) incorrect.

4. **(B)** Lines 45–46 give direct evidence in support of the answer to the previous question, since they state that this time of day was the narrator's favorite time at Rehoboth Beach. Nighttime, after all, is the time when everyone disappears and she finally has the autonomy that she seeks. The other options do not provide such evidence.

5. **(A)** After the mention of "impedimenta" in the sentence, the narrator lists the many things that cluttered the station wagon: sandals, snorkels, and so on. So "clutter" is most appropriate. You may also look at the word root and realize that an "impediment" is a hindrance. Although having a bunch of stuff in a car could be a hardship, choice (B), this is too much of a stretch beyond what is given in the context. It has nothing to do with economic expenses, choice (C). Although a cramped car ride could be a pain, "drudgery" shown in choice (D), like "hardship," is too much of a stretch.

6. **(A)** Lines 7–9 explain that, because she was the second-to-youngest child, the narrator had to sit in the last row of the station wagon. Since her birth order is cited as the only reason for this and since the narrator also mentions that she was surrounded by so much clutter, allowing a smaller person to make do with the seating arrangement, her youngest sibling would most likely join her in the back.

7. **(B)** These lines are the only ones mentioned that focus on where in the car the narrator sat. Even if you did not answer the previous question correctly, you should still be able to choose the right answer.

8. **(B)** In the context of the sentence, the narrator recalls the countless hours she spent wandering the boardwalk. The "save" is most like "except" because it is implicit that the narrator joins the rest of her family for their breakfast and supper meals while spending the rest of her time independently. She is not "preserving" anything, choice (A). She is not ameliorating or helping anyone with her actions, choice (C). Although digestion is obviously associated with meals, choice (D), the sentence focuses on how she spent her time, not on how she processed her food.

9. **(D)** The correct answer is best seen in the second paragraph, where the beach itself is described as "ordinary" while the boardwalk rimming it is described as "special" and "magical." This is like an ordinary plate (the beach) that has a spectacular dessert (the boardwalk) on top of it. Choice (A) is too focused on the natural aspects of the relationship. Choice (B) portrays human activity in a negative light, while the narrator very much enjoys partaking in and observing a variety of human activities. Choice (C) narrowly focuses on enjoyment that the boardwalk provides while neglecting the relationship of the boardwalk to the beach.

10. **(C)** When the person places his hand onto the narrator's shoulder, the narrator is walking about all alone on a pier, which could be very dangerous were she to fall off into the water. The person offers to help by asking the narrator whether she needs someone to reconnect her with her parents. So the motivation is one of "vigilance," or watchfulness. The person is not greedy or avaricious, choice (A), and is not interested in maintaining power over the narrator, choice (B). Also, although the person might be fearful that the narrator could fall into the water, "vigilance" is a better way to describe his calm, helpful interactions with the narrator.

You will have one pair of passages on the PSAT Reading. The passages will address the same general topic but will have different points of view. While reading, pay close attention to the overall relationship between the two passages. If you find this format more challenging, you may want to read Passage 1 and answer the questions about just that passage. Then read Passage 2, and answer the questions about just that passage. Follow up with the more general questions about both passages. This will allow you more time to solidify your overall understanding of the relationship between the passages. Also, the questions generally go in order of where they are in the reading. So it is easy to pick out the Passage 1 questions and the Passage 2 questions, since the Passage 1 questions will come before the Passage 2 ones.

Questions 1–10 are based on the following passages.

Both passages are excerpts from *The World is a Museum*, written in 2014.

Passage 1

Where does art live? Where do we encounter it? Most of us would tend to answer that art belongs in galleries and museums—perhaps even that the limited environmental context of art is part of what defines it. However, many of the most recognizable, impactful, and
Line dynamic pieces of artwork the world over are not contained within the walls of museums,
(5) but out in public, where citizens encounter and engage them every day of their lives. Public art has a rich and storied history, dating at least from the classical era right up into the Renaissance. Consider the iconic *Trevi Fountain* in Rome, or Ghiberti's magnificent *Gates of Paradise*. Both the city of Paris itself and the critical heights of European industrial era ingenuity are epitomized in the unmistakable form of the Eiffel Tower. Even today, public
(10) art continues to evolve.

In 2005, Christo and Jeanne-Claude conceived and executed a massive installation artwork entitled *The Gates*, consisting of 7,503 saffron-colored panels arching over 23 miles of public walkways in New York's Central Park.

Aesthetically, the success of *The Gates* lies in its harmonious interplay of color and
(15) composition. The vibrant saffron-orange fabric conveys energy, which is amplified by the
natural movement of the material in the wind. Further, the orange against the ashen grey
background of Manhattan in the winter is especially fresh and invigorating. In contrast,
The Gates also elicits a serene, calming effect through repetition, with over 7,000 individual
banners blustering in graceful arches. Together, the dynamism of its energy and steadiness
(20) of flow work to keep the viewer engaged and moving—both of which are elemental to a successful work of art.

Beyond the success of its composition, the installation of *The Gates* in a public park
intrinsically influences how we encounter and react to it. Regardless of one's interest in the
work, to any New Yorker passing by Central Park during its display, it could not be avoided
(25) or ignored. It compels the viewer to react, and ponder its purpose and meaning. As public
art, it acts as an ephemeral social equalizer, briefly dissolving the distance between the
homeless man and the business man. Both have free access to *The Gates*; both are equally
entitled to encounter and to interpret it.

Passage 2

Few critics will deny that the transgressive idea for the sake of transgression has often
(30) been the operative principle in the modern evolution of art. And it is not nearly so much the
writerly platitudes and sober dialectics of past eras that embody the trend of visual art in the
20th and 21st centuries as it is the anarchist battle-cry of Mikhail Bakunin that "the passion
for destruction is also a creative passion."

To speak generally, crossing boundaries in order to expand the fields of our conscious-
(35) ness has been accepted in our contemporary culture as a vital component (and indeed, perhaps the only remaining component) demarcating a line between art and object, between
ideation and decoration. However, there is an implied value to this perspective that few—
artists and critics alike—will care to acknowledge. Boundaries matter.

It is well known that this nuance essentially eluded the likes of Marcel Duchamp and
(40) his Dadaist zealots. If we were to accept, as they did, that indeed there is no intrinsic quality—no ineluctable aspect of creation, or innovation, or craft—that defines "art" outside its
being described as exactly that, the very notion of aesthetics collapses upon itself; for such
a world is necessarily predicated on the principle that either everything is art, or else it is
not. And I fear that it must be the latter.
(45) The pluralistic ignorance of our "art-is-whatever-the-artist-says-it-is" society has reached
a new and too infrequently criticized summit in the latest charade of self-described artists
Christo and Jeanne-Claude, *The Gates* of Central Park. The distinctive fabric used in the *The
Gates* was not sewn or dyed by the artists; the posts holding them aloft were not welded or
painted by the artists. In this sense alone, Christo and Jeanne-Claude may be considered
(50) artists to the same extent that one is an artist in selecting new drapes for a sitting room.

But more important (and more brazen) is the setting chosen by Christo and Jeanne-
Claude for their pseudo-aesthetic stunt. Most every person who has walked the paths and
bridges of Central Park—chiefly conceived by Frederick Law Olmstead and Calvert Vaux—
and appreciated both the thoughtfulness and elegance of its design will readily agree that
(55) it is, already, a work of public art. To dress it, even for a day, in the costume of Christo's
and Jeanne-Claude's creatively bankrupt brand of expressionist pretension is tantamount

to drawing a mustache on the Mona Lisa—a ploy, in fact, already executed by Duchamp in his insipid 1919 "objet trouvé," *L.H.O.O.Q.*

It would perhaps make for an apt cautionary tale to Christo and Jeanne-Claude to realize (60) that less than one hundred years later, the sophomoric antics of Duchamp are all but forgotten, whereas after half a millennium, da Vinci's painting remains one of the most iconic works of art in the Western world.

1. The overall attitudes of the authors of Passage 1 and Passage 2 toward the art of Christo and Jeanne-Claude are respectively

    (A) skeptical and critical.
    (B) entranced and morbid.
    (C) grateful and timid.
    (D) appreciative and dismissive.

2. The authors of Passage 1 and Passage 2 use italics throughout their works to denote

    (A) tourist attractions.
    (B) works of art.
    (C) the paintings of Christo and Jeanne-Claude.
    (D) permanent artistic exhibitions in public spaces.

3. As used in line 5, "engage" most nearly means

    (A) pledge.
    (B) fight with.
    (C) interact with.
    (D) create.

4. Lines 5–9 ("Public...Tower.") serve what primary function in Passage 1 as a whole?

    (A) To provide context for an in-depth example that follows
    (B) To give concrete evidence of the types of public artworks that unequivocally inspired Christo and Jeanne-Claude
    (C) To analyze the current state of the placement of modern art in major urban areas worldwide
    (D) To contemplate the evolution of art in all its many forms

5. It can be reasonably inferred from lines 25–28 ("As . . . interpret it.") that artworks other than public art are likely not

    (A) as uniformly accessible.
    (B) as much the subject of ridicule.
    (C) as focused on class struggle.
    (D) as aesthetically pleasing.

6. Which of the following best paraphrases the meaning of the first sentence of Passage 2 (lines 29–30, "Few . . . art.")?

   (A) Critics are overly concerned with public morality.
   (B) There is little agreement on the agenda of modern artists.
   (C) Many artists are motivated by a desire to be offensive.
   (D) Modern artists have strong roots in moral principles.

7. What type of music would a critic with the same philosophical outlook as the author of Passage 2 likely find most appealing?

   (A) Folk music that is currently popular
   (B) Baroque music that has stood the test of time
   (C) Music that is unique for the sake of being unique
   (D) Renaissance chamber music that has been forgotten by scholars

8. Which choice provides the best evidence for the answer to the previous question?

   (A) Lines 29–30 ("Few . . . art.")
   (B) Lines 49–50 ("In this...room.")
   (C) Lines 52–55 ("Most . . . art.")
   (D) Lines 59–62 ("It would . . . world.")

9. As used in line 57, "executed" most nearly means

   (A) done.
   (B) murdered.
   (C) surmised.
   (D) imagined.

10. It can be reasonably inferred that the author of Passage 1 would be more likely than the author of Passage 2 to appreciate which of these events?

    (A) An art festival that attracts entrants from a range of skill levels
    (B) A curated exhibit by a renowned artist at an established museum
    (C) A picnic at the beach on a beautiful summer afternoon
    (D) A walk through Central Park on a blustery autumn morning

Solutions

ANSWER KEY

1.	**D**	4.	**A**	7.	**B**	10.	**A**
2.	**B**	5.	**A**	8.	**D**		
3.	**C**	6.	**C**	9.	**A**		

ANSWERS EXPLAINED

1. **(D)** Passage 1 refers to the artwork of Christo and Jeanne-Claude as a "success" in line 14. Passage 2 dismisses their work as a "charade" in line 46. So you can characterize the general attitudes as "appreciative" and "dismissive," respectively. Choice (A) is wrong because the first passage is hardly skeptical of their work. Choice (B) is wrong because these two words are too extreme in their respective positivity and negativity. Choice (C) is wrong because the second passage is rather bold in dismissing their work.

2. **(B)** The authors use italics to denote the *Trevi Fountain*, the *Gates of Paradise*, *The Gates*, and *L.H.O.O.Q.*—these all fit under the general category of artworks, albeit very different types and styles. Although the *Trevi Fountain* or the *Gates* could be considered tourist attractions, the *L.H.O.O.Q.* and the *Gates of Paradise* cannot reasonably be described as such, making choice (A) incorrect. Works by other artists are italicized, making choice (C) incorrect. Choice (D) does not include works in museums.

3. **(C)** The passage in which "engage" occurs describes citizens coming across public art on a daily basis, making it much more likely that they would "interact with" the art in some way. They are not "pledging" to it or fighting with it, making choices (A) and (B) incorrect. The citizens are not creating it, unless they themselves are the artists, making choice (D) incorrect.

4. **(A)** The author wraps up the introductory paragraph by mentioning other highly influential public artworks over the years. This information shows that what Christo and Jeanne-Claude did was not unprecedented but, instead, another stage in the evolution of public art. Choice (B) is too strong a statement since the passage does not provide evidence that these works "unequivocally" inspired the artists. Choice (C) is incorrect because there is more statement of fact here than an analysis. Choice (D) is not correct because the focus is on public art, not on art in all its forms.

5. **(A)** These lines suggest that no matter what one's social class or background, that person can have access to public art works. Other works of art that are in homes and museums may not be accessible to all members of the public. Passage 2, not Passage 1, considers public artwork to be ridiculous, making choice (B) incorrect. Choices (C) and (D) focus on the subjects and experiences of the works rather than the extent to which people have access to the works.

6. **(C)** A "transgression" is an offensive act. So if artists are trying to be transgressive for the sake of transgression, they are simply trying to be offensive, making choice (C) correct. Choice (A) is incorrect because the critics are merely observing what artists are doing—they do not appear to be taking sides as to the value of modern art. Choice (B) is not right because the sentence begins by saying that few critics would deny this statement. Choice

(D) is wrong because if modern artists had strong roots in moral principles, it is highly unlikely that they would seek to offend people all the time.

7. **(B)** Lines 59–62 argue that while da Vinci's paintings have remained respected for 500 years, Duchamp's modern art has already been forgotten. The general pattern is that the author believes that the best art is that which stands the test of time on account of its aesthetic quality and that inferior art is that which tries to be "different" for its own sake. This is most analogous to music that has stood the test of time. Choice (A) is not correct since music that is currently popular may lose its popularity very quickly. Choice (C) is not the answer because it represents exactly the kind of art the narrator detests. Choice (D) is incorrect because this sort of music would not be considered high in quality by the narrator since it is no longer valued.

8. **(D)** Lines 59–62 give direct evidence that the narrator would prefer artwork that has long-lasting respect rather than art that is temporarily famous on account of its uniqueness. Choice (A) is too broad. Choice (B) does not help you fully grasp what sort of art the narrator would like since it focuses on only what the narrator does not like. Choice (C) focuses on only the kind of art the narrator would like as opposed to what the narrator would both like and dislike.

9. **(A)** The narrator is citing an artwork actually created by Duchamp that he finds mindless and offensive, so "executed" most nearly means "done." Choice (B) gives a common definition of "executed" that is not applicable here. Choices (C) and (D) provide incorrect definitions of "executed."

10. **(A)** The author of Passage 1 is concerned with breaking down boundaries between social classes (lines 25–28) and discussing where and how art can be enjoyed (lines 1–5). The author of Passage 2, however, states that "boundaries matter" in line 38 and believes that there is a clear divide between what is and what is not art. So, it is reasonable to conclude that an art festival that has a wide variety of entrants would appeal to someone more open to breaking down boundaries (Passage 1) rather than to someone who would like the boundaries more firmly established (Passage 2). Choice (B) would appeal more to the author of Passage 2. Choice (C) is too removed from what the passages present for you to draw a conclusion. Choice (D) is something that both authors would likely enjoy.

The PSAT will include a scientific reading passage. Some of the terminology and concepts may be beyond what you have studied. However, enough information will always be given to you in the passage so you can correctly answer the questions. The PSAT will not assume that you have outside knowledge about science topics.

Questions 1–10 are based on the following passage and supplementary material.

This is a passage from a 2013 science blog on the search for the Higgs boson particle, entitled "The God Particle." This particle is considered fundamental to the modern understanding of subatomic physics as it is assumed to give rise to all mass.

In the early 1960's, theoretical physicists were racing to design a consistent and verifiable explanation to the question of how matter becomes massive at the subatomic level. Before the winter of 1964, three similar solutions emerged independently of one another—all of
Line which posited mechanisms that would resolve the issue—but only one of which predicted
(5) a theoretical, undiscovered particle that would mediate such a mechanism. Searching experimentally for this particle—dubbed the Higgs boson in the physics community, and known as the "God Particle" in the media—has been the task of hundreds of physicists since Fermilab's four-mile long Tevatron particle accelerator first came online in 1983.

A satisfying verbal definition for the Higgs boson is difficult to articulate, even for the
(10) theory's founder Dr. Peter Higgs. It is somewhat simpler to first describe how the universe would behave—according to the Standard Model of particle physics—without the activity of the Higgs boson. To begin with, matter would be essentially without mass. Gauge particles,* like photons,** would travel about at the speed of light, colliding occasionally, and sometimes even forming proton-like complexes. However, these complexes would decay
(15) almost instantaneously; the stable, atomic matter that constitutes our material world would be unsustainable.

In rough terms, the Higgs boson's role in imparting mass to the universe involves the propagation of a pervasive "Higgs field," which mediates the collision of subatomic gauge bosons, allowing them to acquire and maintain a mass. It is thought that this occurs because
(20) the Higgs field's non-zero amplitude in a vacuum spontaneously splits the electroweak gauge invariance of W, Z and Higgs bosons and gluons, resulting in a gauge transformation called "the Higgs mechanism." Metaphorically, the Higgs field might be thought of as a pool of molasses, slowing the bosons and gluons, allowing them to become massive, and ultimately reducing the elasticity of their collisions such that they may form larger, stable
(25) subatomic complexes like protons.

The Higgs boson is the only component of the Standard model—a set of physical theories that explain all interactions in the universe apart from gravity—that has yet to be observed experimentally. Because its discovery would mean a tremendous step toward validating the Standard model experimentally, it has often been referred to as a "holy grail" of particle
(30) physics. However, attempts to find the Higgs have proven exceptionally troublesome for scientists.

Together, the world's two largest and most powerful particle accelerators—Tevatron in Illinois, and the Large Hadron Collider in France and Switzerland—have sifted through roughly 70% of the particle's estimated vectors without returning any evidence for its exis-
(35) tence. On one hand this suggests that—if the Higgs exists—its discovery is imminent, as

the remaining "places" to look for it are becoming fewer and fewer. However, the cost of infrastructure and operation at these facilities is becoming, some believe, prohibitively expensive. Reduced federal funding at Fermilab has necessitated the cancellation of many projects involved with the search for the Higgs boson.

(40)   The protracted and arduous search for this singular particle has led some physicists to suspect that, in fact, it does not exist. Several theories competing with the Standard model—including Technicolor, and several extra-dimensional models—have postulated ways to break the electroweak gauge symmetry while maintaining unitarity without the presence of the Higgs boson. Of course, mathematical consistency is only half the battle in particle phys-

(45) ics; without evidence, these models cannot be considered more credible than the Standard. What's more, most physicists remain a far cry from abandoning Higgs boson-reliant models. M-theory, a cutting-edge, theoretical branch of string theory that may someday resolve the mathematical inconsistencies of modern physics, has successfully integrated the Standard and Supersymmetric gauge models—both of which currently rely on the presence of the

(50) Higgs boson.

In any event, the answer looms near on the horizon. Though Tevatron continues to encounter financial setbacks, since coming online in 2009, CERN's seventeen-mile long Large Hadron Collider continues to advance and expand the search for the Higgs boson. At the LHC's current pace of operation, many predict that—if indeed the particle exists—a Higgs

(55) event will be observed and recorded in the very near future. And while it will necessarily require several years of analysis and experimental replication to fully verify such a discovery, the world hasn't much longer to wait for the first firm, material evidence for or against the existence of the elusive "God particle."

*A gauge particle is an elementary particle that carries a fundamental interaction of nature.
**A photon is a gauge particle responsible for electromagnetic radiation and is also known as the particle of light.

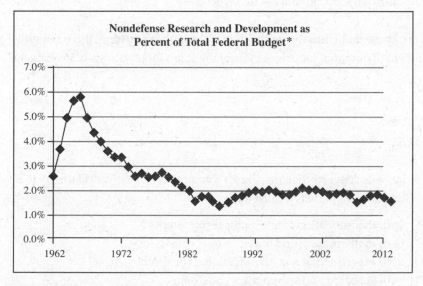

*Source: AAAS estimates based on Budget of the U.S. Government Historical Tables.
http://www.aaas.org/page/historical-trends-federal-rd

1. It can reasonably be inferred that the author's overall stance on the existence of the Higgs boson particle is

    (A) studied neutrality.
    (B) a strong belief in its existence.
    (C) ignorant confusion.
    (D) a strong skepticism about its existence.

2. The passage suggests that at the time the passage was written, the scientific consensus about the existence of the Higgs boson was

    (A) indubitably conclusive.
    (B) generally unsettled.
    (C) worryingly confused.
    (D) unwaveringly skeptical.

3. As used in line 17, "imparting" most nearly means

    (A) breaking.
    (B) defining.
    (C) reproducing.
    (D) bestowing.

4. The primary function of lines 22–25 ("Metaphorically, . . . protons.") in its paragraph as a whole is to

    (A) introduce poetic rhetorical devices to provide aesthetic language.
    (B) summarize the principle argument of the passage.
    (C) explain the mechanism whereby the Higgs particle can be detected.
    (D) clarify an esoteric concept for laypeople.

5. The passage indicates that at the time of the author's writing, there remained about what percent of potential particle vectors of the Higgs for physicists to investigate?

    (A) 30%
    (B) 60%
    (C) 70%
    (D) 95%

6. The passage suggests that in order for a comprehensive physical theory to achieve widespread acceptance, it must have

    (A) both theoretical and philosophical consistency.
    (B) both mathematical and observational consistency.
    (C) both experimental and investigational consistency.
    (D) both standard and symmetrical consistency.

7. Which choice provides the best evidence for the answer to the previous question?

(A) Lines 35–36 ("On the . . . fewer.")
(B) Lines 41–44 ("Several . . . Higgs boson.")
(C) Lines 44–45 ("Of course . . . Standard.")
(D) Lines 55–58 ("And while . . . particle.")

8. As used in line 57, "material" most nearly means

(A) stuff.
(B) physical.
(C) bodily.
(D) theoretical.

9. Scientists eager to confirm or deny the existence of the Higgs boson would most likely want to see the percentage portrayed in the *y*-axis of the graph at

(A) 6.5%
(B) 5.3%
(C) 4.8%
(D) 1.7%

10. Based on the graph, is it possible that overall U.S. government spending on research and development has increased between 2004 and 2006?

(A) No, because research and development decreased as a percent of the overall federal budget
(B) No, because overall governmental spending decreased between 2004 and 2006
(C) Yes, if the growth in overall governmental spending was sufficiently large
(D) Yes, since the percentage of federal spending on research and development increased during this period

Solutions

ANSWER KEY

1.	**A**	4.	**D**	7.	**C**	10.	**C**
2.	**B**	5.	**A**	8.	**B**		
3.	**D**	6.	**B**	9.	**A**		

ANSWERS EXPLAINED

1. **(A)** The author presents a wide range of viewpoints on the plausibility of the existence of the Higgs boson particle and concludes the essay by stating that the world will find out relatively soon whether the Higgs boson exists. So this could best be described as "studied neutrality." The author clearly understands the subject matter well and has adopted a wait-and-see attitude rather than jumping to a conclusion. Choices (B) and (D) are too extreme. Given the author's in-depth analysis of the current status of particle physics, his stance could hardly be described as one of ignorant confusion as stated in choice (C).

2. **(B)** Line 51 states, "In any event, the answer looms near on the horizon," meaning that scientists do not yet definitively know whether or not the Higgs boson exists. If the existence is confirmed, then choice (A) could work. However, that is not the status at the time of the writing of this passage. Although the passage contains some confusion and some skepticism about the Higgs boson, choices (C) and (D) are too extreme in their descriptions.

3. **(D)** Based on the context of the paragraph, the Higgs boson is giving or "bestowing" mass to particles that would otherwise be massless. It is not breaking down particles but slowing them down, making choice (A) incorrect. The Higgs boson is not defining the particles, as in choice (B), since it is helping the particles come into a masslike form rather than giving them their essence. It is not causing more particles to be created from each other, making choice (C) incorrect.

4. **(D)** Immediately before this metaphor is a rather complicated discussion of how the Higgs boson field is thought to operate to give particles mass. The function of these lines is to help clarify this difficult (esoteric) concept for laypeople (nonphysicists) so they can understand a challenging idea in terms they can relate to. Choice (A) is wrong because the objective is to help the reader understand a difficult idea, not to insert a poetic aside. Choice (B) is not correct because this is a minor point of the passage. Choice (C) is incorrect because it focuses on how the Higgs boson provides mass, not on how it can be detected.

5. **(A)** Lines 32–35 report that scientists have sifted through 70% of the particle's estimated vectors, meaning 100% – 70% = 30% of the particle vectors are left for physicists to investigate.

6. **(B)** Lines 44–45 speak of an answer to this. They state that half of the battle in creating a physical theory is mathematical consistency and the other half is experimental evidence. So there will be both mathematical and observational (from experimental observations) consistency. Choice (A) is wrong because the passage does not mention philosophical consistency. Choice (C) is incorrect because investigational and experimental are synonymous. Choice (D) is not right because these terms focus on minor specific names and aspects of theories rather than on their general characteristics.

7. **(C)** Lines 44–45 most directly support the notion that one needs both mathematical and observational consistency to have a sound theory. Choice (A) focuses on the difficulty of finding the Higgs boson. Choice (B) focuses on different theories about the Higgs. Choice (D) focuses on the hope that the Higgs boson will be discovered in the near future.

8. **(B)** The scientists are seeking experimental, observational, *physical* evidence that the Higgs boson exists because they already have a mathematically consistent model for it. Referring to the evidence as "stuff evidence," as in choice (A), would not be appropriate. "Bodily," choice (C), is incorrect because the evidence would come from physical observations of nonliving things, not from humans and other animals. Choice (D) is not right because the theory is already mathematically consistent—the actual observation is lacking.

9. **(A)** In order for scientists to confirm or deny the existence of the Higgs boson particle, they would want to invest as much money as possible into scientific research and development so they could create more experimental opportunities to observe the particle. Choice (A) has the highest percent of the options, so it is correct.

10. **(C)** This question involves thinking critically and creatively about the numbers and statistics presented in the graph. In the graph, the percentage of the budget devoted to research and development remained fairly level, even dropping slightly. Despite this, if the amount from which these percentages are taken goes *up* enough, then the overall amount can increase even though the percentage remains about the same. If you take 10% of 100 dollars and then take 10% of 300 dollars, the value will increase from $10 to $30 even though the percentage remains the same. So if the overall growth in government spending was sufficiently large, it would allow for an increase in research spending even though the percentage remained level. Choices (A) and (B) are incorrect because it is possible that research and development spending increased. Choice (D) is not right because it contradicts the fact that spending on research decreased.

A major change in the new PSAT can be found in excerpts in the Reading Test and in the Writing and Language Test from great global documents about the foundations of democracy. Here is an example of such a passage.

Questions 1–9 are based on the following excerpt.

Excerpt from George Washington's "Farewell Address to the United States of America," 1796.

Against the insidious wiles of foreign influence (I conjure you to believe me, fellow-citizens) the jealousy of a free people ought to be constantly awake, since history and experience prove that foreign influence is one of the most baneful foes of republican government.
Line
(5) But that jealousy to be useful must be impartial; else it becomes the instrument of the very influence to be avoided, instead of a defense against it. Excessive partiality for one foreign nation and excessive dislike of another cause those whom they actuate to see danger only on one side, and serve to veil and even second the arts of influence on the other. Real patriots who may resist the intrigues of the favorite are liable to become suspected and odious, while its tools and dupes usurp the applause and confidence of the people, to surrender
(10) their interests.

The great rule of conduct for us in regard to foreign nations is in extending our commercial relations, to have with them as little political connection as possible. So far as we have already formed engagements, let them be fulfilled with perfect good faith. Here let us stop. Europe has a set of primary interests which to us have none; or a very remote relation. Hence she
(15) must be engaged in frequent controversies, the causes of which are essentially foreign to our concerns. Hence, therefore, it must be unwise in us to implicate ourselves by artificial ties in the ordinary vicissitudes of her politics, or the ordinary combinations and collisions of her friendships or enmities.

Our detached and distant situation invites and enables us to pursue a different course.
(20) If we remain one people under an efficient government, the period is not far off when we may defy material injury from external annoyance; when we may take such an attitude as will cause the neutrality we may at any time resolve upon to be scrupulously respected; when belligerent nations, under the impossibility of making acquisitions upon us, will not lightly hazard the giving us provocation; when we may choose peace or war, as our interest, guided
(25) by justice, shall counsel.

Why forego the advantages of so peculiar a situation? Why quit our own to stand upon foreign ground? Why, by interweaving our destiny with that of any part of Europe, entangle our peace and prosperity in the toils of European ambition, rivalship, interest, humor or caprice?

(30) It is our true policy to steer clear of permanent alliances with any portion of the foreign world; so far, I mean, as we are now at liberty to do it; for let me not be understood as capable of patronizing infidelity to existing engagements. I hold the maxim no less applicable to public than to private affairs, that honesty is always the best policy. I repeat it, therefore, let those engagements be observed in their genuine sense. But, in my opinion, it is unnecessary and would be unwise to extend them.

(35) Taking care always to keep ourselves by suitable establishments on a respectable defensive posture, we may safely trust to temporary alliances for extraordinary emergencies.

1. The principle thesis of the passage is best summarized in

   (A) lines 2–3 ("since . . . government.").
   (B) lines 12–13 ("So far . . . stop.").
   (C) lines 23–24 ("belligerent . . . provocation.").
   (D) line 36 ("we may . . . emergencies.").

2. The passage suggests that Washington's primary concern is which of the following sorts of foreign interactions?

   (A) The U.S. is invaded by land from European aggressors, who quickly dismantle the fragile early republic.
   (B) The U.S. is drawn into a foreign war based not on our inherent interests but on treaty obligations.
   (C) The U.S. is taken over by foreign saboteurs who infiltrate the federal government and assume positions of power.
   (D) The U.S. is enmeshed in a long-lasting trade war over tariffs and fees on exports and imports.

3. Lines 7–10 ("Real . . . interests.") most directly warn against what potential outcome?

   (A) Devoted, capable Americans are impugned while gullible Americans become pawns.
   (B) Patriotic, reputable Americans are praised while less capable Americans are impoverished.
   (C) Traitorous, clever Americans rise to power while lower-class Americans are disregarded.
   (D) Meddling, crafty Europeans successfully invade the U.S. while Americans surrender easily.

4. Paragraph 2 (lines 11–18) suggests that the principle aim of America's foreign relations should be

   (A) to encourage the development of new allies.
   (B) to isolate the U.S. from European interactions.
   (C) to promote commerce without alliance.
   (D) to seize new territories unchecked.

5. Washington postulates that the major domestic threat to American independence and prosperity is

   (A) patriotism.
   (B) disunity.
   (C) political isolationism.
   (D) impartiality.

6. Which choice provides the best evidence for the answer to the previous question?

   (A) Lines 11–12 ("The great . . . possible.")
   (B) Lines 14–16 ("Hence . . . concerns.")
   (C) Lines 20–21 ("If we . . . annoyance.")
   (D) Lines 32–34 ("I repeat . . . them.")

7. As used in line 24, "hazard" most nearly means

   (A) endanger.
   (B) confuse.
   (C) chance.
   (D) stop.

8. As used in line 26, "peculiar" most nearly means

   (A) distinct.
   (B) strange.
   (C) undesirable.
   (D) eccentric.

9. Suppose that at the time of the passage's writing, the United States had a trade pact with a European country that had been in place for some time. We can reasonably infer that Washington would suggest what should be done to this pact?

   (A) It should be maintained.
   (B) It should be renegotiated.
   (C) It should be abandoned.
   (D) It should be built upon with political agreements.

Solutions

ANSWER KEY

1.	**A**	4.	**C**	7.	**C**
2.	**B**	5.	**B**	8.	**A**
3.	**A**	6.	**C**	9.	**A**

ANSWERS EXPLAINED

1. **(A)** The overall argument of the passage is that the young United States should avoid alliances with foreign powers and focus instead on its own affairs. This is best summarized by lines 2–3, which state that "history and experience prove that foreign influence is one of the most baneful foes of republican government." This means that being influenced by other countries will hurt governments elected by the people. Choice (B) is incorrect because it is addressing a potential objection. Choice (C) is not right because it is making a related point but not the primary point of the passage's argument by advocating a stronger military posture to thwart potential invaders. Choice (D) is incorrect because it is noting an exception.

2. **(B)** Lines 11–18 state that European powers are likely to engage in frequent conflicts and that the U.S. should not entangle itself with "artificial ties," i.e., treaties that would oblige it to fight in wars in which the U.S. has no interest. So choice (B) is the best option. Choice (A) is incorrect. Although it is a concern, the primary argument of the excerpt is focused on avoiding foreign obligations, not on preparing for foreign invasion. Choice (C) is not right because internal treason is not a focus of the passage. Choice (D) is wrong because Washington advocates foreign economic interaction in lines 11–12.

3. **(A)** In lines 7–10, Washington expresses concern that "real patriots" will be considered suspicious simply because they side with a different foreign power, while "tools and dupes" will receive unwarranted praise. So Washington is expressing his concern that highly capable Americans truly devoted to the U.S. will be condemned, while easily manipulated Americans will become pawns for European powers. Choices (B) and (C) are incorrect because there is no discussion of economic status. Choice (D) is not right because Washington is not concerned with whether or not Americans can fight but with whether or not Americans will unnecessarily turn against one another.

4. **(C)** Washington uses this paragraph to argue that the U.S. should extend "commercial relations" but should not implicate itself "by artificial ties" to foreign powers that would require the U.S. to fight foreign wars. Choice (A) is wrong because Washington wants to avoid alliances. Choice (B) is not correct because trade is an interaction with Europe that Washington does want. Choice (D) is incorrect because Washington does not discuss American territorial expansion in this paragraph.

5. **(B)** Lines 20–21 state that if Americans remain "one people," they will be able to fend off foreign threats. So by implication, if Americans are disunited, they will encounter major threats to their independence and prosperity. Choice (A) is not correct because these statements about unity would serve to encourage patriotism as a helpful virtue to American independence. Choices (C) and (D) are not right because Washington advocates avoiding "artificial ties" (line 16) with other countries by being more neutral and isolated.

6. **(C)** Lines 20–21 provide the most direct evidence that Washington thought of disunity as a major threat to American independence and prosperity since they mention the need to be "one people." Choice (A) is incorrect because these lines do not focus on threats. Choice (B) is wrong because these lines focus more on Europe. Choice (D) is wrong because these lines discuss how the U.S. can balance treaty obligations.

7. **(C)** Washington argues that the U.S. should get to a point where other countries will not take war with the U.S. lightly, thereby not wishing to "hazard" (risk or chance) war. Choices (A), (B), and (D) are all incorrect. Stating that other countries do not want to "endanger," "confuse," or "stop" giving the U.S. provocation does not make sense. These words do not have the secondary definition of "risk" that "chance" does.

8. **(A)** In ordinary usage, "peculiar" is something strange, eccentric, or even undesirable. In this context of antiquated English, though, Washington is arguing that the United States should not give up the advantages of its unique, or distinct, situation by making alliances with other countries.

9. **(A)** Washington states in lines 32–33 that when it comes to existing treaty obligations, he wishes for "those engagements" to be observed since doing otherwise would be dishonest. So Washington would want to maintain an existing trade treaty (pact). Choice (A) is also supported by Washington's advocacy of economic interactions with other nations.

The PSAT may include a literature selection from an older piece of fiction. The language in such a passage may be a bit more challenging since it is from an earlier era. Take things slowly at the beginning so you develop a feel for the writer's style. Then read at a normal pace as the story develops.

Questions 1–9 are based on the following passage.

The following passage is an excerpt from the 1877 novel *The American*. Christopher Newman, a civil war hero and self-made millionaire, is visiting Europe for the first time. In Paris, he meets and dines with the wife of an old friend, Mrs. Lizzie Tristram.

She had an especial wish to know whether he had ever been in love—seriously, passionately—and, failing to gather any satisfaction from his allusions, at last closely pressed him. He hesitated a while, but finally said, "Hang it then, no!" She declared that she was
Line delighted to hear it, as it confirmed her private conviction that he was a man of no real
(5) feeling.
"Is that so?" he asked, very gravely. "But how do you recognize a man of real feeling?"
"I can't make out," said Mrs. Tristram, "whether you're very simple or very deep."
"I'm very deep. That's a fact."
"I believe that if I were to tell you with a certain air that you're as cold as a fish, you would
(10) implicitly believe me."
"A certain air?" said Newman. "Well try your air and see."
"You would believe me, but you would not care," said Mrs. Tristram.
"You've got it all wrong. I should care immensely, but I shouldn't believe you. The fact is I have never had time to 'feel' things. I have had to *do* them, had to make myself felt."
(15) "Oh, I can imagine indeed that you may have sometimes done that tremendously."
"Yes, there's no mistake about that."

"When you're in one of your furies it can't be pleasant."

"I am never in a fury."

"I don't, nevertheless, see you always as you are now. You've *something* or other behind,
(20) beneath. You get harder or you get softer. You're more pleased—or you're more displeased."

"Well, a man of any sense doesn't lay his plans to be angry," said Newman, "and it's in
fact so long since I have been displeased that I've quite forgotten it."

"I don't believe," she returned, "that you're never angry. A man ought to be angry
sometimes, and you are neither good enough nor bad enough always to keep your temper."

(25) "I lose it perhaps every five years."

"The time is coming round, then," said his hostess. "Before I've known you six months I
shall see you in a magnificent rage."

"Do you mean to put me into one?"

"I should not be sorry. You take things too coolly. It quite exasperates me. And then
(30) you're too happy. You have what must be the most agreeable thing in the world: the consciousness of having bought your pleasure beforehand, having paid for it in advance. You
have not a day of reckoning staring you in the face. Your reckonings are over."

"Well, I suppose I am happy," said Newman, almost pensively.

"You've been odiously successful."

(35) "Successful in copper," said Newman, "but very mixed in other ventures. And I've had to
take quite a back seat on oil."

"It's very disagreeable to know how Americans have come by their money," his companion sighed. "Now, at all events, you've the world before you. You've only to enjoy."

"Oh, I suppose I'm all right," said Newman. "Only I'm tired of having it thrown up at
(40) me. Besides, there are several drawbacks. I don't come up to my own standard of culture."

"One doesn't expect it of you," Mrs. Tristram answered. Then in a moment: "Besides,
you do come up. You *are* up!"

"Well, I mean to have a good time, wherever I am," said Newman. "I am not cultivated, I
am not even educated; I know nothing about history, or art, or foreign tongues, or any other
(45) learned matters. But I am not a fool, either, and I shall undertake to know something about
Europe by the time I have done with it. I feel something under my ribs here," he added in
a moment, "that I can't explain—a sort of a mighty hankering, a desire to stretch out and
haul in."

"Bravo!" Mrs. Tristram cried; "that's what I want to hear you say. You're the great Western
(50) Barbarian, stepping forth in his innocence and might, to gaze a while at this poor corrupt
old world before swooping down on it."

"Oh come," Newman protested; "I'm not an honest barbarian either, by a good deal. I've
seen honest barbarians; I know what they are. "

"There are different shades."

(55) "I have instincts—have them deeply—if I haven't the forms of a high old civilization,"
Newman went on. "I stick to that. If you don't believe me, I should like to prove it to you."

Mrs. Tristram was silent a while. "I should like to make you prove it," she said at last. "I
should like to put you in a difficult place."

"Well, put me!" said Newman.

(60) "Vous ne doutez de rien!" his companion rejoined.

"Oh," he insisted, "I've a very good opinion of myself."

"I wish I could put it to the test. Give me time and I will."

1. Based on the passage as a whole, Newman is best characterized as

   (A) easily flustered and emotionally vulnerable.
   (B) even tempered and business savvy.
   (C) odiously successful and frighteningly barbaric.
   (D) innocently optimistic and personally intimidating.

2. The conversation between Mrs. Tristram and Newman is essentially a/an

   (A) philosophical dialogue.
   (B) insulting accusation.
   (C) complimentary platitude.
   (D) playful exchange.

3. As used in line 7, "deep" most nearly means

   (A) profound.
   (B) engrossed.
   (C) extended.
   (D) saturated.

4. It can be inferred from the passage that Mrs. Tristram most strongly believes that she can bear witness to a greater emotional range from Newman if she has sufficient

   (A) money.
   (B) culture.
   (C) time.
   (D) empathy.

5. Which choice provides the best evidence for the answer to the previous question?

   (A) Lines 9–10 ("I believe . . . me.")
   (B) Lines 13–14 ("You've . . . felt.")
   (C) Lines 26–27 ("The time . . . rage.")
   (D) Lines 30–32 ("You have . . . over.")

6. When Newman says "I'm tired of having it thrown up at me" (lines 39–40) he most likely means that he is

   (A) sorry that he continues to fall ill.
   (B) annoyed with European culture.
   (C) wishful that he could be more successful.
   (D) weary of being reminded of his wealth.

7. As used in line 47, "hankering" most nearly means

   (A) confusion.
   (B) cultivation.
   (C) appreciation.
   (D) desire.

8. Newman's opinion of his capacity to understand higher culture is

(A) drearily pessimistic.
(B) unquestionably recognized.
(C) intuitively confident.
(D) jealously guarded.

9. Which choice provides the best evidence for the answer to the previous question?

(A) Lines 41–42 ("One . . . up.")
(B) Lines 43–48 ("Well . . . haul in.")
(C) Line 52 ("Oh . . . deal.")
(D) Line 55 ("I have . . . civilization.")

Solutions

ANSWER KEY

1.	**B**	4.	**C**	7.	**D**
2.	**D**	5.	**C**	8.	**C**
3.	**A**	6.	**D**	9.	**D**

ANSWERS EXPLAINED

1. **(B)** Tristram describes Newman as someone without "real feeling" in lines 3–5. Tristram continues to try to press Newman's emotional buttons to demonstrate that her assumptions about his even-tempered nature are correct. Also, Newman has been "successful in copper" (line 37), which allows him to live a more free and luxurious life. So he must have business savvy (know-how or smarts). Choice (A) is incorrect because Newman does not demonstrate much emotion. Choices (C) and (D) are incorrect because Newman is in no way a frightening or intimidating person.

2. **(D)** Throughout the conversation, Tristram playfully attempts to touch on the emotions of Newman, while Newman eagerly engages her with thoughtful responses. This is best described as a "playful exchange." Choice (A) is incorrect because the conversation is more superficial, preventing it from being considered philosophical. Choice (B) is wrong because they are getting along well with one another. Choice (C) is not the answer because Tristram is trying to find Newman's emotional vulnerability. A complimentary platitude would involve her saying nice yet meaningless things to him.

3. **(A)** In this context, they are referring to feelings. So "deep" refers to Newman's capacity for feeling. It would by synonymous in this context to call his feelings "profound." Choice (B) is incorrect because "engrossed" would be more applicable in describing one's intellectual focus. Choice (C) is incorrect because "extended" would refer more to breadth than depth. Choice (D) is wrong because "saturated" would refer to having a great deal of some quality but not necessarily having it in depth.

4. **(C)** Lines 26–27 state that Tristram believes that surely by the time she has known Newman for at least six months, she will have seen him demonstrate great emotional passion. There is no indication that her lack of money or her European culture contributes to this. She seems to have plenty of empathy already, given how she is able to read his emotions quite well.

5. **(C)** Lines 26–27 provide the most direct support for the idea that if Mrs. Tristram has more time to get to know Newman, she will see him demonstrate passion. Choice (A) is wrong because these lines refer to Mrs. Tristram's belief in her own capacities. Choice (B) is wrong because it gives Newman's reasoning as to why he does not demonstrate much feeling. Choice (D) is incorrect because it states that Newman is financially prosperous.

6. **(D)** Considering the context before answering this is critical. Prior to line 38, Tristram and Newman are discussing Newman's success in business. So following this discussion, it makes the most sense to infer that the meaning of "I'm tired of having it thrown up at me" is referring to Newman's weariness at hearing that he is quite wealthy. Choice (A) is incorrect because it has nothing to do with physical illness. Choice (B) is wrong because Newman cannot get enough of European culture. Choice (C) is not correct because Newman is satisfied with the business success he has had.

7. **(D)** Immediately after mentioning the word "hankering," Newman clarifies that he has a "desire to stretch out and haul in." Therefore, "desire" is the correct answer. Although he cannot precisely explain his feelings, he is certain that he does have them, making "confusion," choice (A), incorrect. Choices (B) and (C) are incorrect because Newman is working on cultivating his cultural awareness and appreciation—he does not yet have such awareness and appreciation.

8. **(C)** Newman states that he has deep instincts for high civilization even though he does not have the forms of it quite yet. So he is "intuitive" (instinctive) in his confidence that he will someday be able to master European culture. Choice (A) is wrong because Newman is optimistic. Choice (B) is not correct because his capacity is not recognized by others or even explicitly and fully by himself. Choice (D) is not right because Newman is very forthcoming about his opinions.

9. **(D)** Line 55 provides the best evidence that Newman is intuitively confident about his ability to understand the "higher cultures" he is studying. Choice (A) focuses on Tristram's opinion of Newman. Choice (B) gives us only an introduction to Newman's self-assessment. Choice (C) responds to Tristram's playfully insulting comments immediately beforehand.

This is an historical analysis passage. As mentioned previously, you will not need to use outside knowledge to answer the accompanying questions—all of the answers will be provided in the text.

Questions 1–10 are based on the following passage.

The following excerpt is from a 2013 history article titled "The Great Seal."

In the wake of the wild and lucrative conspiracy theories that swept through our nation's popular culture in the last decade, widely disseminated misinformation seems still to haunt an alarming portion of our national symbols. Yet in many cases the reality behind
Line these symbols is far richer in meaning and profundity than any farfetched tale spun by a
(5) Hollywood screenwriter; and while the truth may not ensnare our sense of fantasy, it can still capture our imaginations with an illuminating insight into our nation's history, and the minds of early American patriots.

Take for instance the Great Seal of the United States, which was first commissioned by the Continental Congress on the very day that they declared independence from Great (10) Britain (though it was not fully completed for another six years). For the most part, the symbolism of the obverse side is readily discernible to those versed in the story of the American Revolution; the bald eagle—our ubiquitous symbol for natural power and majesty—is displayed with a striped escutcheon and splayed wings in a formation that echoes (but is distinct from) English heraldry. The eagle was selected over the traditional heraldic animal of (15) power—the lion—both because it is native to North America, and to avoid the overtones of kingship historically associated with the lion. The thirteen red and white stripes (or Pieces) and single blue cap (or Chief) of the escutcheon are described by Charles Thomson—who presented the final design of the Seal before Congress in 1782—as representing "the several states all joined in one solid compact entire, supporting a Chief, which unites the whole (20) and represents Congress."

The constellation of thirteen stars in a blue field above the eagle also signifies the colonies, and their capacity to shine independently while remaining integral components of a larger structure. The number appears again in the thirteen arrows and thirteen leaves of the olive branch clutched, respectively, in the left and right talons of the eagle. Together, (25) the branch (which is said to derive from the Judeo-Christian symbol of peace in the story of Noah) and arrows represent a dichotomy—a national preparedness in both times of war and peace. Surrounding the stars above the eagle is a design described in heraldry as "clouds and glory," another symbol of religious origin (meant to invoke the Saint's Halo of Judeo-Christian iconography) that alludes to a belief held by many American revolutionar- (30) ies that the victory of their new nation was the result of "divine providence." The arrangement of the stars themselves mimics the geometry of the Star of David.

The reverse side of the Great Seal is slightly more esoteric in its significance, and as such has been more vulnerable to exploitation at the hands of those who would popularize baseless myth at the expense of obscuring our national symbols. The "Eye of Providence"— (35) which floats near the top of the Seal—is admittedly a derivative of the ancient Egyptian symbol for the Eye of Horus (which stood for royal power and good health), but it is also a symbol of tremendous distribution that has meant many different things to many different cultures. The incarnation of the Eye that appears on the Great Seal emerges from the far more recent Christian tradition of the European Renaissance, in which the eye symbolized (40) the universal presence of the Judeo-Christian God, and the triangle surrounding it the Holy Trinity. If one takes into account the motto above the Eye—"Annuit Cœptis," or "[He] has approved our undertakings"—as well as the prevalent belief among those American revolutionaries of the Christian persuasion that the founding of the United States was a literal act of Providence, there is little room for doubt that the Eye of Providence itself is meant (45) to symbolize the "grace of God" as it were, and not, by any means, the nobility of ancient Egyptian monarchy.

The absurd suggestion that the Eye is meant to invoke Horus would likely never have been uttered but for the inclusion of an unfinished pyramid—consisting of thirteen steps— at the Seal's base. However, Charles Thomson describes the pyramid explicitly as signifying, (50) "Strength and Duration," while, "the Eye over it & the Motto allude to the many signal interpositions of providence in favour of the American cause." In light of these words, one can surmise that the pyramid was selected because it is a worldwide symbol for a remarkable and enduring civilization—a thing manmade that stands the test of unfathomable time. In contrast to the pyramid's (in this case) wholly secular implications, the Eye of Providence

(55) hovers above it near the heavens; together they constitute another symbolic duality: the secular and spiritual foundations of our nation as envisioned by many of the Founding Fathers. The true symbolic beauty of the Seal's pyramid lies rather in its unfinished aspect; it demonstrates that—for all their accomplishments—the American Revolutionaries recognized that their work was but a beginning. To achieve its full splendor, the pyramid would

(60) require the equally impactful contributions of countless generations, building a still greater nation onward throughout time.

1. The author's overall purpose in writing the essay is to

    (A) analyze public opinion.
    (B) dispel misconceptions.
    (C) postulate a hypothesis.
    (D) confirm widespread views.

2. The passage primarily uses which of the following to make its argument?

    (A) Primary source quotations
    (B) Religious dogma
    (C) Symbolic analysis
    (D) Archaeological findings

3. As used in line 6, "illuminating" most nearly means

    (A) enlightening.
    (B) bright.
    (C) shiny.
    (D) creative.

4. Lines 10–14 suggest that a viewer of the Great Seal could generally understand it with some

    (A) in-depth scholarly investigation.
    (B) basic historical knowledge.
    (C) background information about bird anatomy.
    (D) familiarity with English heraldry.

5. Which symbol in the Great Seal of the United States does the author suggest was chosen in an effort to differentiate the U.S. from more aristocratic countries?

    (A) The eagle
    (B) The olive branch
    (C) The "Eye of Providence"
    (D) The unfinished pyramid

6. Which choice provides the best evidence for the answer to the previous question?

   (A) Lines 14–16 ("The eagle . . . lion.")
   (B) Lines 24–25 ("Together . . . peace.")
   (C) Lines 34–38 ("The . . . cultures.")
   (D) Lines 47–49 ("The absurd . . . base.")

7. As used in line 19, "compact" most nearly means

   (A) small.
   (B) firm.
   (C) grouping.
   (D) union.

8. It can reasonably be inferred that the author believes the "Eye of Providence" is widely mis-interpreted on account of the presence of what other symbol on the Great Seal?

   (A) The eagle
   (B) The triangle of the Holy Trinity
   (C) The unfinished pyramid
   (D) The Star of David

9. The author suggests that many early Americans believed that divine power had what role in the formation of the United States?

   (A) A negative and revolutionary role
   (B) A neutral and removed role
   (C) A positive and instrumental role
   (D) A helpful yet tangential role

10. Which choice provides the best evidence for the answer to the previous question?

   (A) Lines 1–7 ("In the . . . patriots.")
   (B) Lines 21–27 ("The constellation . . . peace.")
   (C) Lines 41–46 ("If one . . . monarchy.")
   (D) Lines 57–61 ("The true . . . time.")

Solutions

ANSWER KEY

1. **B**	4. **B**	7. **D**	10. **C**
2. **C**	5. **A**	8. **C**	
3. **A**	6. **A**	9. **C**	

ANSWERS EXPLAINED

1. **(B)** The first sentence of the passage refers to the widespread presence of "misinforma-tion" about the national symbols of the United States. The essay goes on to dispel a number of misconceptions readers may have about the Great Seal of the United States. Choice (A) is incorrect because the passage does not focus on what the public as a whole thinks. Choice

(C) is wrong because the excerpt is sharing information, not making a hypothesis. Choice (D) is not right because the information refutes commonly held views.

2. **(C)** The passage makes its argument by thoroughly analyzing the symbols in the Great Seal of the United States, from its eagle to its constellation. Choice (A) is wrong because the visual images of the Seal are primarily analyzed. Choice (B) is not correct because religion is mentioned only as an aside, not as the primary focus of the argument. Choice (D) is not correct. Although this is an historical symbol, it is one still in use today, so it does not involve archaeology.

3. **(A)** In this context, "illuminating" is describing the type of insight that people may gain from learning the true history of American symbols. Since this has to do with learning, it can best be described as "enlightening." The word in this context does not mean "bright" or "shiny" because it does not refer to the physical aspects of the symbol. The word does not mean "creative" because the insight we have is more informational and factual.

4. **(B)** Lines 10–12 state that "the symbolism of the obverse side is readily discernible to those versed in the story of the American Revolution." This means that if someone has basic historical knowledge about U.S. history, he or she will be able to make sense of the symbolism. Choice (A) is wrong because such in-depth knowledge is not necessary. Choice (C) is wrong because it is too narrowly focused on the eagle. Choice (D) is not correct because the Great Seal of the United States is "distinct from" English heraldry according to lines 13–14.

5. **(A)** Lines 14–16 indicate that the eagle was chosen because it would avoid the "overtones of kingship" that the more common lion symbol would have. Although the other symbols are on the Great Seal, they are not as clearly present in order to differentiate the U.S. from more aristocratic countries.

6. **(A)** Lines 14–16 discuss the eagle in the Great Seal of the United States. The other choices refer to the symbols in each of the incorrect answers to the previous question.

7. **(D)** "Compact" in this context refers to the "union" of the different states joined into one country. It is not referring to size as in choice (A) or to texture as in choice (B). Also, a "grouping," found in choice (C), is too weak a word to describe the joining of states together into a country.

8. **(C)** Lines 57–59 explain that the suggestion that the Eye on the Great Seal refers to an Egyptian deity is based on the unfinished pyramid underneath the Great Seal. The other symbols, although present on the Great Seal, do not contribute to the misinterpretation of the Eye.

9. **(C)** Lines 41–46 report the belief of many American revolutionaries that "the grace of God" contributed to the founding of the United States. This can best be described as positive and instrumental since they believed divine power was vital to the formation of the country. This belief would not then be described as negative or neutral as in choices (A) and (B). The word "helpful" in choice (D) could be applicable. However, "tangential" is not correct since the definition of tangential is "diverging from the main topic."

10. **(C)** Lines 41–46 address the role that many American revolutionaries believed divine providence played in the founding of the country. Choice (A) gives an introduction to the essay. Choice (B) touches on only religion. Choice (D) focuses on the contributions of future generations of Americans.

Profanity

Profanity is a curious phenomenon in human speech—it exists in most every language and consists of a small subset of words that carry inside them some incredible social power. Distinct from pejoratives and slurs—which are derived from traditions of racism, jingoism,
Line homophobia, and gross, general ignorance—true profanity encompasses only those pre-
(5) cious few lexemes that might be applied to and by any individual within a given linguistic culture. They are, in a sense, universals. By and large, they derive from elemental human experiences, none more so than those concerning sexuality and egesta.*

In the sense of Ferdinand Saussure's theory of Semiotics, one might suggest that the use of literal profanity—as opposed to figurative, which possesses only social sway based on its
(10) proximity to the literal—garners part of its power by being the closest available union of signifier and signified in subjects that, as a culture, we tend to avoid in polite and formal conversations. That is, the word is rude because the thing itself—in a general context—is also considered rude. In English, we tend to use either circumlocution or euphemisms to avoid the literal forms of our profanity in informal settings where swearing would be inappropri-
(15) ate. In formal conversations, we turn to the Latin derivatives—words like "intercourse" and "excrement," which are tolerated socially, albeit with some reluctance, because they represent the mother language of both medical science and the Christian church. Our infamous "four-letter words," meanwhile, are almost exclusively descended from the Germanic components of English. Even without an expertise in linguistics, one might sense this simply
(20) by the way they sound—phonically, most profanity in English is composed of short, terse syllables and rounds off abruptly with a hard consonant.

Many accounts from people immersed in a language that is not their own have, throughout several centuries, pointed to profanity as by far the most difficult aspect of a novel language to master. There is, in our profanity, a high cultural learning curve that demands
(25) intimate knowledge and sensitivity to the subtleties of social interactions. Swearing is, in its own way, a kind of national art—one shared and apprehended almost exclusively by the members of a particular language community. Ernest Hemingway speaks of the artistry of another culture's profanity with admiration in his celebrated novel *For Whom the Bell Tolls*, wherein the narrator bears witness as obscenities and insults build to a high formalism and
(30) eventually collapse upon themselves, leaving the profanities implied rather than stated.

At least for the Western languages, it is impossible to ignore an additional—albeit wholly separate—source of profanity; and that is the Christian church. The word "profane" itself is a classical Latin derivative meaning "outside the temple." In early use, it referred to anything belonging to the secular world. By the Middle Ages, it had come to represent anything
(35) that demonstrated an active or passive indifference to the "religious" and the "sacred"—no longer was a thing profane if it did not belong to the Church but also if it did not belong in the Church. This included, as we have noted, the age-old obscenities of sex and excrement—whose profane statuses predate the church by several thousand years—as well as a kind of profanity that, while certainly not invented by the church, is preserved more or less
(40) intact within our languages to this day.

*"Egesta" refers to matter excreted from the body.

1. The passage suggests that a randomly selected human culture would most likely have some version of profane words for

   (A) technical and scientific terminology.
   (B) social practices prohibited by religion.
   (C) digestive waste and human reproduction.
   (D) the implied meaning conveyed by formal art.

2. As it is used in line 6, "elemental" most nearly means

   (A) molecular.
   (B) essential.
   (C) environmental.
   (D) experiential.

3. Based on lines 8–13, one can reasonably conclude that Ferdinand Saussure believes that a major factor that gives profanity its power is

   (A) the real-life things the profanity represents.
   (B) profanity's representation of conflict between symbolism and clarity.
   (C) the rarity with which profanity's ideas are encountered.
   (D) the use of profanity by the socially dominant classes.

4. According to lines 19–21, a newly formed profane English word would most likely have which of the following suffixes?

   (A) -lah
   (B) -ock
   (C) -soo
   (D) -aly

5. As it is used in line 23, "novel" most nearly means

   (A) new.
   (B) literary.
   (C) wordy.
   (D) challenging.

6. The phenomenon described in lines 27–30 is most similar to

   (A) an aqueduct that is constructed in ancient times only to crumble as the centuries pass.
   (B) the development of architectural technology enabling ever higher construction.
   (C) the prohibition of subversive political meetings by an authoritarian dictator.
   (D) the evolution of painting from realistic portraiture to abstract expressionism.

7. The passage suggests that modern English speakers feel more comfortable discussing the ideas represented by profanity if the terminology used has roots in what areas?

   (A) Sexuality and human waste
   (B) German and Latin
   (C) Science and religion
   (D) Works of medieval literature

8. Which choice provides the best evidence for the answer to the previous question?

    (A) Lines 6–7 ("They are . . . egesta.")

    (B) Lines 15–17 ("In formal . . . church.")

    (C) Lines 19–21 ("Even without . . . consonant.")

    (D) Lines 37–40 ("This included . . . this day.")

9. A teacher of high school foreign language could most successfully use what selection in the text to pacify students who were eager to learn "swear words" in the new language immediately?

    (A) Lines 3–6 ("Distinct from . . . linguistic culture.")

    (B) Lines 13–17 ("In English . . . Christian church.")

    (C) Lines 22–25 ("Many accounts . . . interactions.")

    (D) Lines 37–40 ("This included . . . to this day.")

Solutions

ANSWER KEY

1.	**C**	4.	**B**	7.	**C**
2.	**B**	5.	**A**	8.	**B**
3.	**A**	6.	**D**	9.	**C**

ANSWERS EXPLAINED

1. **(C)** Lines 6–7 best support this answer. They state that profane words largely represent "universals" concerning "sexuality" and "egesta" (i.e., human waste products). Profanity is not associated with scientific terminology, making choice (A) incorrect. Although the passage describes a connection to the religion of the West, not enough support is provided to state that any randomly selected culture would have a religion that prohibits certain social practices. Choice (D) is incorrect because the reference to formal art is very small in the passage, and not all cultures in the world have "formal" art.

2. **(B)** "Essential" is the most logical definition. Without human reproduction, or sexuality, people would not exist. Without producing bodily waste products, people would not survive. Therefore, these processes are essential to humans. Although reproduction does include "molecular," "environmental," and "experiential" aspects, these words do not capture the intended meaning of "essential" in this context.

3. **(A)** This is best seen by considering lines 12–13, in which the author clarifies that "the word is rude, because the thing itself . . . is also considered rude." In other words, profane words derive much of their power by standing for profane things. Choice (B) is not correct because conflict between symbolism and clarity is not discussed in the passage. Choices (C) and (D) are incorrect because profane ideas are encountered frequently by a variety of social classes.

4. **(B)** The suffix "-ock" is the only possible option because it has a short syllable coupled with a hard consonant ending.

5. **(A)** "New" makes the most sense because the author refers to people who have been immersed in a different language, i.e., a new language. The other options are not strongly associated with this newness.

6. **(D)** The lines mentioned refer to a process in which words become less and less literal. The evolution of painting from realism to abstraction is a similar shift away from literal or obvious meaning to a meaning that is implied. Choice (A) is about the gradual decay of human constructions due to time. Choice (B) is about the development of technology. Choice (C) is about stopping free expression.

7. **(C)** Lines 15–17 mention that words that have a religious or scientific basis have a general tendency to be "tolerated socially." The author does not associate the other options with social comfort.

8. **(B)** Lines 15–17 best support the notion that English speakers feel more comfortable discussing profanity when it has its basis in science and religion. Choice (A) provides a general introduction. Choice (C) focuses on the sound of profane words. Choice (D) describes the longevity of profanity.

9. **(C)** The teacher could refer to lines 22–25 because they justify that students of a new language take many years to master the subtleties that allow one to use profanity properly. The other options do not give helpful information that would reassure students who want to learn profane words in a foreign language.

Questions 1–9 are based on the following passage.

A Quiet Revolutionary

Though today the familiar names of French impressionism—Degas, Pissarro, Cézanne, Renoir, and Monet—are nearly synonymous with what we may inscrutably refer to as "great art," in its own time the impressionist movement was often identified with artistic
Line dissidence, the avant-garde, and painterly provocateurs. In its development, the impres-
(5) sionist style boldly challenged the entrenched principles of French painting and ultimately transformed art for most of the Western world.

There is one linchpin name, however, too frequently omitted from surveys of early impressionism. Eugène Boudin—a friend and contemporary of the Paris impressionists—never described himself as an innovator or revolutionary, and yet his work tremendously
(10) influenced the transmigration of impressionism from the walls of radical art galleries to those of homes and businesses throughout Europe.

Primarily, Boudin painted beach scenes on the shores of Brittany and Normandy. Alongside Monet, he was among the first of the impressionists to embrace painting *en plein air*, and he was also one of very few artists to show canvases in all eight of the
(15) Paris Impressionist Exhibitions. Despite his proximity to the avant-garde, Boudin's work remained, for the most part, conspicuously marketable throughout his career.

Employing slightly subtler brushstrokes than most of his counterparts, Boudin focused his labors on capturing the tranquil, shoreside recreations of bourgeois vacationers. Around this time it was becoming fashionable among the middle class to possess com-
(20) memorative depictions of the places one had traveled, and Boudin managed to fill this niche masterfully.

By painting the idle vacationers from behind and obscuring any visible faces in the impressionist-landscape style, his patrons could purchase premade a work articulating the mood, activity, colors, and locale of their holiday without the monetary and temporal
(25) obstacles of a traditional, commissioned painting. For comparison, Renoir's painting of

models from the rear—far from making the work more commercially viable—was executed as a stylistic affront to classical notions of portraiture. Suffice to say that Boudin's mercantile techniques were, at least among the impressionists, rather unique.

(30) Boudin's beachscapes made French impressionism not only familiar to the masses but pleasing and even preferable. That is not to say that his talents were inferior to those of the other preeminent impressionists. During his lifetime, Boudin's work was well respected among the artistic elite; fellow landscape painter Jean-Baptiste Corot described him as "the master of the sky," and the poet Baudelaire was a lifelong admirer of his paintings. Monet himself cited Boudin as a profound influence on his early work.

(35) More recently, Boudin has garnered attention for his less common—and far less popular—paintings depicting the seaside labors of working-class men and women. Though these works brought him very little financial profit, it is known that he was exceptionally fond of them. Having worked as a bay fisherman in his youth, it has been claimed that Boudin was perhaps somewhat ashamed of his reputation as painter of "les gens de la mode." In any
(40) case, these works provide us with a compelling contrast to those of the languorous, well-to-do beachgoers; and together they provide a rare, panoptical insight into the full social spectrum of French life by the sea in the mid-to-late 19th century.

1. It can reasonably be inferred that the narrator's general attitude toward impressionism can best be characterized as

    (A) warm appreciation.
    (B) awestruck reverence.
    (C) dispassionate objectivity.
    (D) mild contempt.

2. Which choice provides the best evidence for the answer to the previous question?

    (A) Lines 4–6 ("In its . . . world.")
    (B) Lines 19–21 ("Around . . . masterfully.")
    (C) Lines 26–27 ("was . . . portraiture.")
    (D) Lines 35–36 ("More . . . women.")

3. The overall structure of the passage is best described as

    (A) a historical survey followed by an artistic critique.
    (B) a fictitious flashback followed by a factual discussion.
    (C) an overall introduction followed by an in-depth analysis.
    (D) a general impression followed by a studied introspection.

4. As used in line 7, "linchpin" most nearly means

    (A) artistic.
    (B) essential.
    (C) commercial.
    (D) improvisational.

5. The author uses what to denote that a different language is being used?

   (A) Italics only
   (B) Quotation marks only
   (C) Both italics and quotation marks
   (D) Neither italics nor quotation marks

6. Which of the following labels applied toward Boudin would be most unjustified based on lines 15–16 ("Despite . . . career.")?

   (A) "Savvy businessman"
   (B) "Starving artist"
   (C) "Skillful impressionist"
   (D) "Independent thinker"

7. As used in line 19, "fashionable" most nearly means

   (A) tailored.
   (B) popular.
   (C) leisurely.
   (D) economical.

8. Lines 22–25 suggest that the primary aspect of Boudin's work that made it distinct from those of his contemporaries was its

   (A) economic viability.
   (B) impressionist style.
   (C) focus on natural landscapes.
   (D) affront to common sensibilities.

9. A painting in the High Renaissance style that would give a similar insight into society as the one found in Boudin's paintings as described in lines 39–42 ("In any . . . century.") would most likely have

   (A) an emphasis on characters from the lower echelons of society.
   (B) an explicit message of social and economic justice.
   (C) a contrast between seafarers and land lovers.
   (D) subjects from a variety of socioeconomic classes.

Solutions

ANSWER KEY

1. **A**	4. **B**	7. **B**
2. **A**	5. **C**	8. **A**
3. **C**	6. **B**	9. **D**

ANSWERS EXPLAINED

1. **(A)** The narrator has an attitude of warm appreciation. This is especially evidenced by the first paragraph of the essay. The narrator describes impressionist art as "boldly" challenging

the older principles of art, transforming it into something new. Choice (B) is too positive, choice (C) too neutral, and choice (D) too negative.

2. **(A)** Lines 4–6 most clearly support the author's warm appreciation toward impressionist art since they cite the boldness and transformative power of impressionism. Choice (B) is too vague with respect to the narrator's attitude. Choice (C) focuses on the specific approach of Renoir. Choice (D) mentions increasing interest by others in Boudin without mentioning the narrator's attitude.

3. **(C)** The narrator starts with an overall introduction of impressionism in the first paragraph and then provides an in-depth analysis of Boudin's artistic approaches. The passage does not critique the works as described in choice (A). It does not have a fictitious flashback as listed in choice (B). It does not look inward to the author's own attitudes as described in choice (D).

4. **(B)** "Essential" is most fitting since the paragraph goes on to discuss Boudin's tremendous influence on the artistic scene, making a history of impressionism severely lacking without mentioning him. The other words do give descriptions that can be associated with impressionism, but they do not fit this context.

5. **(C)** Line 14 refers to *en plain air*, while line 39 refers to "les gens de la mode." Both of these are French phrases.

6. **(B)** The narrator asserts that Boudin's works were "conspicuously marketable," which means that consumers were willing to purchase them. Hence, referring to him as a "starving artist" does not make sense since he was able to make money off his paintings. The other options properly characterize Boudin in the eyes of the narrator.

7. **(B)** "Fashionable" refers to the popularity of travelers placing paintings of their travel destinations in their homes. "Tailored" implies a level of customization not present in these works. "Leisurely" refers to the scenes in the paintings. "Economical" could apply to the practice of saving money by using more general scenes than customized ones, but the focus in the sentence is on the increased interest in this practice.

8. **(A)** Boudin's works were economically viable, i.e., they could be sold to consumers successfully, because he painted the vacationers and locations in a way that enabled the paintings to capture the essence of the people and their destinations without having to pay the added expense of a customized painting. Choices (B) and (C) could be widely applied to almost all impressionist art. Choice (D) could apply to certain artists other than Boudin.

9. **(D)** Lines 41–42 refer to the "full social spectrum" portrayed in Boudin's paintings, including lowerclass fisherman to well-to-do beachgoers. So a painter of the High Renaissance style would also portray a variety of social classes in the paintings. Choice (A) has too narrow of a focus on the poor. Choice (B) would be too direct a message. Choice (C) emphasizes individual preferences instead of social classes.

Writing and Language

2

The PSAT Writing and Language Test is part of the "Evidence-Based Reading and Writing" half of the test. The Writing and Language Test is set up as follows:

- 1 section
- 35 minutes long
- 4 passages
- 11 questions per passage, with 44 questions total
- Questions are in a random order of difficulty

This chapter includes the following:

- Reviews of the key grammar concepts for the PSAT Writing and Language Test
- 12 Writing and Language Test strategies
- "Putting It All Together" section with example problems and explanations
- In-depth practice for the types of questions and passages you will encounter:

    - Four passage types: careers, humanities, social science/history, science
    - Expression of ideas questions: development, organization, and effective language use
    - Standard English conventions questions: sentence structure, conventions of usage, and conventions of punctuation

REVIEW OF KEY GRAMMAR CONCEPTS

Sentence Basics

A sentence expresses a complete thought and contains both a subject and predicate, i.e., a subject and a verb. A subject is either a noun—a person, place, or thing—or a pronoun. The predicate contains a verb—a word that expresses an action, such as *is, are, ate, swam,* or *lifted.* Here are some examples of complete sentences:

> I am going to swim.
> When are we going to have dinner?
> Stop right there.
> Johnny is excited about going to the game.

A sentence fragment expresses an incomplete thought and includes only a subject or only a predicate. Here are some examples of sentence fragments:

> Is going to win.
> Franklin, my favorite pet dog.
> The first thing I am going to do on vacation.

Here are some possible ways the above sentence fragments could be fixed:

She is going to win.
Franklin is my favorite pet dog.
That is the first thing I am going to do on vacation.

A run-on sentence consists of two or more complete sentences that are *not* joined together with appropriate punctuation or transitions. Here are some examples of run-on sentences:

Eloise went for a nap, she was very tired as a result of not sleeping the previous day.
Why can't you clean up the dishes it would be really nice if you could be more courteous.
Once upon a time, the princess was rescued by the prince, he was a very helpful young man.

Here are some possible ways the above sentences could be fixed:

Eloise went for a nap; she was very tired as a result of not sleeping the previous day.
Why can't you clean up the dishes? It would be really nice if you could be more courteous.
Once upon a time, the princess was rescued by the prince. He was a very helpful young man.

PRACTICE

Determine whether each of the following is a complete sentence, a sentence fragment, or a run-on sentence.

1. When you turn in your homework.

   _____

2. It is so hot today, I am going to cool off in the pool.

   _____

3. Who are you?

   _____

4. It is high time that someone did something about the problem with the landfill.

   _____

5. Between you and me a great time.

   _____

6. I dare you.

   _____

7. From here to there, from near to far, from high to low.

   _____

8. How I won the big race.

_____

9. Chocolate is delicious, I am going to eat some for a snack.

_____

10. In years past, people did not have access to the instantaneous communication now afforded us by social media.

_____

ANSWERS WITH POSSIBLE CORRECTIONS

1. **Fragment**. _Turn in your homework._ Sometimes you will need to omit wording to change something from a fragment to a sentence.
2. **Run-on**. _It is so hot today; I am going to cool off in the pool._
3. **Complete**.
4. **Complete**.
5. **Fragment**. _You and I had a great time._
6. **Complete**.
7. **Fragment**. _They travel from here to there, from near to far, and from high to low._
8. **Fragment**. _I won the big race._
9. **Run-on**. _Chocolate is delicious, so I am going to eat some for a snack._
10. **Complete**.

Sentence Flow and Structure

To be correct, sentences must be more than complete—they must be logically and consistently written. Here are some major things to look out for as you edit the material on the PSAT Writing and Language Test.

COORDINATION AND SUBORDINATION

Parts of sentences must coordinate and subordinate. In other words, the different parts of sentences must be joined by logical, connecting words as shown in Table 1. Note that the corrections shown are only examples. Each incorrect sentence can be fixed in multiple ways.

Table 1. Coordination and Subordination

Incorrect	Correct
There was a big fire at our house, and we moved into a hotel while the house was being fixed.	There was a big fire at our house, **so** we moved into a hotel while the house was being fixed.
I ordered too much food, and I had to take some home.	**Since** I ordered too much food, I had to take some home.
She won the student council presidency, and most people think she did not win fairly.	She won the student council presidency, **but** most people think she did not win fairly.

LOGICAL COMPARISONS

Make sure that the sentence compares the correct number and types of things so that the comparison is logical as shown in Table 2. Note that the correct comparisons shown are only examples. Each incorrect sentence can be fixed in multiple ways.

Table 2. Logical Comparisons

Incorrect	Correct
I am better at math problems than everybody in my class.	I am better at math problems than everybody **else** in my class.
The coach of the football team is stronger than the baseball team.	The coach of the football team is stronger than the **coach of** the baseball team.
My neighbor's yard is always greener than me.	My neighbor's yard is always greener than **mine.**

MODIFIER PLACEMENT AND CLARITY

Place descriptions in logical spots in the sentence so that the object of discussion is clear. Clarify modifiers if they are vague. Table 3 shows how to correctly place modifiers. Note that the corrections shown are only examples. Each incorrect sentence can be fixed in multiple ways.

Table 3. Modifier Placement and Clarity

Incorrect	Correct
The kitten nuzzled up against my leg, purring softly.	**While purring softly,** the kitten nuzzled up against my leg.
Marie Curie was world-renowned for her scientific expertise, winner of two Nobel Prizes.	Marie Curie, **winner of two Nobel Prizes,** was world-renowned for her scientific expertise.
While hiking through the woods, a large bear crossed my path.	While **I was** hiking through the woods, a large bear crossed my path.
Their group project was unsatisfactory, not having worked together well.	The group project was unsatisfactory, **because the students** had not worked together well.
After learning about the product, the commercial remains unpersuasive.	After learning about the product, **I remain unpersuaded by the commercial.**

WORDINESS

Quality writing demands clear descriptions, but a longer sentence is not necessarily a better one. You must remove repetitive and irrelevant wording, as shown in Table 4.

Table 4. Wordiness

Incorrect	Correct
The meeting is going to last for the duration of 5 hours.	The meeting is going to last for ~~the duration of~~ 5 hours.
Be careful that trespassers, those who may intrude on your property without permission, do not enter your house.	Be careful that trespassers~~, those who may intrude on your property without permission,~~ do not enter your house.
Synecdoche, a literary device in which a part represents the whole or vice versa, is something this author uses frequently.	Fine as is. Since *synecdoche* is not a commonly understood word, clarifying its meaning is helpful.

PARALLELISM

Excellent writing requires more than just the necessary information. The information must be presented in a way that is consistent, flowing, and parallel. See Table 5 for examples of correct parallelism. Note that the corrections shown are only examples. Each incorrect sentence can be fixed in multiple ways.

Table 5. Parallelism

Incorrect	Correct
The blizzard was snowy, had wind, and icy.	The blizzard was snowy, **windy**, and icy.
Drink your milk and eating your food to earn dessert.	Drink your milk and **eat** your food to earn dessert.
When responding to the interview, answer each question accurately and with completeness.	When responding to the interview, answer each question accurately and **completely**.

VERB USE

Be sure that the tense, mood, and voice of the verbs are properly used. See Table 6 for examples of the correct usage of verbs. Note that the corrections shown are only examples. Each incorrect sentence can be fixed in multiple ways.

Table 6. Verb Use

Incorrect	Correct
Susan had been working on her research up to the present day.	Susan **has been** working on her research up to the present day.
The assignment was completed by me.	**I completed** the assignment. (Don't use the passive voice—use the active voice instead.)
If you was here, I would give you your keys.	If you **were** here, I would give you your keys.

PRACTICE

Correct the sentence—not all sentences will need to be fixed. The sentences can be corrected in multiple ways. So when you are reviewing the solutions, make sure that you at least understand why the given solution is correct.

1. When you go to the amusement park, enjoy riding, eating, and to go for a swim.

_____

2. The dishes were washed by Andy.

_____

3. Terri lost her keys, and she couldn't start her car.

_____

4. The year 1999, the last year of the past millennium, was filled with both excitement for and nervous anticipation of what was to come.

_____

5. The conductor of the symphony was better than the other symphony.

_____

6. I caught a fish, I had something for dinner.

_____

7. Pam is an excellent speaker and also quite skillful at writing.

_____

8. To the bathroom, please take the dog outside to go.

_____

9. Once he had completed the computer program, he is ready for the next project.

_____

10. Each year, there is an annual company picnic.

_____

11. Between Bill and Tanner, Bill was the best at playing golf.

_____

12. The weather forecast was for a windy, blustery, and breezy day.

_____

ANSWERS WITH POSSIBLE CORRECTIONS

1. When you go to the amusement park, enjoy riding, eating, and **swimming**.
2. **Andy washed the dishes.**
3. Terri lost her keys, **so** she couldn't start her car.
4. *Fine as is.*
5. The conductor of the symphony was better than the other **symphony's conductor**.
6. **After** I caught a fish, I had something for dinner.
7. Pam is an excellent speaker and also a **quite skilled writer**.
8. **Please take the dog outside to go to the bathroom.**
9. Once he had completed the computer program, he **was** ready for the next project.
10. Each year, there **is a company** picnic. *Omit "annual" since it is repetitive.*
11. Between Bill and Tanner, Bill was **better** at playing golf.
12. The weather forecast was for a **windy day**. *Omit* blustery *and* breezy *since they are repetitive.*

Clarifying Singular and Plural

Matching subjects and verbs would be easy if they were always placed next to one another. On the PSAT, determining correct number agreement among nouns, pronouns, adjectives, and verbs will often be challenging. Table 7 shows some examples of clarifying whether a sentence is singular or plural. Note that the corrections shown are only examples. Each incorrect sentence can be fixed in multiple ways.

Table 7. Clarifying Singular and Plural

Incorrect	Correct
If one is looking for a job, you should find solid references.	If one is looking for a job, **one** should find solid references.
The teacher who has read many good books are instructing my class.	The teacher who has read many good books **is** instructing my class.
Neither John nor Mitchell are going to the mall.	Neither John nor Mitchell **is** going to the mall. *(Both "either/or" and "neither/nor" are considered singular in this sentence, because the nouns "John" and "Mitchell" are singular. When nouns of different numbers are connected by "or/nor," the verb agrees with the noun closest to it.)*
Each present for Sarah were great.	Each present for Sarah **was** great.
Hannah and Caitlin were excited to visit her family.	Hannah and Caitlin were excited to visit **Caitlin's** family. *(The sentence could refer to either one's family—the "her" needs to be clarified.)*
Everyone who is coming to the party are bringing a present.	Everyone who is coming to the party **is** bringing a present. *(Words like* everybody, *anyone, and* nobody *are singular.)*
The group of junior and senior members vote at weekly meetings.	The group of junior and senior members **votes** at weekly meetings. *("Group" is the singular subject, not "members.")*

PRACTICE

Correct the sentence—not all sentences will need to be fixed. The sentences can be corrected in multiple ways. So when you are reviewing the solutions, make sure that you at least understand why the given solution is correct.

1. When the teacher forgets their grading, it is difficult to obtain feedback.

   _____

2. How many euros do it cost to go on the trip?

   _____

3. The lead singer in the band did an excellent job at the concert.

   _____

4. Everybody who is selected by the principal are worthy of recognition.

   _____

5. The girl who left their calculator at school need to be more careful.

   _____

6. The team of athletes have 60 members.

   _____

7. The boat that travels to the Hawaiian Islands are quite colorful.

   _____

8. No matter whether you win or lose, one should be respectful of the officials.

   _____

9. Social media chatting—one of the most frequent ways we now communicate with friends—are sometimes distracting.

   _____

10. Jacob was excited to invite Mary over to his apartment.

   _____

11. The collection of rare coins were highly valued.

   _____

12. Due to the fact that it is a culturally vibrant place to visit, New York and Chicago are must-see destinations.

ANSWERS WITH POSSIBLE CORRECTIONS

1. When the teacher forgets **his or her** grading, it is difficult to obtain feedback.
2. How many euros **does** it cost to go on the trip?
3. *Fine as is.*
4. Everybody who is selected by the principal **is** worthy of recognition.
5. The girl who left **her** calculator at school **needs** to be more careful.
6. The team of athletes **has** 60 members.
7. The boat that travels to the Hawaiian Islands **is** quite colorful.
8. No matter whether you win or lose, **you** should be respectful of the officials.
9. Social media chatting—one of the most frequent ways we now communicate with friends— **is** sometimes distracting.
10. *Fine as is.*
11. The collection of rare coins **was** highly valued.
12. Due to the fact that **they are** culturally vibrant **places** to visit, New York and Chicago are must-see destinations.

Proper Wording

The PSAT tests your fluency with the English language by assessing your skill in picking proper wording. Here are some sentences that properly use some of the most commonly confused words.

> Like any language, English is full of unusual idiomatic expressions. Do not overthink when deciding which expression is correct—trust your instincts.

Accept vs. Except: I **accept** most of his apology, **except** for his claim that he had good intentions all along.

Affect vs. Effect: The **effect** of a great leader is that he or she has the ability to **affect** people's opinions.
Affect *is typically a verb, and* effect *is typically a noun.*

I vs. Me: **I** love it when she talks to **me**.
Use I *as a subject and* me *as an object.*

Its vs. It's: **It's** important, when you purchase a car, that you check **its** warranty.

Less vs. Fewer: There is **less** happiness because there are **fewer** toys.
Less *typically refers to things that CANNOT be easily counted, while* fewer *typically refers to countable items.*

Lie vs. Lay: When you **lie** down on the couch, try to **lay** your head on a soft cushion.
Lie *means "to recline," and* lay *means "to place." An easy way to remember this is both* lie *and* recline *contain the letter "i." Both* lay *and* place *contain the letter "a."*

Than vs. Then: If one team scores more points **than** the other, **then** obviously that team will win.

Than *is for comparisons, and* then *is for time.*

There vs. Their vs. They're: Whenever **they're** on vacation over **there**, they always forget **their** passports.

To vs. Too vs. Two: Since the **two** cows ate **too** much food, they have **to** go to the veterinarian.

Your vs. You're: While **you're** sleeping, try to close **your** eyes.

Who vs. Whom: Who is the person from **whom** you received that message?

Use who *as a subject and* whom *as the object. An easy way to keep this straight is to use* who *when you would use* he *and use* whom *when you would use* him.

Example: He is eating. → Who is eating?

Example: I am talking to him. → To whom am I talking?

Who vs. Which vs. That: The babysitter **who** forgot the toys, **which** she had left in the car, was disappointed **that** she had left them. The toy **that** the child most wanted was not available.

In addition to commonly confused words, watch that you properly use common expressions and prepositions such as those that appear in the following examples.

It is good to do things in moderation.
The traitor was in collaboration with the enemy.
My tutor and I meet on a regular basis.
I will fill out the contract on behalf of my client.
Sometimes it can be helpful to pick answers by process of elimination.
For the good of the group, keep your negative opinions to yourself.
He is of the opinion that this book is well written.

PRACTICE

Choose the better option based on the context of the sentence.

1. I would (**have** or **of**) finished the movie if it had been interesting.

   _____

2. When swimming close to a shark, watch out for (**its** or **it's**) sharp teeth.

   _____

3. The magician made an (**allusion** or **illusion**) to his past awards.

   _____

4.   To (**who** or **whom**) are you sending your test scores?

_____

5.   There are simply (**to** or **too**) many things to do today.

_____

6.   The coach's son is truly a chip (**of** or **off**) the old block.

_____

7.   (**Between** or **Among**) all the U.S. Presidents, Washington was the first.

_____

8.   There was much (**less** or **fewer**) anger between us after we apologized to one another.

_____

9.   They will finish the house once (**their** or **they're**) paid.

_____

10. Dogs (**which** or **that**) bark quite a bit keep me up at night.

_____

ANSWERS

1. **have**	4. **whom**	7. **Among**	10. **that**
2. **its**	5. **too**	8. **less**	
3. **allusion**	6. **off**	9. **they're**	

Punctuation

On the PSAT, punctuation is highly emphasized. Although proper English uses many specific punctuation rules, here are some essential guidelines to help you succeed on the PSAT.

COMMAS

The rules concerning proper comma usage could fill an entire chapter of a grammar book! Do not worry, though. Table 8 gives you the general guidelines to the most commonly used comma rules tested by the PSAT.

Table 8. Commas

Appropriate Use	General Guideline
When I want to go to sleep, I have a glass of warm milk.	Separate a phrase (dependent clause) when it comes before a complete sentence (independent clause).
My favorite television show was going to be on, so I recorded it.	Join two complete sentences when there is a transition word, like *so, and,* or *but.*
The grandfather clock in the living room, which was twenty years old, had a delightful chime.	Separate extra information (parenthetical phrases) from the rest of the sentence.
In order to bake the cake, be sure you have eggs, sugar, flour, and milk.	Separate items in a list with commas.*
The plane that just took off is already at 20,000 feet in altitude.	Don't use commas to separate parts of a sentence if everything in the sentence is needed to make it clear and logical. (In this case, clarifying that is was the plane "that just took off" is necessary in order to specify the subject).
The signing of the Declaration of Independence was truly one of the most significant events in early American history.	Just because a sentence is long doesn't mean that it needs a comma. Look more at the structure of the sentence than at its length.
A Nobel Prize winning author, Toni Morrison has written several novels with epic themes and vivid imagery.	A clarifying phrase (appositive) can sometimes come after a subject, but in this case it comes before. A comma is required to separate the subject from its description.

*The SAT has traditionally preferred using the Oxford comma, i.e., having a comma between the second-to-last and last items in a list. Since there is not a universally accepted rule about whether the Oxford comma should be used, it is extremely unlikely that the PSAT would include a test question about it.

SEMICOLONS

Many students are not sure when semicolons should be used. By learning the general guidelines for semicolon usage shown in Table 9, you will have an advantage over other students taking the PSAT.

Table 9. Semicolons

Appropriate Use	General Guideline
It was a beautiful day outside; we decided to go for a long hike.	You can use a semicolon to separate two complete, related sentences.
We need to mail invitations to Brooklyn, New York; Chicago, Illinois; and Los Angeles, California.	Use a semicolon to separate items in a list when each item has a comma within it.

COLONS

Table 10 lists some general guidelines concerning the appropriate usage of colons.

Table 10. Colons

Appropriate Use	General Guideline
Be sure to bring the following items to the PSAT: a watch, pencils, and a calculator.	Use a colon after a complete sentence to set off a list.
If you are going to cook paella, don't forget the key ingredient: saffron.	Use a colon after a complete sentence to set off a clarification.

DASHES

Table 11 lists some general guidelines concerning the appropriate usage of dashes.

Table 11. Dashes

Appropriate Use	General Guideline
Don't exceed the speed limit—it's a speed maximum, not a speed minimum.	Although other punctuation can often work (in this case a colon could work instead of the dash) the dash can provide variety in your writing when you need to indicate an interruption or change of thought.
She didn't ground me—I was completely shocked—but she did take away my phone for a week.	A dash can be used to interrupt a sentence and provide a change of voice.
Paris—home of the Louvre, Eiffel Tower, and Picasso Museum—is famous for its culture.	Dashes can set off a parenthetical phrase. If you start with a dash at the beginning of the phrase, you need to use a dash at the end of it for consistency.

APOSTROPHES

Table 12 lists some general guidelines concerning the appropriate usage of apostrophes.

Table 12. Apostrophes

Appropriate Use	General Guideline
The cow's field was covered with grass.	Use an apostrophe before the "s" to indicate that a singular entity possesses something.
My classmates' reunion was not to be missed.	Use an apostrophe after the "s" to indicate that a plural entity possesses something.
When they're running quickly, they need to monitor their hydration.	Use an apostrophe to indicate a contraction with pronouns (*they're, it's, you're, who's*). Do not use an apostrophe to indicate possession (*their, its, your, whose*).
The children's museum has a number of interactive exhibits.	Use an apostrophe before the "s" to indicate possession after an already-plural noun.

PRACTICE

Pick whichever choice, (A) or (B), is better suited given the context.

1. Phillip, Chief of the Police (A) Department, or (B) Department enjoyed serving his community.

   _____

2. Send me a (A) postcard, or (B) postcard; I want to hear about your trip.

   _____

3. (A) Stop we or (B) Stop—we need to ask for directions.

   _____

4. Drivers who are (A) well-rested typically or (B) well-rested, typically have fewer accidents.

   _____

5. My girlfriend told me what she wants me to wear to the (A) prom; a tuxedo or (B) prom: a tuxedo that matches her dress.

   _____

6. Their high school is not as good as (A) your's or (B) yours.

   _____

7. When I am on vacation, I love to watch Channel (A) 8, the sports station; Channel 54, the music video network; and Channel 63, the science fiction station. or (B) 8, the sports station, Channel 54, the music video network, and Channel 63, the science fiction station.

   _____

8. I am looking forward to doing the following this (A) summer, catching or (B) summer: catching up on sleep, reading good books, and going to the pool.

   _____

9. Please pick up (A) Ryan's or (B) Ryans video games.

   _____

10. To (A) Dylan fishing or (B) Dylan, fishing was everything.

    _____

ANSWERS

1. **A**	4. **A**	7. **A**	10. **B**
2. **B**	5. **B**	8. **B**	
3. **B**	6. **B**	9. **A**	

12 PSAT WRITING AND LANGUAGE STRATEGIES

1. Take Your Time

Most students will have no trouble finishing the PSAT Writing and Language Test. Although your fellow test takers may be rushing along, do not get caught up in that. If you are going to edit well, you must be very thorough.

2. Pace Yourself to Finish When Time Is Called

It is much more likely that you will pick up on a grammar issue if you do the questions one time well as opposed to rushing to the end so that you can double-check your work. You will have nearly 9 minutes to work on each passage. So you may want to plan on checking your pace at the end of each passage so that you do not work too quickly or too slowly.

3. Underline and Circle Key Information as You Read Long Questions

If you miss even one word on one of the writing and language questions that actually asks you a direct question, you may very well miss the entire point of what is being asked. Take advantage of the fact that you can write all over the test. Underline and circle anything that seems especially important as you read through the questions.

4. Try to "Hear" as You Read by Silently Mouthing Things

One of the best ways to edit a paper is to hear what is written as opposed to only reading the words. While there is no substitute for knowing the fundamental rules of grammar, silently mouthing what is written will help you pick up on a variety of things, such as necessary pauses for punctuation, parallel phrasing, and proper idiom usage. Hearing the words will help you tap into your intuitive knowledge about what sounds right in the English language. You simply need to answer the question correctly; you do not need to justify why you have chosen your answer. Do be careful that while hearing the words, you are not too casual in your tone. The PSAT writing is formal. So the style may, at times, differ from the way you may informally talk. For example, "I knew it was she" is correct while "I knew it was her" is not. While the writing you encounter will be more formal, it will not be stuffy. For example, you should say, "The teacher tried to stop the fight," as opposed to "The teacher endeavored to terminate the belligerence."

5. Think About the Meaning

Many writing errors will involve small-scale issues, like punctuation and subject-verb agreement. Other errors will involve large-scale issues, like conforming to a given writing objective or making an appropriate transition. As a result, you must focus not just on looking for minor grammar errors, but also on carefully considering how you can make the writing as logical as possible.

6. Consider Relevant Context

Most grammar errors are not problematic when considered in isolation. Consider the surrounding context when looking for bigger-picture problems, like logical transitions, tense agreement, and tone consistency. When in doubt about whether a selection is consistent with the rest of the passage, take the time to check out the selection.

7. Maybe Read the Passage Through Once Before Answering Questions

With nearly 9 minutes available per passage and a little under 1 minute per question, you should have plenty of time to work through the problems. Rather than having time at the end of the Writing and Language Test to double-check and possibly do nothing, you can instead use your time to read the passage with an eye on its overall flow and meaning. This will enable you to do well on questions involving big-picture analysis of the passage and proper transitions.

8. Try to Create Your Own Answer Before Looking at the Choices

All of the choices on the PSAT writing will be well written, and many will be quite persuasive. Prior to jumping into the choices, do your best to come up with a general idea of what you think the answer should be. This will put you in control rather than letting the test control you. Sometimes, it may be difficult to formulate an answer without considering the choices. If and when this happens, be open-minded as you carefully evaluate your options.

9. Do Not Hesitate to Come Back to Questions

If you are having difficulty determining the answer to a question, skip it. Let your subconscious mind take over solving the question while you consciously move on to other problems. While you are working through the other problems, your subconscious mind will likely piece together what makes the most sense on the problem you skipped. Then with fresh eyes, you can come back to the questions you previously skipped. You will likely find the correct answer more easily than before.

10. Use Similarities Among Answers to Eliminate Choices

If you have a multiple-choice question and the following choices, what is the answer?

(A) &
(B) &
(C) @
(D) &

The answer is choice (C) because it is different from the other options. Pretend you have a PSAT writing and language question with choices like these:

(A) Additionally
(B) Also
(C) In contrast
(D) Moreover

You can use the similarities among the answers to eliminate possibilities. "Additionally," "also," and "moreover" mean that you are giving further discussion or examples along the same lines as before. "In contrast" means you have something that is the opposite of what came previously. So the answer would be choice (C). This technique can be particularly helpful when sorting out wordiness, punctuation, transitions, and other issues. Use this technique as a useful supplement to thinking through the question, not as your primary approach.

11. If You Must Guess, Be Smart About It

There is no penalty for guessing on questions as there was in the past. So be certain you have filled in an answer for every question. Instead of picking a random answer, keep the following tips in mind:

- The PSAT will often have a few of the same answer choices in a row. Do not avoid picking an answer choice simply because you have used it on the previous question.
- "NO CHANGE" has just as much of a chance of being correct as the other options. Do not feel that you must make edits to every single question.
- These questions do not have tricks or gimmicks. If you are picking an answer because of some trick (e.g., thinking the PSAT will always prefer shorter answers), you will be incorrect. If you pick an answer because it represents well-written English, you will be right.
- Once you have made a thoughtful decision, don't second-guess. There is only so much you can do—read the context, consider the answers carefully, and pick the best option. If you have done these things, be comfortable picking your answer and moving on.

12. Realize That These Are Grammar Rules, Not Merely Preferences

You have likely had a teacher who has had certain pet peeves about how you should write your essays. Maybe you have had a teacher who insisted you use only the formal, third-person voice in your essays. Maybe your teacher marked off points for starting sentences with "but" or "because." The PSAT will not care about such things. Any issues you encounter will be clear problems, the answers to which are based on widespread English practice, not on the personal preferences of particular editors. As a result, do not overthink what you encounter on the PSAT Writing and Language Test.

PUTTING IT ALL TOGETHER: APPLYING GRAMMAR CONCEPTS AND STRATEGIES

Let's use this short writing sample to review how you can use the strategies discussed above to answer questions on the Writing and Language Test as correctly as possible.

The College Essay

When applying ❶ to colleges you will need to write at least one application essay. In your essay, it is critical that you speak with an authentic voice to express what makes you an interesting person who will contribute ❷ to the overall atmosphere of the college. Most of the time, you will have a few essay prompts from which to choose; sometimes you can even make your own topic. ❸ When your schedule allows you to do so, go ahead and begin the brainstorming process.

1. (A) NO CHANGE
   (B) to colleges: you will
   (C) to colleges; you will
   (D) to colleges, you will

2. (A) NO CHANGE
   (B) for the overall atmosphere at
   (C) on the overall atmosphere with
   (D) through the overall atmosphere in

3. If the author wishes to express that readers should begin the college essay right away, which choice would be most effective?

   (A) NO CHANGE
   (B) If you are interested in pursuing higher education,
   (C) As soon as you have a chance to review the essay topics,
   (D) Once you have decided what you are interested in studying in college,

Solutions

1. **(D)** Punctuation will be a major focus of the writing questions. You must consider the context surrounding the underlined portion to determine what sort of punctuation works the best. In this case, an introductory phrase, "When applying to colleges," begins the sentence. Then an independent clause follows, "You will need to write at least one application essay." To join the introductory dependent clause to the main independent clause, a comma is required. Using a colon or semicolon would be correct only if a complete sentence came right before the punctuation mark. The original option does not have any needed break. So the correct answer is choice (D).

2. **(A)** This question involves determining the correct prepositions (words like "to," "of," "from") based on the particular situation. The English language would be much easier if it consistently used prepositions and idioms. Like nearly all languages, however, English has exception after exception that truly fluent English speakers know by heart. The underlined portion is fine as originally written because you "contribute to" something, not "contribute for," "contribute on," or "contribute through" something. Additionally, it is appropriate to say that a physical setting has an "atmosphere of" something—not that it has an "atmosphere at," an "atmosphere with," or an "atmosphere in." You will overthink questions like these if you seek to justify your answer in the same way you can logically justify a more straightforward issue, like subject-verb agreement. The fact of the matter is that particular uses of prepositions are correct because they are commonly accepted as such.

3. **(C)** A great approach on a question like this is to underline and circle the key words as you read through the question. That way, you will be certain that you fully understand what is being asked and do not make any careless mistakes. This question is asking you to pick that choice most consistent with the author's belief that readers should begin the college essay process sooner rather than later. Although all of the answer choices are in some way related to the college application, choice (C) is the only one that focuses on the need to start the essay process quickly, encouraging readers to begin writing their essays immediately after they review the essay topics. Choice (A) does not express urgency. Instead, it suggests that readers begin the essay writing passage when it is convenient for them. Choices (B) and (D) focus more on the reader's general educational goals and interests rather than highlight the need to begin the essay quickly as the question requests. Grammatically, all of the options are perfectly fine. However, choice (C) best accomplishes what the question asks.

PRACTICE PASSAGES WITH EXPLANATIONS

On the PSAT Writing and Reading Test, you will see 4 passages. Each one will be from a different content area: careers, history/social sciences, humanities, and science. One passage from each of these categories is presented below, giving you the same number of passages/questions you will have on the actual PSAT Writing and Reading Test. After each passage, detailed solutions to the questions follow.

Electroconvulsive Therapy

Despite its sinister and somewhat Draconian reputation, electroconvulsive therapy ❶ (ECT) is making a rather magnificent return in the treatment of chronic clinical depression. Like many of its pharmaceutical counterparts, the exact physiological mechanism responsible for ECT's alleviation of the symptoms of depression remains fairly elusive, ❷ and its results are inarguably remarkable. The idea itself—which in many ways seems like the fever dream of a 19th-century medical quack—was in fact spawned from the careful observation by two Italian physicians in the 1930s of patients who suffered from both depression and epilepsy. Doctors Lucio Bini and Ugo Cerletti ❸ noted that with, startling consistency, many of their patients experienced an extended reprieve from their depression symptoms following a grand mal seizure. Concluding that seizures and depression were, somehow, pathologically incompatible—and after some extensive animal testing—the two cautiously began experimenting ❹ in the treatment of severely depressed patients.

1. Should the underlined phrase be kept or deleted?

   (A) Kept, because it defines the term immediately before it.
   (B) Kept, because it clarifies the abbreviation that will be used throughout the passage.
   (C) Deleted, because it provides an unnecessary parenthetical reference.
   (D) Deleted, because it restates an acronym that is widely present elsewhere in the passage.

2. (A) NO CHANGE
   (B) since
   (C) with
   (D) but

3. (A) NO CHANGE
   (B) noted that, with startling, consistency many
   (C) noted that, with startling consistency, many
   (D) noted that with startling consistency many

4. (A) NO CHANGE
   (B) for the treating on
   (C) of the treatment for
   (D) to the treating with

The procedural sophistication of ECT has evolved tremendously in the past 25 years. Innovations in muscle relaxants have eliminated the violent, involuntary spasms that contributed to ECT's notorious character. **⑤** The administration of ECT which once required heavy restraints and at least six orderlies to prevent the patient from causing harm to himself or others can now be carried out by as few as two medical **⑥** professionals: one to operate the equipment, another to monitor the patient's vitals and electroencephalogram. Theories seeking to explain the physiological cause for ECT's impressive outcomes **⑦** is limited by the impossibility of directly observing a patient's brain activity during and immediately following treatment. However, the prevailing consensus suggests that the induced electrical current stimulates a release of certain neurotransmitters in the brain—perhaps endorphins—and temporarily **⑧** overwhelm the chemical imbalances of depression.

More contentious than ECT's neurological mechanism **⑨** are their potential to produce long-term or permanent results. Despite its essentially immediate results following treatment, roughly half of the patients who undergo an ECT relapse within six months. Some proponents of the therapy have suggested that this is in part due to the severity and chronicity of the depression typical of patients following a course of treatment

5. (A) NO CHANGE
   (B) The administration of ECT—which once required heavy restraints and at least six orderlies to prevent the patient from causing harm to himself or others—can now
   (C) The administration of ECT; which once required heavy restraints and at least six orderlies to prevent the patient from causing harm to themselves or others, can now
   (D) The administration of ECT, which once required heavy restraints, and at least six orderlies to prevent the patient from causing harm to themselves or others can now

6. (A) NO CHANGE
   (B) professionals one to operate the equipment, another
   (C) professionals—one to operate the equipment another
   (D) professionals, one to operate the equipment another

7. (A) NO CHANGE
   (B) is limiting
   (C) are limiting
   (D) are limited

8. (A) NO CHANGE
   (B) overwhelms
   (C) overwhelming
   (D) provides an overwhelming effect on

9. (A) NO CHANGE
   (B) is their
   (C) are its
   (D) is its

in ECT; ❿ scientists are hopeful that ECT will, in the not too distant future, provide a long-term solution for most types of mental illness. Perhaps one day—with its surprising efficacy and minimal side effects—ECT will become as commonplace as the pharmacological giants Prozac and Zoloft in the treatment of depression. However, until the skeptical public perception of ECT catches up with its modern medical reality, we can do little more than ⓫ speculate.

10. Which choice would give an optimistic and logical clarification of the first part of the sentence that is supported by the information in this paragraph?

(A) NO CHANGE
(B) there is a scientific consensus that further experiments will demonstrate that ECT is a lasting cure for victims of the most intense depression.
(C) it is possible that the treatment will prove more effective in the long term for patients suffering from milder cases of depression.
(D) many researchers contend that due to this ineffectiveness, ECT should be abandoned in all its forms in favor of therapeutic approaches.

11. (A) NO CHANGE
(B) convert.
(C) venture.
(D) optimize.

Solutions

ANSWER KEY

1.	**B**	4.	**A**	7.	**D**	10.	**C**
2.	**D**	5.	**B**	8.	**B**	11.	**A**
3.	**C**	6.	**A**	9.	**D**		

ANSWERS EXPLAINED

1. **(B)** Later in the passage, the author uses "ECT" to refer to electroconvulsive therapy. If this underlined portion were deleted, the meaning of the abbreviation would not be clear. Choice (A) is not correct because it provides an abbreviation, not a definition. Choices (C) and (D) are incorrect because without including this abbreviation in the passage, the reader would be confused by its subsequent use throughout the essay.

2. **(D)** The word "but" is the appropriate transition. The sentence contains a contrast—scientists do not know exactly how ECTs work, but they do know that the results are remarkable. The transitions in choices (A), (B), and (C) do not indicate a contrast.

3. **(C)** It is best to place the breaks around the clarifying parenthetical phrase "with startling consistency." The sentence can function as a logical sentence without this phrase, so the phrase can be set aside, although it does provide an important clarification. Choices (A) and (B) break up the phrase "with startling consistency," and choice (D) does not have any needed pauses.

4. **(A)** Choice (A) uses the correct prepositions given the context since it is proper to say "experimenting in." Additionally, this choice uses the proper wording of "treatment." Choices (B) and (D) use improper prepositions ("for" and "to") to introduce the phrase, and they also use "treating" instead of "treatment." Choice (C) uses the incorrect preposition since it is improper to say "began experimenting of" something.

5. **(B)** Choice (B) uses dashes to set apart the long parenthetical phrase from the rest of the sentence. The sentence can function without this parenthetical phrase, so the phrase can be placed aside. In addition, since "patient" is singular, "himself" must be used in order to have singular numerical agreement. The word "themselves," although often used in conversation in such a context, does not work in this situation because it is plural. Choice (A) does not set aside the parenthetical phrase. Choices (C) and (D) improperly use "themselves" instead of "himself."

6. **(A)** Choice (A) uses the colon to set off a list that clarifies the medical professionals used to carry out the procedure. Choice (B) does not have a pause before the list. Choices (C) and (D) do not have a comma separating the two items listed.

7. **(D)** Choice (D) correctly matches the plural subject of "theories" by using "are." This answer also uses the proper verb since it is correct to say "are limited by" instead of "are limiting by." Choices (A) and (B) use the singular "is." Choice (C) is incorrect since saying "they are limiting by" is improper while saying "they are limited by" is proper.

8. **(B)** "Overwhelms" matches up with the singular subject of "current." Choice (A) is for a plural subject. Choice (C) does not maintain the parallel structure with "suggests" and "stimulates" from earlier in the sentence. Choice (D) is too wordy.

9. **(D)** "Is" matches with the singular subject of "potential," and "its" matches with the singular noun of "ECT." Choices (A) and (B) both improperly use the plural "their." Choices (A) and (C) improperly use the plural "are."

10. **(C)** Prior to this statement, the author gives a hypothetical explanation as to why so many of the patients who undergo ECT go back to having the illness they previously had—the fact that so many ECT patients had severe, long-term depression, skewing the results toward negativity. If ECT is used on patients who have more mild depression, perhaps research will demonstrate that ECT is much more effective. Choices (A) and (B) are incorrect because the paragraph indicates that researchers have found this treatment does not work for many patients since so many relapse. Choice (D) is not correct because although many patients relapse, some do benefit, making this option far too pessimistic.

11. **(A)** The author does not know whether ECT will one day become as widespread as other mental illness treatments. Therefore, the author can only "speculate" (guess) about what might happen in the future. The author is not going to "convert" anything from one form to another, making choice (B) incorrect. If choice (C) had said "venture a guess," it could work. However, the word "venture" alone is insufficient. Choice (D) is incorrect because although scientists might want to optimize their understanding, they can hardly do so given the status of public perception.

Summer Break

Why is it that our modern schools still operate on a preindustrial calendar? How many students need to spend three months of the year helping the family with the crop harvest? ❶ <u>Only about two percent of the U.S. population is involved in agriculture.</u> The modern school calendar should be updated to reflect our modern lifestyles, and summer break should be ended in favor of several longer breaks throughout the school year.

❷ <u>Teachers spend approximately two months, out of the nine-month school year on reviewing the material from the last academic year.</u> If school were operated on a year-round basis, student retention of material would be strengthened since it is much easier to forget material over a three-month break ❸ <u>then</u> over a two-week one. Material retention is especially vital for subjects like math and foreign language in which more advanced units will not make sense without a sound basis in the earlier material. ❹ <u>However,</u> if students have more frequent breaks from the rigors of school, they are less likely to burn out. This will help minimize behavioral issues due to student fatigue and maximize student learning since students will be more physically rejuvenated throughout the academic year.

Some will argue that students need time to do sports and camps over the ❺ <u>summer why</u> can't camps and sports adjust to take advantage

1. Which choice most specifically builds upon the argument of the previous sentence?

   (A) NO CHANGE
   (B) Not very many students are familiar with raising crops themselves, having familiarity with food only from groceries and restaurants.
   (C) Three months is far too long to spend farming; instead, time could be better focused on academic learning.
   (D) Although many students might do gardening as a hobby, few students plan on pursuing agriculture as their primary career.

2. (A) NO CHANGE.
   (B) Teachers spend approximately two months, out of the nine-month school year, on reviewing the material, from the last academic year.
   (C) Teachers spend, approximately two months out of the nine-month school year on reviewing the material from the last academic year.
   (D) Teachers spend approximately two months out of the nine-month school year on reviewing the material from the last academic year.

3. (A) NO CHANGE
   (B) than
   (C) moreover
   (D) for

4. (A) NO CHANGE
   (B. Consequently,
   (C) Additionally,
   (D) On the other hand,

5. (A) NO CHANGE
   (B) summer. Why
   (C) summer, why
   (D) summer, why,

of breaks throughout the year? ❻ It makes no sense that camps cannot shift to accommodate the needs of the new school calendar. Some sports and activities, like football, do benefit from having summer to prepare for the fall season. ❼ Other sports and activities however, are primarily done in the winter like basketball. Basketball players could greatly benefit from having a 2–3 week break from academics to focus on their practice. Also, not all students are financially able to benefit from being able to do summer camps and the like. ❽ When he or she is not in school, they are not going to academic enrichment camps; odds are, they are spending time at home watching television and letting their minds deteriorate. For students who cannot afford summer enrichment, a year-round school schedule would be especially helpful in keeping them from falling ❾ from their peers.

6. The writer is considering deleting the underlined sentence. Should the sentence be kept or deleted?

(A) Kept, because it elaborates on the argument of the previous sentence.
(B) Kept, because it provides specific details that demonstrate how camps will adjust to the new circumstances.
(C) Deleted, because it contradicts information presented elsewhere in the passage.
(D) Deleted, because it unnecessarily repeats the idea presented in the previous sentence.

7. (A) NO CHANGE
(B) Other sports and activities, however, are primarily done in the winter like basketball.
(C) Other sports and activities, however, are primarily done in the winter, like basketball.
(D) Other sports and activities however are primarily done in the winter, like basketball.

8. (A) NO CHANGE
(B) When he or she is not in school, he or she is not
(C) When they are not in school, they are not
(D) When one is not in school, one is not

9. (A) NO CHANGE
(B) down
(C) beneath
(D) behind

10 [1] When adults have full-time jobs, they take periodic breaks during the year. [2] By having a year-round school calendar, students will be preparing for the real-world schedules they will face as grown-ups. [3] It is time that our society moves from a calendar based on a nineteenth-century schedule to one based on a twenty-first–century schedule and shifts to year-round school.

10. The writer would like to insert this sentence into the paragraph.

"Doing so helps them refresh and recharge so that they are able to perform their occupational tasks well when they return."

What would be the best placement of this sentence?

(A) Before sentence 1
(B) Before sentence 2
(C) Before sentence 3
(D) After sentence 3

11. Suppose the author presents her paper to her colleagues. They argue that, rather than eliminating summer break in favor of the same amount of vacation throughout the year, the school board should merely add hours of instruction to the school year in order to improve academic performance. The author could best dispute this counterargument by citing information about which two states from the table?

State*	Hours of Elementary School Instructional Time in a Year	Average SAT Reading Score	Average SAT Math Score
California	840	501	516
Florida	900	496	498
New York	900	484	499
Texas	1,260	484	505
Massachusetts	900	512	526

*Sources: *http://www.centerforpubliceducation.org/Main-Menu/Organizing-a-school/Time-in-school-How-does-the-US-compare http://www.publicagendaarchives.org/charts/state-state-sat-and-act-scores*

(A) California and Florida
(B) Massachusetts and New York
(C) Texas and Massachusetts
(D) New York and California

Solutions

ANSWER KEY

1.	**A**	4.	**C**	7.	**C**	10.	**B**
2.	**D**	5.	**B**	8.	**C**	11.	**C**
3.	**B**	6.	**D**	9.	**D**		

ANSWERS EXPLAINED

1. **(A)** The previous sentence rhetorically argues that since very few people are involved in agriculture, building the school calendar around the old agricultural economy does not make sense. Choice (A) most specifically builds on this argument by giving statistical evidence in support. Choice (B) is specific but does not directly relate to the argument. Choice (C) repeats information from the previous sentence. Although choice (D) is relevant to the argument, it is not as specific as choice (A).

2. **(D)** Choice (D) deletes the unnecessary comma. Just because this is a long sentence does not mean that a comma is required. Choices (A) and (B) break up the phrase "two months out of the nine-month school year." Choice (C) breaks up the phrase "spend approximately." This is a good example of a problem where quietly mouthing the words will help you determine when a pause is needed.

3. **(B)** The word "than" properly compares how it is easier to forget something over a longer break *than* over a shorter one. Choice (A) incorrectly uses "then," which refers to time, not comparison. Choice (C), "moreover," is synonymous with "also." Choice (D), "for," provides more of a direct connection rather than a separation between compared terms. So out of the options, choice (B) is the only one that can be used in this context to provide a comparison.

4. **(C)** The word "additionally" correctly indicates that this sentence builds upon the argument in the previous sentences. Choice (B), "consequently," indicates a cause-and-effect relationship. Choice (A) "however," and choice (D), "on the other hand," both indicate a contrast.

5. **(B)** Without a period between the two independent clauses (i.e., complete sentences), this is a run-on sentence. All of the other choices would form run-ons because two independent clauses are joined by either nothing, as in choice (A), or by a comma, as in choices (C) and (D). A comma without a conjunction, like "but" or "and," is insufficient to join two independent clauses.

6. **(D)** The previous sentence rhetorically asks, "Why can't camps and sports adjust to take advantage of breaks throughout the year?" This is the same general point made by the underlined sentence, so the underlined sentence should be deleted in order to avoid repetition. Choices (A) and (B) both incorrectly leave this redundant sentence in the paragraph. Choice (C) is incorrect because the idea in the underlined portion is repetitive, not contradictory.

7. **(C)** Choice (C) properly sets aside a transitional word, "however," and a clarifying phrase, "like basketball," with commas since the sentence would function as a complete and logical sentence without these two insertions. Choices (A) and (B) do not have a needed pause before "like basketball." Choice (D) does not set aside the word "however."

8. **(C)** "They" correctly refers to the "students," which is plural. Choices (A) and (B) both use "he or she," which would be fine if the paragraph was referring to each student as an individual. However, the paragraph is referring to them as a group. Choice (D) uses "one," which is also singular.

9. **(D)** The phrase "falling behind" refers to people's failure to keep up with something, which is applicable to academic progress in this sentence. Falling "from," "down," or "beneath" indicate falling in a physical sense.

10. **(B)** This sentence should be placed before sentence 2 because it clarifies how taking periodic breaks helps adults perform better in their jobs. Choice (A) is not correct because the phrase "doing so" would lack the intended meaning without sentence 1 coming beforehand. Choices (C) and (D) are incorrect because "occupational tasks" more appropriately refers to the work of adults, not the schooling of children.

11. **(C)** Comparing the SAT results of Texas and Massachusetts would best counter this argument. Texas provides significantly more hours of instructional time than Massachusetts, yet the average SAT reading and math scores for students in Texas are lower than those of students in Massachusetts. The data for the states in choices (A), (B), and (D) are all too similar to one another with respect to the hours of elementary school instructional time, making citing any of these pairs unhelpful to countering the argument.

The Sur-Surrealist

Easily one of the most distinctive painters associated with the surrealist movement of the early 20th century, Frida Kahlo ❶ consequently insisted adamantly throughout her career that she was by no means a surrealist herself. It is true enough that she had personal contact with many brazen members of the movement, and her work is ❷ soundly featured as a triumph in any compilation study of surrealist imagery. However, Kahlo sought to distinguish herself from artists such as Dali and de Chirico, ❸ affirming that rather than painting from dreams or imagination she explored exclusively her own reality.

The infamous social eccentricities of her surrealist counterparts are, perhaps, partly responsible for why so many scholars have too frequently taken ❹ Kahlos self-proclaimed distinction so lightly—a superficial glance at her work exposes a world where skyscrapers erupt from volcanoes, electric lamps possess umbilical cords, and ❺ a shattered Roman Column is the thing which replaces the human spine. These are, one might easily suppose, undeniably the stuff of dreams. However, a more ❻ biased evaluation of the works coupled with a little knowledge of Kahlo's life history may help to reveal how such fantastical and, often, unsettling images became intertwined with Kahlo's personal reality. So inward was her artistic focus that she often dismissed the work, saying that her paintings were "all small and unimportant, with the same personal subjects that only appeal to me

1. (A) NO CHANGE
   (B) moreover
   (C) accordingly
   (D) nonetheless

2. Which choice best expresses the great renown of Kahlo's work in a tone consistent with the context?

   (A) NO CHANGE
   (B) somewhat respected by scholars
   (C) plainly disregarded as mediocrity
   (D) really liked a lot

3. (A) NO CHANGE
   (B) affirming that, rather than painting from dreams or imagination she
   (C) affirming that, rather than painting from dreams or imagination, she
   (D) affirming that rather than painting, from dreams or imagination, she

4. (A) NO CHANGE
   (B) Kahlo's self proclaimed
   (C) Kahlo's self-proclaimed
   (D) Kahlos' self-proclaimed

5. (A) NO CHANGE
   (B) by a shattered Roman Column is the human spine substituted.
   (C) the human spine was being replaced with a destroyed Roman Column.
   (D) the human spine is replaced with a shattered Roman column.

6. (A) NO CHANGE
   (B) sober
   (C) troublesome
   (D) confusing

and nobody else." **7** Kahlo was in fact able to create images that were rather physically large in size.

The fantastical elements of her paintings are invariably symbolic of Kahlo's personal experiences; this distinguishes her, to some degree, from so many surrealists **8** who sought to distort reality for the sheer sake of invention. It is well known that throughout her life, Kahlo suffered tremendously both physically and emotionally. At the age of eighteen, Kahlo was involved in a bus accident that left her with significant permanent damage to her spinal column and reproductive organs, and caused frequent relapses into chronic pain throughout her life. Emotionally, the injuries caused further distress later in life when Kahlo suffered three consecutive miscarriages, the last of which left her completely sterile. Kahlo's embattled relationship with her husband, artist **9** Diego Rivera was another source of inner turmoil: some of Kahlo's most despairing works can be traced to the time of their brief divorce in 1939. Recurring symbols of these **10** tribulations—such as blood, dry and cracked landscapes, and even orthopedic corsets—are prevalent throughout her work, though their correlation should seem perfectly natural to one familiar with Kahlo's life and her need to express a synthesis of her emotional and physical pain. To the untrained eye, such juxtapositions may easily betoken the randomness of a **11** weird and odd dream.

7. Which choice would best express a view that is contradictory toward Kahlo's sentiments about her own paintings?

(A) NO CHANGE
(B) Kahlo was greatly mistaken in supposing her powerful images would resonate with no one but herself.
(C) Kahlo is a shining example of an artist who looked to her own inner thoughts for creative inspiration.
(D) Kahlo was truly despondent about her personal abilities, much like many perfectionists have a tendency to be.

8. Should the underlined portion be kept or deleted?

(A) Kept, because it provides a helpful clarification.
(B) Kept, because it details the experiences of the surrealists.
(C) Deleted, because it is irrelevant to the focus of the paragraph.
(D) Deleted, because it shifts the discussion to other artists instead of Kahlo.

9. (A) NO CHANGE
(B) Diego Rivera, was another source of inner turmoil, some of
(C) Diego Rivera was another source of inner turmoil. Some of
(D) Diego Rivera, was another source of inner turmoil; some of

10. (A) NO CHANGE
(B) tribulations—such as blood, dry and cracked landscapes, and even orthopedic corsets, are prevalent
(C) tribulations, such as blood dry and cracked landscapes, and even orthopedic corsets, are prevalent
(D) tribulations: such as blood, dry and cracked landscapes, and even orthopedic corsets, are prevalent

11. (A) NO CHANGE
(B) pitiful
(C) surreal
(D) evil

Solutions

ANSWER KEY

1.	**D**	4.	**C**	7.	**B**	10.	**A**
2.	**A**	5.	**D**	8.	**A**	11.	**C**
3.	**C**	6.	**B**	9.	**D**		

ANSWERS EXPLAINED

1. **(D)** "Nonetheless" is used to show a contrast between the fact that Frida Kahlo is considered a surrealist by society yet she did not consider herself a surrealist. Choice (A), "consequently," and choice (C), "accordingly," show cause and effect. Choice (B), "moreover," is synonymous with "also." This is a good example where you can use the similarities among choices (A) and (C) to eliminate them.

2. **(A)** "Great renown" refers to significant respect, and stating that something is "soundly . . . a triumph" best captures the feeling of respect for Kahlo's work. Choice (B) does not go far enough in its praise. Choice (C) is far too negative based on the context. Choice (D) is inconsistent with the tone since "really liked a lot" is far too informal.

3. **(C)** Choice (C) properly uses commas to surround the parenthetical phrase that contrasts with the rest of the sentence. Choice (A) has no pauses at all. Choice (B) has only one comma at the start of the parenthetical phrase and does not have a comma at the end of the phrase. Choice (D) has a comma that interrupts the phrase "painting from dreams."

4. **(C)** Kahlo is a singular person who possesses the "distinction," so there should be an apostrophe before the "s." In addition, "self-proclaimed" is an adjective describing the distinction, so it should be hyphenated. Choice (A) does not show possession. Choice (B) lacks hyphenation. Choice (D) places the comma where it would be placed with a plural noun.

5. **(D)** Choice (D) puts the words in the most logical order, making clear that the human spine is replaced by the column in the painting. It also correctly lowercases "column." Choices (A) and (C) are too wordy, and Choice (B) is inverted.

6. **(B)** "Sober" in this context means "serious" and "careful." This is the best fit given that the essay argues that if one gets past the initial notion that Kahlo's paintings are merely the stuff of dreams, one will find a much deeper meaning. If we evaluated Kahlo's work in a "biased," "troublesome," or "confusing" way, we would not have these insights.

7. **(B)** The previous sentence states that Kahlo thought that her work would appeal only to herself. To contrast with this, choice (B) is the best since it points out that many people actually do find her work interesting. Choices (A) and (C) do not relate to Kahlo's attitude toward her paintings. Choice (D) further develops the sentiment Kahlo expresses in the previous sentence rather than contradicting it.

8. **(A)** Without this information, we would not fully understand what distinguished Kahlo's paintings from those of other surrealist painters—she symbolized her personal experiences, while many surrealists painted unrealistically just to be unrealistic. Choice (B) is incorrect because we do not see details about what surrealists experienced. Choices (C) and (D) are not correct because this phrase needs to stay in the sentence for clarification.

9. **(D)** Choice (D) properly places a comma after Rivera, which is needed since it is an appositive (a helpful yet not essential clarification of a title). Choice (D) also puts a needed semicolon between the two independent clauses. Choices (A) and (C) do not place a comma after the appositive. Choice (B) makes this a run-on sentence.

10. **(A)** Choice (A) places dashes around the parenthetical description of what the symbols were. It clearly distinguishes among the individual symbols by separating each item in the list with commas. Choice (B) does not finish the parenthetical phrase in the same way it started—it uses a dash at the beginning and a comma at the end. Choice (C) does not separate "blood" with a comma from the next item in the list. Choice (D) improperly and inconsistently uses a colon to start off the parenthetical phrase and uses a comma to finish it.

11. **(C)** The paragraph describes Kahlo's images with words like "randomness" and refers to unusual symbols, like an orthopedic corset. Such visuals are best described as "surreal" since they are imaginative rather than realistic. Choice (A) is incorrect because these words are too informal in tone and are repetitive. Choice (B) is not correct because Kahlo's images most likely do not arouse pity but do evoke imaginative musings. Choice (D) is incorrect because although many negative things happened to Kahlo in her life, "evil" takes the description of these images to a negative extreme since evil is not necessarily associated with "randomness."

Resumes

A professional and error-free resume helps you stand out ❶ <u>in a sea of applicants.</u> How a resume should be organized and presented is fairly static across fields, with the notable exception being the art and design industries. For these positions, it may be acceptable to ❷ <u>conform with</u> the traditionally accepted format to showcase your individual design skills and creativity.

For all other ❸ <u>fields; however, resume</u> structure for recent graduates is very much the same. Paper should be white or cream, and ink should be black. Choose a commonly used font, such as Times New Roman or Arial. Headings should be a visually pleasing mix of capitalization and bolded font. ❹ <u>Most jobs to which people will apply will have a similar resume-writing format.</u>

Begin with contact information, including ❺ <u>name, phone number, address, e-mail</u> address, and, if appropriate, professional networking information. Objectives or goal statements are not typically used. Your resume should make your qualifications clear, and any other job-related topics can be addressed in the cover letter. List education and major educational accomplishments beginning with your most recent school. If your grade point average overall or within your major is impressive, include it.

❻ <u>Finally include</u> clinical experience or specialized training programs if you have any. Then move on to work experience. Begin with either the most recent experience and work backward chronologically, or begin with the most relevant work experience and list from most relevant to least relevant experience. For each position, include the name of the company, dates you worked there, your position, and two or three bullet points about your

1. (A) NO CHANGE
   (B) between the different applications.
   (C) among applications submitted by students worldwide.
   (D) OMIT the underlined portion.

2. Which choice would most logically build upon the previous sentence?

   (A) NO CHANGE
   (B) try
   (C) break with
   (D) seize upon

3. (A) NO CHANGE
   (B) fields, however, resume
   (C) fields: however, resume
   (D) fields, however resume

4. The writer is considering deleting the underlined sentence. Should the underlined sentence be kept or deleted?

   (A) Kept, because it elaborates on common resume-writing techniques.
   (B) Kept, because it clarifies the general characteristics of well-written resumes.
   (C) Deleted, because it repeats an idea previously stated in the paragraph.
   (D) Deleted, because it diverges from the primary focus of the paragraph.

5. (A) NO CHANGE
   (B) name phone number, address, e-mail
   (C) name, phone, number, address e-mail
   (D) name, phone number address, e-mail

6. (A) NO CHANGE
   (B) Finally, include
   (C) Next include
   (D) Next, include

responsibilities. Begin your bullet points with active verbs such as **7** "implemented" or "managed" instead of less-impressive words such as "helped" or "worked on."

If you have more experience related to the position but it is not quite as important, put it under an "Additional Experience" heading. Here, list the **8** company and organization the dates, and your position.

If you have still more relevant and important awards or activities, choose the most important ones and put them under an "Additional Selected Activities, Leadership, and Honors" heading. **9** The word "selected" emphasizes that you have earned these prestigious honors due to being "selected" by outside organizations for your professional excellence. Include the organization or award, the date, and any leadership position held.

When **10** your finished, review your resume for visual appeal. It should not look cluttered and should be a mix of white space and black text. If your resume looks cluttered, continue on to a second page. Make sure you have enough information to fill **11** at least half of the second page. If you do not, review the information you have included and reduce it until your resume fits on one page.

7. The writer is considering removing the quotation marks from the words in the underlined sentence. Should the writer make this change?

   (A) Yes, because these are not quotations from actual people.
   (B) Yes, because these words do not possess other items and so do not require quotations.
   (C) No, because the writer is referring to the words themselves rather than to what the words represent.
   (D) No, because they are referring to formal titles that must be placed in quotations.

8. (A) NO CHANGE
   (B) company and organization,
   (C) company or organization
   (D) company or organization,

9. Which sentence should be used in the underlined portion to logically support why the writer uses "selected" in the heading discussed in the previous sentence?

   (A) NO CHANGE
   (B) The use of "selected" is important as it shows the person reading your resume that this is just a sample of your most important honors.
   (C) Writing "selected" indicates that you have confidence in your abilities to get the job done.
   (D) Specifying that these are "selected" honors demonstrates that you have a masterful command of the English language, impressing potential companies with your ability to communicate.

10. (A) NO CHANGE
    (B) you were
    (C) you are
    (D) you felt

11. (A) NO CHANGE
    (B) half at least with
    (C) of least at half
    (D) at least of half

Solutions

ANSWERS EXPLAINED

1. **(A)** Choice (A) gives a grammatically proper and concise clarification of how exactly a resume will help you stand out. Choice (B) is incorrect because "between" is used when comparing just two things—there would surely be more than two applicants for a typical job. Choice (C) is too wordy. Choice (D) is incorrect because without this phrase, the sentence would be unclear about how a well-crafted resume would help you stand out.

2. **(C)** "Break with" is the best option since it establishes a contrast between the recommended resume styles for traditional career fields and for more creative ones. The other options all keep with the traditional resume format, which do not make sense given that art and design are described as exceptions to how resumes should be organized.

3. **(B)** A semicolon or colon would not work, as in choices (A) and (C), since there is not a complete sentence beforehand. Choice (B) correctly sets aside the transitional "however" with commas, unlike choice (D), which has a comma only before the word.

4. **(C)** The underlined sentence repeats the idea expressed in the first sentence of the paragraph, i.e., that resumes are mostly formatted in the same way across career fields. Choice (D) is not correct because the sentence is focused on the topic of the paragraph. In fact, it repeats a point already made in the paragraph, which is problematic. Choices (A) and (B) are not correct because these would both keep this redundant sentence in the paragraph.

5. **(A)** Choice (A) places commas at the appropriate spots between each whole item in the list. Choice (B) makes "name phone number" into one object. Choice (C) makes "address e-mail" into one object. Choice (D) makes "phone number address" into one object.

6. **(D)** As the second major point in the body of the essay, "next" is more appropriate than "finally." Also, a comma is needed immediately after the introductory transition of "next" to provide a small pause.

7. **(C)** When you refer to a word itself, put quotation marks around the word. When you refer to what the word actually represents, no quotation marks are needed. For example, *I drive a car* vs. *"Car" rhymes with "star."* The writer is describing what words should be placed on a resume, so quotation marks are appropriate. Choice (D) is incorrect because these words are not formal titles of things like books or people. Choices (A) and (B) are not correct because they would unnecessarily remove the quotation marks.

8. **(D)** Since you would list either the company or the organization, depending on whether you worked for a business or a nonprofit, it is correct to say "or" and not to separate the two terms with commas. So you will list three things: the group for which you worked (company/organization), the dates, and the position. Choices (A) and (B) are incorrect because these use "and" while you would have either a company or an organization but not both. Choice (C) is not correct because the needed pause between "company or organization" and "the dates" would be missing.

9. **(B)** The reader might wonder why the author recommends that you write "selected" in the previous sentence. Choice (B) provides the most logical support. It clarifies that you have many awards that you could mention but that you are choosing to list only some of the most significant or selected ones. Choice (A) does not make sense, because the idea that you were given these awards by outside organizations would still be expressed without "selected" in the title. Choice (C) does not make sense. If you said you had been selected for something, you would be expressing confidence. However, this use of "selected" pertains to choosing which awards to mention, not directly to your confidence in your abilities. Choice (D) does not make sense. There is no strong reason that inserting this word primarily demonstrates mastery of the English language.

10. **(C)** This should be in the present tense to be consistent with the rest of the essay, making choices (B) and (D) incorrect. It also should be a subject and verb, not possession, making choice (A) incorrect since "your" indicates possession. "You are" is in the correct tense and gives the proper subject and verb.

11. **(A)** Choice (A) puts the words into the most logical order since the correct expression is "fill at least half." The other options make this phrase nonsensical and inconsistent with common practice.

Math

The PSAT Math Test is composed of two subsections:

- 45-minute calculator permitted section, consisting of 31 questions total

  - 27 multiple-choice
  - 4 grid-ins

- 25-minute no calculator permitted section, consisting of 17 questions total

  - 13 multiple-choice
  - 4 grid-ins

The questions generally become *more difficult* as you go through a section. This chapter contains the following:

- 27 concepts you need to know for the PSAT
- 18 math strategies
- "Putting It All Together" section with example problems
- In-depth practice for all four types of questions:

  - Heart of algebra
  - Problem solving and data analysis
  - Passport to advanced math
  - Additional topics in math

THE MATH CONCEPTS YOU MUST KNOW

Although the PSAT Math Test primarily involves application of the quantitative critical thinking skills you have developed over the years, you do need to know several key concepts. This section lists the 27 most critical math concepts to know for the PSAT.

1. Use Substitution to Solve Equations

A common way to solve equations with two variables is by *substitution* of one variable in terms of the other.

➥ Example _____

Solve for x in the system of equations below.

$$2x = y$$
$$y - 3x = -5$$

Solution

Substitute $2x$ for y in the second equation:

$$(2x) - 3x = -5$$
$$-x = -5$$
$$x = 5$$

2. Use Elimination to Solve Equations

When two equations are written in similar formats, *elimination* of terms and variables may be the easiest way to solve for the variables. Multiply one of the equations by a number that allows you to add or subtract the equations easily to eliminate one of the variables.

> Two equations will have infinitely many solutions if the equations are identical. For example, when $x + y = 2$ and $2x + 2y = 4$ are a system of equations, they have infinitely many solutions. This occurs because the equations are simply multiples of one another. Some equations, like $x + y = 2$ and $2x + 2y = 10$, have no solutions. They do not intersect at all because the lines are parallel to each other.

➡ Example

Solve for both x and y in the system of equations below.

$$3x + 2y = 7$$
$$2x - y = 0$$

Solution

Multiply the second equation by 2.

$$3x + 2y = 7$$
$$4x - 2y = 0$$

Then add the equations to eliminate the y-variables.

$$3x + 2y = 7$$
$$\underline{+ (4x - 2y = 0)}$$
$$7x + 0 = 7$$

Divide both sides by 7 to get the answer: $x = 1$.

Then solve for y by plugging 1 in for x in the first equation:

$$3x + 2y = 7 \ \rightarrow$$
$$(3 \times 1) + 2y = 7 \ \rightarrow$$
$$3 + 2y = 7 \ \rightarrow$$
$$2y = 4 \ \rightarrow$$
$$y = 2$$

3. Use the Quadratic Formula to Solve an Equation

A second-degree equation containing the variable x, the constants a, b, and c, and written in the form $ax^2 + bx + c = 0$ can be solved using the *quadratic formula*:

$$x = \frac{-b \pm \sqrt{b^2 - 4ac}}{2a}$$

➥ Example

What are the values of x in the equation $7x^2 + 4x - 5 = 0$?

Solution

The values of the constants are $a = 7$, $b = 4$, and $c = -5$. Solve for x by plugging a, b, and c into the quadratic formula:

$$x = \frac{-b \pm \sqrt{b^2 - 4ac}}{2a} \rightarrow x = \frac{-4 \pm \sqrt{4^2 - 4 \cdot 7 \cdot (-5)}}{2 \cdot 7} \rightarrow x = \frac{-4 \pm \sqrt{156}}{14} \rightarrow$$

$$x = \frac{-4 \pm 2\sqrt{39}}{14} \rightarrow x = \frac{-2 \pm \sqrt{39}}{7}$$

4. Use Factoring to Simplify Expressions

When simplifying an equation, take out any *common factors*.

➥ Example

Factor $nx + ny$.

Solution

$nx + ny$ can be expressed as $n(x + y)$ by factoring out the n.

➥ Example

Factor $\dfrac{2x^3 + 6x}{3x}$.

Solution

$\dfrac{2x^3 + 6x}{3x}$ can be expressed as $\dfrac{2x(x^2 + 3)}{3x}$ since you can factor $2x$ out of the numerator.

Then you can cancel out an x from the numerator and denominator:

$$\frac{2x(x^2 + 3)}{3x} = \frac{2\cancel{x}(x^2 + 3)}{3\cancel{x}} = \frac{2}{3}(x^2 + 3)$$

You also should know how to factor equations like $x^2 - x - 12 = 0$. Try to express it as two binomials that are multiplied by each other. The factored form looks like:

$$(x + \text{something})(x - \text{something}) = 0.$$

In the case of $x^2 - x - 12 = 0$, you can rewrite it as $(x + 3)(x - 4) = 0$. If you used FOIL to multiply the left-hand side (i.e., multiply the <u>F</u>irst terms together, then the <u>O</u>uter terms, then the <u>I</u>nner terms, and finally the <u>L</u>ast terms), you will get the original equation:

$$(x + 3)(x - 4) = 0 \longrightarrow x^2 - 4x + 3x - 12 = 0 \longrightarrow x^2 - x - 12 = 0$$

5. Common Factoring Patterns

Memorize these patterns so you can recognize them on the PSAT Math Test and save time.

The first three patterns multiply binomials. Note the differences in each pattern:

$(a+b)(a+b) = a^2 + 2ab + b^2$
Example:
$(x+3)(x+3) = x^2 + 6x + 9$

$(a+b)(a-b) = a^2 - b^2$
Example:
$(m+2)(m-2) = m^2 - 4$

$(a-b)(a-b) = a^2 - 2ab + b^2$
Example:
$(3-y)(3-y) = 9 - 6y + y^2$

Sum of Cubes
$(a+b)(a^2 - ab + b^2) = a^3 + b^3$
Example:
$(2+x)(4-2x+x^2) = 8 + x^3$

Difference of Cubes
$(a-b)(a^2 + ab + b^2) = a^3 - b^3$
Example:
$(y-4)(y^2 + 4y + 16) = y^3 - 4^3 = y^3 - 64$

6. Slope-Intercept Form

Determine the graph of a line by putting it in *slope-intercept form*:

$$y = mx + b$$

m = slope of the line, the "rise" over the "run"

b = y-intercept of the line, i.e., where the line intersects the y-axis

> Since the PSAT includes quite a few problems that don't allow you to use a calculator, be sure you don't have to rely on your calculator to graph a line.

⮕ Example _____

Graph the following equation:

$$y = 3x + 2$$

Solution

Based on the slope-intercept formula, the line has a slope of 3 and a y-intercept of 2.

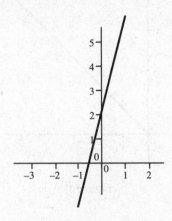

7. Slope Formula, Positive and Negative Correlations

To find the slope between two points, (x_1, y_1) and (x_2, y_2), plug the coordinates of the points into this formula:

$$\text{Slope} = \frac{\text{Change in } y}{\text{Change in } x} = \frac{(y_2 - y_1)}{(x_2 - x_1)}$$

⮕ Example _____

If a line includes the points (6, 4) and (2, 9), what is the slope of the line?

Solution

You can determine the slope as follows:

$$\frac{(y_2 - y_1)}{(x_2 - x_1)} = \frac{(9-4)}{(2-6)} = -\frac{5}{4}$$

You can examine the slope of a line to see whether the variables have a positive or a negative correlation. If the x-values and y-values both increase or both decrease, the variables have a *positive correlation*. The line has a *positive slope*. If the x-values increase while the y-values decrease, or vice versa, the variables have a *negative correlation*. The line has a *negative slope*.

8. Linear, Quadratic, and Exponential Models to Interpret Functions

A *linear relationship* between two variables is represented by a graph with a *constant slope*. For example, the equation $y = x$ represents a linear relationship between x and y, as you can see in the graph in Figure 1 below

> If a question says that some quantity is increasing at a "constant rate," realize this is code for a linear relationship.

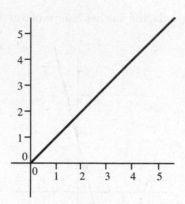

Figure 1

A *quadratic relationship* between two variables, x and y, is generally represented by an equation of the form $y = kx^2$ or $y = ax^2 + bx + c$, in which k, a, b, and c are constants. It is called a quadratic relationship because *quad* means *square*. Figure 2 shows a portion of the graph of $y = x^2$, in which x and y have a quadratic relationship.

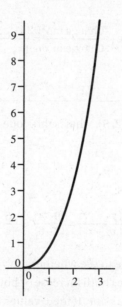

Figure 2

An *exponential relationship* between two variables, x and y, is generally expressed in the form $y = cb^x$ or $y = ab^x + c$, in which a, b, and c are constants. Figure 3 shows a portion of the graph of $y = 3^x - 1$, which is an exponential function.

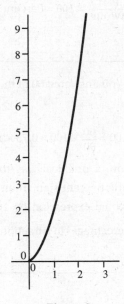

Figure 3

Keep in mind that functions can have *negative* linear, quadratic, and exponential relationships. In other words, these functions can express *decay* rather than growth. For example, the function $y = 20 \times 0.5^x$ shows decay because as x increases to infinity, the y-value decreases. The graph of the function is shown in Figure 4.

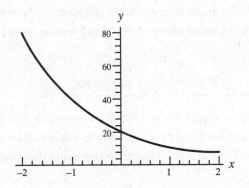

Figure 4

Generally, the most rapid growth or decay is found using an exponential function. The least rapid growth or decay is found using a linear function.

9. Percentages

The following shows the general formula for percentages:

$$\frac{\text{Part}}{\text{Whole}} \times 100 = \text{Percent}$$

➡ Example

You took a test with 80 questions, and you answered 60 of them correctly. What percentage of the questions did you answer correctly?

$$\frac{\text{Part}}{\text{Whole}} \times 100 = \frac{60}{80} \times 100 = 0.75 \times 100 = 75\%$$

On the calculator-permitted section, a practical way to work with percentages is to convert them to decimals. First remove the percent sign. Then move the decimal point 2 spots to the left. Finally, multiply the last decimal expression by 100. Note that on the noncalculator section, you may want to convert the percentages to a fraction, like $\frac{1}{2} = 50\%$.

➡ Example

What is 45 percent of 300?

> **Tip**
>
> Common Fractions and % Conversions:
>
> $\frac{1}{4} = 25\%$
>
> $\frac{1}{2} = 50\%$
>
> $\frac{3}{4} = 75\%$

Solution

Convert the percentage to a decimal and multiply the result by 300:

$$45\% \text{ of } 300 = 0.45 \times 300 = 135$$

When doing multistep percentage calculations, be very careful that you are considering the increases or decreases from previous steps in your later calculations.

➡ Example

A book is regularly $20, but it is on sale for 10% off. A customer also has a coupon for 30% off the price of the book in addition to any sale discounts. What will be the price of the book the customer pays first using the sale and then the price also using the coupon? Ignore any sales tax.

Solution

First determine the sale price of the book by subtracting the 10% discount from the original price:

$$\$20 - (0.1 \times \$20) = \$20 - \$2 = \$18$$

Then subtract 30% of the new price from the new price to find the fully discounted price:

$$\$18 - (0.3 \times \$18) = \$18 - \$5.40 = \$12.60$$

Alternatively, you could calculate 90% of the original amount and then calculate 70% of that new amount. This method takes away the need to do subtraction:

$$\$20 \times 0.9 = \$18 \ \rightarrow \ \$18 \times 0.7 = \$12.60$$

10. Ratios and Proportions

Recognize when ratios and proportions can be used. This will most frequently occur with word problems.

➡ Example _____

A cookie recipe calls for 6 cups of sugar and 4 cups of milk. Brendan has 18 cups of sugar. If Brendan wants to use all of that sugar, how many cups of milk will he need?

Solution

Set up a ratio:

$$\frac{4 \text{ cups milk}}{6 \text{ cups sugar}} = \frac{x \text{ cups milk}}{18 \text{ cups sugar}} \rightarrow \frac{2}{3} = \frac{x}{18} \rightarrow$$

$$\text{Cross Multiply} \rightarrow 2 \cdot 18 = 3x \rightarrow$$

$$\text{Divide both sides by } 3 \rightarrow \frac{2 \cdot 18}{3} = x \rightarrow \frac{36}{3} = 12 = x$$

Brendan will need 12 cups of milk.

11. Unit Conversion

Convert an expression in one unit to another by canceling out the units you do not want.

➡ Example _____

Sam wants to exchange 400 U.S. dollars for euros; the U.S. dollar is currently valued at 0.92 euros. How many euros will Sam receive if he makes this exchange? Assume no transaction fees.

Solution:

$$\$400 \times \frac{0.92 \text{ euros}}{\$1} = 368 \text{ euros}$$

The dollars cancel out from the top and bottom, leaving only euros.

12. Scientific Notation

Scientific notation enables you to express extremely large or extremely small numbers without having to write out a bunch of zeros. For example, rather than writing 3,600,000,000,000, you can simply write 3.6×10^{12}.

So how do you easily express a number in scientific notation? Move the decimal point so the first number is greater than or equal to 1 but less than 10. Then that number will have to be multiplied by 10 raised to a power. If you have moved the decimal point to the left, count the number of spots you have moved it. That number becomes the exponent of the 10. However, if you have moved the decimal point to the right, the negative of the number of spots you have moved it becomes the exponent of the 10.

➡ Example _____

Express 5,438 in scientific notation.

Solution

First move the decimal point to the left 3 spots to get 5.438. Then multiply that number by 10^3. When expressed in scientific notation, 5,438 is 5.438×10^3.

➡ Example _____

Express 0.00476 in scientific notation.

Solution

First move the decimal point to the right 3 spots to get 4.76. Then multiply that number by 10^{-3}. When expressed in scientific notation, $0.00476 = 4.76 \times 10^{-3}$.

13. Inequalities

An inequality is an expression that indicates if something is less than or greater than something else. The open end of the ">" goes toward the larger number. For example, $4 < 8$ and $7 > 2$.

When an inequality sign has a line underneath the greater/less than sign, the terms on either side can also equal one another. For example, $x \leq 5$ means that x is less than or equal to 5.

When working with inequalities, generally solve them just like you would regular equations EXCEPT for this common situation: **When you multiply or divide by a negative number, change the direction of the inequality sign**.

➡ Example _____

The inequality sign should also be flipped when taking a reciprocal.

$$x > 7 \rightarrow \frac{1}{x} < \frac{1}{7}$$

➡ Example _____

Solve for x:

$$-5x > 2$$

Solution

Divide both sides by –5 and turn the > around to <.

$$-5x > 2$$

$$\frac{-5x}{-5} < \frac{2}{-5}$$

$$\frac{\cancel{-5}x}{\cancel{-5}} < \frac{2}{-5}$$

$$x < -\frac{2}{5}$$

When graphing inequalities on the number line, a hollow circle indicates < or > and a solid circle indicates ≤ or ≥. Figure 5 shows the graph of two inequalities.

$n > 2$ is

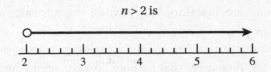

$n \leq 5$ is

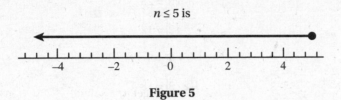

Figure 5

14. Exponents

Table 1 shows the most important exponent rules along with some concrete examples. It also includes ways to remember these rules.

Table 1. Exponent Rules

Exponent Rule	Concrete Example	Way to Remember
$x^a x^b = x^{(a+b)}$	$x^3 x^4 = x^{(3+4)} = x^7$	Remember the acronym **MADSPM**. Multiply exponents,
$\dfrac{x^a}{x^b} = x^{a-b}$	$\dfrac{x^7}{x^2} = x^{7-2} = x^5$	Add them. Divide exponents, Subtract them.
$(x^a)^b = x^{ab}$	$(x^3)^5 = x^{15}$	Parentheses with exponents, Multiply them.
$x^{-a} = \dfrac{1}{x^a}$	$x^{-5} = \dfrac{1}{x^5}$	If you are "bad" (negative), you are sent down below!
$x^{\frac{a}{b}} = \sqrt[b]{x^a}$	$x^{\frac{2}{7}} = \sqrt[7]{x^2}$	The root of a tree is on the bottom. Similarly, the root is on the bottom and on the left-hand side!

15. Absolute Value

Absolute value is the distance that a number is from zero along the number line. Both –3 and +3 are the same distance from zero. Therefore, both have an absolute value of 3.

If you want the absolute value of 9, express it like this: $|9|$.

When computing the value of an absolute value expression, start by determining the value of what is inside the two bars. Then make that number positive, no matter whether it is originally positive or negative. Here are some examples:

$$|25| = 25$$
$$|-12| = 12$$
$$|-3 + 8| = 5$$
$$|-2 \cdot 9| = 18$$

When solving an absolute value equation, rewrite it as two equations. In one equation, set the absolute value portion equal to a positive value. In the other equation, set the absolute value portion equal to a negative value.

➥ Example

Solve for x in the following absolute value equation.

$$|x + 2| = 4$$

Solution

Rewrite the equation as two different equations since what comes inside the absolute value signs can have either a positive or a negative value. Then solve for x.

$$x + 2 = 4$$
$$x + 2 = -4$$

So x could be either –6 or 2.

16. Probability Basics

Probability is the *likelihood that a given event will happen*, expressed as a fraction, decimal, or percentage. If there is no chance an event will occur, it has a probability of 0. If there is a 100% chance something will happen, it has a probability of 1.

To calculate probability, take the number of cases of a success and divide it by the total number of possible outcomes:

$$\text{Probability} = \frac{\text{Number of successes}}{\text{Number of possible outcomes}}$$

➥ Example

If Janice has 3 red marbles out of the 200 total marbles in her collection, what is the probability that she will randomly pick a red marble?

Solution

The number of successes is 3. The number of possible outcomes is 200.

$$\frac{\text{Number of red marbles}}{\text{Number of total marbles}} = \frac{3}{200} = 0.015 = 1.5\%$$

17. Independent/Dependent Counting Problems

Counting problems are either independent or dependent.

INDEPENDENT COUNTING PROBLEMS (DRAWING WITH REPLACEMENT)

These types of problems involve drawing an object and then replacing it before drawing again. In independent counting problems, each choice is computed *independently*. In other words, what you pick the first time has *no impact* on what you pick the second time, which has no impact on what you pick the third time, and so on. Such problems include flipping a coin several times because the flip of one coin has no impact on the later coin flips.

➡ Example

John is choosing a 3-letter combination for his safe. Whether or not the letters are repeated does not matter. How many unique combinations can John make?

Solution

What John picks for one letter does not impact what he picks for another letter. Since there are 26 letters in the alphabet, calculate the total number of possible combinations as follows:

$$26 \times 26 \times 26 = 17{,}576 \text{ possible combinations}$$

DEPENDENT COUNTING PROBLEMS (DRAWING WITHOUT REPLACEMENT)

These types of problems involve drawing an object and not replacing it before drawing again. In dependent counting problems, each choice *depends* on what was previously chosen. In other words, what you pick the first time *has an impact* on what you pick the second time, which has an impact on what you pick the third time, and so on. Such problems include drawing a name out of a hat because you do not want to pick the same name more than once.

➡ Example

John is choosing a 3-letter combination for his safe. The letters cannot be repeated. How many unique combinations can John make?

Solution

What John picks for the first letter does impact what he picks for the second, which impacts what he picks for the third. So he will have one fewer possible letter for each subsequent choice. He can compute the total number of unique 3-letter combinations with no repeating letters as follows:

$$26 \times 25 \times 24 = 15{,}600 \text{ possible combinations}$$

18. Distance, Rate, and Time

When considering the relationship among distance, speed/rate, and time, use the following formula:

$$\text{Distance} = \text{Rate} \times \text{Time}$$

For example, biking 80 miles at 10 miles per hour would take you 8 hours. See how this scenario fits into the equation:

$$80 \text{ miles} = 10 \frac{\text{Miles}}{\text{Hour}} \times 8 \text{ hours}$$

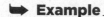 **Example** _____

If Fred has to drive 200 miles in 5 hours, at what average speed should he drive?

Solution

Insert the given information into the formula and solve for rate (speed):

$$\text{Distance} = \text{Rate} \times \text{Time}$$

$$200 \text{ miles} = \text{Rate} \times 5 \text{ hours}$$

$$\frac{200}{5} = 40 \text{ miles per hour}$$

19. Measures of Center

Table 2 describes the 3 most common measures of center.

Table 2. Types of Measures of Center

	Definition
Mean	$\dfrac{\text{Sum of Items}}{\text{Number of Items}} = \text{Mean}$ What you usually think of when you calculate the average.
Median	The middle term of a set of numbers when lined up from smallest to largest. When the number of terms is even and the two terms in the middle are not the same, take the mean of the two middle terms to find the median.
Mode	The most frequent term in a set of numbers. In a set of numbers, if each number appears only once, there is no mode. However, if 2 or more numbers are tied for appearing the most times, that set has multiple modes.

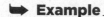 **Example** _____

Compute the mean, median, and mode for the following set of numbers:

$$\{1, 4, 4, 5, 8, 13, 22\}$$

Solution

Calculate each center of measure.

The mean:

$$\frac{1 + 4 + 4 + 5 + 8 + 13 + 22}{7} = \frac{57}{7} \approx 8.14$$

The mean is 8.14.

The median:

The numbers are already in order from smallest to largest. There are 7 numbers in the set. The median is 5 since it is in the middle of the set.

The mode:

The most frequent term is 4, so it is the mode.

20. Range and Standard Deviation

The PSAT will emphasize analyzing data sets. So be comfortable with the important concepts of "range" and "standard deviation."

RANGE

Range is defined as the difference between the smallest and largest values in a set of data.

STANDARD DEVIATION

Standard deviation measures how spread out or varied the data points are in a set. It can be calculated using the following equation:

$$\text{Standard deviation} = \sqrt{\text{Average of the squared differences of the data points from their mean}}$$

Rather than having you conduct elaborate calculations to find the standard deviation of a set of data, you will need to have a feel for what the standard deviation represents.

If the standard deviation is small, the data points have little variation.

If the standard deviation is large, the data points have great variation.

➥ Example

Compare the ranges and standard deviations of Set A and Set B.

Set A: {1, 3, 4, 6, 8}
Set B: {1, 8, 50, 200, 380}

Solution

The range and standard deviation of Set B are greater than the range and standard deviation of Set A. Why? The values in Set A range from only 1 to 8 and do not vary much from the average of Set A (4.4). The values in Set B range from 1 to 380 and vary quite a bit from the average of Set B (127.8). The sets are simple enough that you can likely determine the general trends with standard deviation and range without doing detailed calculations.

The most common graph involving standard deviation is the *normal distribution*—the typical distribution of a large sampling of values in a bell curve shape. Figure 6 shows a normal distribution. About 68% of the values are within 1 standard deviation of the mean. About 95% of the values are within 2 standard deviations of the mean. About 99.7% of the values are within 3 standard deviations of the mean.

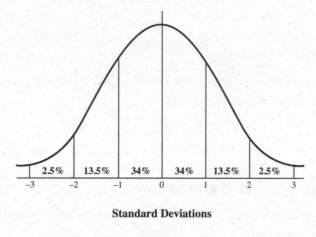

Standard Deviations

Figure 6

21. Margin of Error, Confidence Intervals

When collecting a sample of data from a population, you need to be sure that the results give a true snapshot of the population as a whole. Two important terms are associated with the quality of data sampling: confidence interval and margin of error.

> Use common sense when thinking about data. To get an accurate snapshot of public opinion, ask as MANY RANDOM people your questions as you can!

CONFIDENCE INTERVAL

The confidence interval is a range of values defined so that there is a pre-determined probability that the value of an unknown parameter that is under investigation will fall within the range. (The higher the confidence level, the more likely the parameter will fall within the interval.)

➥ Example

Suppose a stockbroker has research indicating a 95% confidence interval that a company's stock will have a return between –7.8% and +9.5% during the next year. What does this mean?

Solution

In this case, the unknown parameter is the average stock return for the year. This means that if all economic conditions remain the same, there is a 95% chance that the stock will have an average return in this interval.

MARGIN OF ERROR

The margin of error is the maximum expected difference between the actual (unknown) parameter and the estimate for that parameter obtained through a sample. (The smaller the margin of error, the more accurate the survey results.)

➥ **Example** _____

Suppose that a survey has a margin of error of plus or minus 5% at 96% confidence. What does this mean?

Solution

This means that 96% of the time the survey is repeated, the results are within plus or minus 5% of the amount reported in the original survey.

You do not need to know the details of calculating margin of error and confidence level for the PSAT. Instead, you need to have a feel for what will make survey results more reliable. The margin of error and confidence level for survey results are interrelated. If you want a smaller margin of error, you may have to have less confidence in the results. If you want to be more confident in your results, you should allow for a larger margin of error. In order to maximize confidence in the results and minimize the margin of error, make sure that the sample is as *large and as random* as possible.

22. Parabola Equation

Sometimes you will need to look at the equation of a U-shaped curve, known as a parabola, and determine certain properties of it.

- The vertex form of a parabola is $y = a(x - h)^2 + k$.
- The vertex (the bottom point of the U-shape) has the coordinates (h, k). If the parabola is facing down, the vertex will be the top of the curve.
- The x-coordinate of the vertex provides the *axis of symmetry* for the parabola.

➥ **Example** _____

A parabola with the equation $y = (x - 1)^2 + 2$ has a vertex of $(1, 2)$. The equation for the axis of symmetry for the parabola is $x = 1$. The parabola is graphed below:

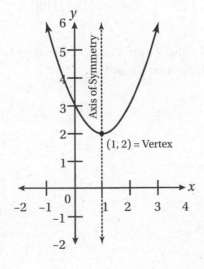

23. Function Solutions

The *root* or *zero* of a function is the value for which the function has a value of zero. A function can have more than one root/zero. To find the root(s) of a function, either examine the equation of the function or look at the function's graph.

➡ Example

What are the zeros of $y = x^2 - 10x + 21$?

Solution

The equation is graphed below:

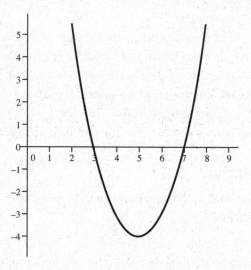

The function has roots/zeros at 3 and 7 since that is where the function intersects the x-axis. Since the function intersects the x-axis twice, it has 2 solutions.

You can also determine the roots/zeros of the function by factoring it and setting the function equal to zero. Then solve for x. Let's do that with the above function:

$$y = x^2 - 10x + 21$$
$$0 = (x - 3)(x - 7)$$
$$(x - 3) = 0 \text{ and } (x - 7) = 0$$
$$x = 3 \text{ and } 7$$

The values of x that give a y-value of 0 are 3 and 7. Depending on the situation, use the graph or a simplified equation to determine roots/zeros.

Alternatively, you can use the quadratic formula to determine the roots:

$$y = x^2 - 10x + 21$$

$$x = \frac{-b \pm \sqrt{b^2 - 4ac}}{2a} \rightarrow$$

$$x = \frac{-(-10) \pm \sqrt{(-10)^2 - 4(1)(21)}}{2(1)} \rightarrow$$

$$x = \frac{10 \pm \sqrt{100 - 84}}{2} \rightarrow$$

$$x = \frac{10 \pm \sqrt{16}}{2} \rightarrow$$

$$x = \frac{10 \pm 4}{2} \rightarrow$$

$$x = 5 \pm 2 \rightarrow$$

$$x = 3 \text{ or } 7$$

24. Imaginary Numbers

A complex number involves the square root of a negative number, and will be expressed using i, which is $\sqrt{-1}$. Some examples of imaginary numbers:

$$\sqrt{-64} = 8i$$

$$\sqrt{-4} = 2i$$

$$7i + 4i = 11i$$

$$i \times i = -1$$

$$\frac{7i^3}{3i} = \frac{7}{3}i^2 = -\frac{7}{3}$$

> Imaginary numbers have a recurring pattern when they are in exponential form:
>
> $$i^1 = i$$
> $$i^2 = -1$$
> $$i^3 = -i$$
> $$i^4 = 1$$
> $$i^5 = i$$
> $$i^6 = -1$$
> and so on

25. Sine, Cosine, Tangent

The three sides in a right triangle (a triangle with a 90° angle) each have special names that are based on the angles, as shown in Figure 7.

- **HYPOTENUSE:** This side is always the longest and is across from the 90° angle.
- **OPPOSITE:** This side depends on the location of the angle you are using. It is always *directly opposite* the angle.
- **ADJACENT:** This side also changes depending on the location of the angle you are using. It is always *adjacent* (next to) the angle you are using. People often confuse the adjacent with the hypotenuse. Just remember that the hypotenuse is always the longest side in a right triangle.

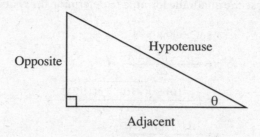

Figure 7

Use the acronym *SOH-CAH-TOA* to remember the key trigonometric ratios, as shown in Table 3.

Table 3. A Trick to Remember Trigonometric Ratios

SOH	CAH	TOA
$\sin\theta = \dfrac{opposite}{hypotenuse}$	$\cos\theta = \dfrac{adjacent}{hypotenuse}$	$\tan\theta = \dfrac{opposite}{adjacent}$

➨ **Example** _____

A triangle has side lengths of 3, 4, and 5. The angle θ is opposite from the side with length 3. What are the different trig values for angle θ?

Solution

Draw the triangle to see what the different trig values are.

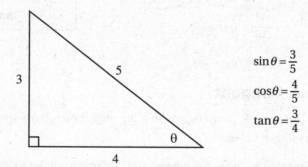

$$\sin\theta = \frac{3}{5}$$

$$\cos\theta = \frac{4}{5}$$

$$\tan\theta = \frac{3}{4}$$

To cover all of your bases, you may also want to memorize these two trigonometric identities:

$$\sin^2 x + \cos^2 x = 1$$

$$\tan x = \frac{\sin x}{\cos x}$$

26. Circle Formula

This formula provides the graph of a circle in the x-y coordinate plane:

$$(x - h)^2 + (y - k)^2 = r^2$$
$$h = x\text{-coordinate of center}$$
$$k = y\text{-coordinate of center}$$
$$r = \text{radius}$$

➡ Example

What are the center and radius of the following equation? What is its graph?

$$(x - 3)^2 + (y - 2)^2 = 9$$

Solution

$(x - 3)^2 + (y - 2)^2 = 9$ has a center at $(3, 2)$ and a radius of 3. Its graph is shown:

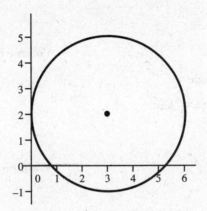

27. Miscellaneous Geometry and Trigonometry

The PSAT WILL PROVIDE you with the following facts and formulas.

> It is a good idea to memorize these formulas, even though they are provided to you when you take the test.

Radius of a circle = r
Area of a circle = πr^2
Circumference of a circle = $2\pi r$

Area of a rectangle =
length × width = lw

Area of a triangle =
$\frac{1}{2}$ × base × height = $\frac{1}{2}bh$

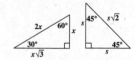

Pythagorean theorem: $a^2 + b^2 = c^2$

Volume of a box =
length × width × height = lwh

Volume of a cylinder = $\pi r^2 h$

Volume of a sphere = $\frac{4}{3}\pi r^3$

Volume of a cone = $\frac{1}{3}\pi r^2 h$

Volume of a pyramid =
$\frac{1}{3}$ × length × width × height = $\frac{1}{3}lwh$

Special right triangles: 30-60-90
and 45-45-90

KEY FACTS:

- A circle has 360 degrees.
- There are 2π radians in a circle.
- There are 180 degrees in a triangle.

18 PSAT MATH STRATEGIES

1. The PSAT Math Test Is More Straightforward than It Used To Be

On the old PSAT, you had to worry about whether drawings were to scale and whether you should leave questions blank. On the updated PSAT, all drawings will be to scale unless they state otherwise. You should answer every question since there is no guessing penalty. All in all, you will be able to spend more time thinking through the problems and less time playing mind games with the test.

2. The PSAT Math Test Is Curved, So Do Your Best to Keep Levelheaded

The PSAT is the one chance juniors have to qualify for a National Merit Scholarship. As much as we can try to predict ahead of time the precise difficulty of the test, even the College Board does not know ahead of time exactly how difficult the test is—that is why they will curve it. So no matter if the PSAT seems more challenging or less challenging than you anticipated, do your best to keep a level head and not get too confident or too worried. Everyone taking the PSAT will be in the same situation, and the curve will reflect the relative difficulty of the test on that particular day.

3. Do Not Overthink the Questions

Especially at the beginning of the test, do not allow yourself to overthink the questions. The questions will generally become more difficult within each section. The PSAT questions may all be solved in fairly straightforward ways once you get past the surface. Since the PSAT mainly tests algebra, many advanced students who are taking calculus or precalculus may overthink relatively easy questions. You do not need higher-order math to solve the questions on the PSAT—you just need a firm grounding in the basics.

4. Rely More on Your Thinking, Less on Your Knowledge

You will be presented with concepts and situations on the PSAT Math Test that may intimidate you due to their unfamiliarity. Do not respond by quickly giving up because you were never officially taught the concept. Instead, use your intuition and reasoning to think through the problems. Your job is to get the right answer, not to explain your thought process to someone else. If you can devise a clever way to work through the problem, go with it. The PSAT is designed to assess your general mathematical thinking skills, not your memorization of formulas.

5. Do Not Rush Through the PSAT Math

When compared to other major standardized tests, like the ACT, the PSAT will be easier to finish. Practice your pacing on the practice math tests in this book, and go into the test ready to be thorough rather than hasty.

6. Do the Questions One Time Well Instead of Double-Checking

On many math tests, it makes all the sense in the world to finish quickly and then go back and check your answers. This is especially true on tests where all you need to do is to plug your answers back into the equations given in the questions. The PSAT Math Test is not like this since you cannot easily plug your answers back into the problem. Instead of rushing through the questions, second-guessing yourself, and having to spend time double-checking your work, focus on doing the questions *one time well*. If you misread a math question because you are going too quickly and then quickly read the question again while double-checking, you are much more likely to answer it incorrectly than if you simply take the necessary time to read and answer the question and do not double-check.

7. Focus on What the Question Is Asking

Try to underline and circle key words in the question as you go to ensure you do not miss anything important. Rather than going on autopilot and quickly jumping into solving the question, really pay attention to what the question is asking you to do. Unless you are mindful about focusing on what the questions are asking, you will get tunnel vision and tune out vital information in the questions.

8. Approach the Questions as Puzzles, Not as Typical School Math Problems

Challenging school math questions often require long calculations and cover tough concepts. The PSAT Math Test questions will not be difficult in these ways. In contrast, the tough questions will involve the patient and creative mindset needed to solve puzzles. When you try to do a Sudoku puzzle, a jigsaw puzzle, or a challenging video game, you succeed by setting up the puzzle well instead of going full-speed ahead and doing unnecessary steps. The same applies to answering tough PSAT Math Test questions.

9. When You Solve for *X*, Watch Out!

On many math tests, the incorrect answers are random numbers. On the PSAT, though, the incorrect answers are carefully designed to be answers to the most likely ways of incorrectly solving the problems. Simply because an answer is on your calculator is no guarantee that it is correct. For example, in math class you typically solve for x and the answer is a given solution. On the PSAT, however, the question may be asking for the value of an expression, like $-2x^2 - x$.

> If you have absolutely no idea what the correct answer is to a question, then guess. There is no guessing penalty. The PSAT does not consistently favor one answer choice letter over another. So before you take the test, choose a letter at random. When you have to guess and have absolutely no idea what the answer is, just use that letter. Choosing a particular letter ahead of time and always using it when you are blindly guessing will help you avoid wasting time during the test deciding which letter to pick.

10. Write Out Your Work

Bright students often take pride in solving all their math problems in their heads. Don't be prideful—be correct! The more that you write as you work through the problems, the more likely that you will answer the question correctly. Why? First, you will more easily visualize the appropriate setup for solving the question. Second, you will avoid making careless mistakes, such as missing a negative sign or incorrectly multiplying numbers, if you carefully visualize the calculations step-by-step on the paper.

11. Don't Overuse Your Calculator

The PSAT Math Test has a whole section in which you are not allowed to use your calculator. Even on the section that does allow calculator use, do not let your calculator be a crutch. PSAT math problems will not require elaborate calculations, and having a bunch of sophisticated programs on your calculator will not make a difference. In fact, many of the answers to the problems will keep radicals and fractions in their nondecimal form. So calculating too far ahead could set you behind. Use the calculator when necessary. However, rely on your critical thinking first and on your calculator second.

12. Use the Choices to Sharpen Your Thinking

Although you do not want to jump to an answer prematurely or eliminate answers too quickly, checking out the answers can often be helpful. Be open to plugging numbers back into expressions when possible, starting with choices (B) or (C) since the choices are typically arranged from small to large. That way you minimize plugging in numbers. (If your first attempt is too small, you simply try the larger answers and vice versa). Considering the answer choices may also help you develop a sense of what the question is asking, empowering you to break through roadblocks in your initial thinking.

13. Mistakes Can Lead to Success

If the PSAT math problems each involved 20–30 steps of calculations, a simple mistake would jeopardize your entire problem-solving process and waste valuable time. In actuality, solving the PSAT math problems will not require a great number of steps. So making a small mistake will not be catastrophic. As long as you make mistakes quickly and recover quickly, you will be fine.

14. Careless Mistakes Are Still Mistakes

Bright students often dismiss careless errors as ones that should not concern them while preparing to take a test. However, if you make careless mistakes while preparing for the PSAT, you will likely make those same mistakes when taking the real PSAT. Although it may be nice to focus your preparation on learning to solve the most challenging questions elegantly, realize that making a couple of careless errors on easier problems may be more detrimental than having conceptual difficulties on a challenging question.

15. Come Back to Questions You Do Not Understand

Do not underestimate the power of your subconscious mind to work through a previous problem while your conscious mind is focused on a different problem. If you have given a problem a decent attempt but still do not know the answer, circle the question and come back. While you are working on other problems, your subconscious mind will be unlocking possible approaches to the problem you left behind. Come back to the problem later and with fresh eyes. That problem may seem much easier than it did before. Since the math problems gradually increase in difficulty, you will likely want to return to the earlier problems rather than the later ones in the test if you want to attempt them again. Whatever you do, do not allow yourself to become bogged down on a single problem—you can still earn a top score while missing questions.

16. Give the Questions the Benefit of the Doubt

The College Board spends a couple of years developing the materials you will see on the PSAT. It has extensively field tested possible questions on students to ensure the fairness and accuracy of the questions. As a result, when you encounter a tough problem on the PSAT Math Test, do not immediately assume that it is an unfair or a stupid question. Instead, know that quite a bit of work and care went into crafting the question. Instead, try to reexamine *your* understanding of the question.

17. Be Prepared for the Unexpected

Since the PSAT is testing your ability to think critically and solve challenging problems, do not let unusual questions surprise you. If you encounter anything that seems different from what you have seen while preparing, do not worry. Since the PSAT wants to test your ability to think on your feet, it will give you questions that may throw you off a bit.

18. What About the Additional Topics in Math?

Do not worry about the "Additional Topics in Math" section while studying unless you are aiming for a perfect score or National Merit recognition. The PSAT has only 2 questions from this wildcard series of topics. So do not worry too much about thoroughly studying this section for the PSAT unless you are trying to ensure that you can definitely answer all sorts of problems. Note that the SAT will have a greater percentage of questions from this area. So studying this section for the PSAT can benefit your long-term SAT performance.

PUTTING IT ALL TOGETHER WITH EXAMPLE PROBLEMS

Let's carefully break down some sample math questions using the above strategies.

➡ Example 1 _____

When measuring temperature, the equation to convert degrees Celsius, C, to degrees Fahrenheit, F, is $\frac{9}{5}C + 32 = F$. For the same actual temperature, what is the range of degrees Fahrenheit for which the given number is greater than the given number of degrees Celsius?

(A) $F > -40$

(B) $F < 26$

(C) $F < -78$

(D) $F > 30$

Solution

Although this problem seems as though you may need to incorporate outside knowledge from chemistry, everything you need to figure it out is right in front of you. First paraphrase what the question is asking, "For what temperatures will F be bigger than C?" To determine this, find a value for C and F that is identical. Why? Because if you know the point at which the values are equal to one another, you can then test values greater than or less than that value to determine the direction of the inequality sign.

Let x equal the value for which C and F are the same. Plug it into the equation and solve:

$$\frac{9}{5}C + 32 = F \rightarrow$$

$$\frac{9}{5}x + 32 = x \rightarrow$$

$$32 = -\frac{4}{5}x \rightarrow$$

$$x = -40$$

Since C and F are equivalent at –40 degrees, plug in a simple number for F to see if the expression should be $F > -40$ or $F < -40$. Try 0 for F since it is easy to plug in:

$$\frac{9}{5}C + 32 = F \rightarrow$$

$$\frac{9}{5}C + 32 = 0 \rightarrow$$

$$\frac{9}{5}C = -32 \rightarrow$$

$$C \approx -17.8$$

From this, you can see that when the F value is 0, it is greater than the value of C, which is a negative number. So the values for which F are greater than the values of C when both numbers represent the actual temperatures are $F > -40$, making the answer choice (A).

Instead, you can use an alternative algebraic approach. Since the answers are in terms of F, first solve for C in terms of F:

$$\frac{9}{5}C + 32 = F \rightarrow$$

$$\frac{9}{5}C = F - 32$$

$$C = \frac{5}{9}(F - 32)$$

Then you can make $F > C$ and solve the inequality:

$$F > \frac{5}{9}(F - 32) \rightarrow$$

$$F > \frac{5}{9}F - \left(\frac{5}{9}\right)32 \rightarrow$$

$$\frac{4}{9}F > -\left(\frac{5}{9}\right)32 \rightarrow$$

$$F > -\left(\frac{9}{4}\right) \times \left(\frac{5}{9}\right) \times 32 \rightarrow$$

$$F > -\frac{5}{4} \times 32 \rightarrow$$

$$F > -40$$

If you did not notice the algebraic approaches to solving the problem, an alternative would be to take the time to test out the different answers by trying sample values from their ranges to see what would make them true. This approach can work, but it may take you more time than if you can recognize an algebraic solution.

➥ Example 2

What are the real number value(s) of x in this equation?

$$x = \sqrt{2x+15}$$

    (A) –3 only

    (B) 5 only

    (C) –3 and 5

    (D) Cannot determine with the given information.

Solution

Although this looks fairly easy to solve, more is here than meets the eye. You have to be careful that what seems to be a solution actually is a solution. Start by squaring both sides and determining the potential values for x:

$$x = \sqrt{2x+15} \rightarrow x^2 = 2x+15 \rightarrow x^2 - 2x - 15 = 0 \rightarrow (x+3)(x-5) = 0$$

So if $(x + 3) = 0$ or if $(x - 5) = 0$, the entire expression equals 0. That means –3 can be a solution since you can set $(x + 3)$ equal to 0 and solve for x:

$$(x + 3) = 0 \rightarrow \text{subtract 3 from both sides} \rightarrow x = -3$$

You can do the same procedure for $(x - 5)$:

$$(x - 5) = 0 \rightarrow \text{add 5 to both sides} \rightarrow x = 5$$

So it appears that both –3 and 5 work as solutions since they both cause $(x + 3)(x - 5)$ to equal 0. When you try these in the original equation, however, only 5 works. Why? Because –3 cannot be the principal square root of 9, since –3 cannot equal the positive square root of a number. So, –3 is an "extraneous solution," making **B** the answer.

➥ Example 3

Consider a set of 25 different numbers. If two numbers are added to the set, one that is larger than the current median of the set and one that is smaller than the current median of the set, which of the following quantities about the set MUST NOT change?

    (A) Range

    (B) Mean

    (C) Mode

    (D) Median

Solution

On a problem like this, try visualizing what will happen by making up some sample values. Suppose you have a simple set of numbers something like this:

$$\{1, 1, 2, 3, 4, 5, 6, 7, 8, 9, 10, 11, 12, 13, 14, 15, 16, 17, 18, 19, 20, 21, 22, 23, 24\}$$

The range of the set is 23, which is the difference between the smallest value (1) and the largest value (24).

The mean for this set is all of the above numbers added together and then divided by 25.

The mode is 1 since it appears the most frequently.

The median is 12 since it is the middle value when the numbers are placed in order from smallest to largest.

If you can come up with even one set of values that will make one of these quantities change, that answer is out as a possibility.

If you add –5 and 100 to the set, the range of the set will become much larger—it will be 105. So choice (A) is not correct.

If you add 2 and 1,000 to the set, the mean will change because the average will shift significantly upward. So choice (B) is not correct.

If you add 7 and 17 to the set, it will have 3 different modes instead of just having 1 as the only mode. So choice (C) is not correct.

Choice (D) is correct. As long as you add any number less than 12 and any number greater than 12, the median will remain the same because 12 will still be in the middle of the set of numbers when they are all placed in order from smallest to largest.

You could also solve this more intuitively if you have a solid understanding of the concept of the median of a set. When given a particular median, if you add one number greater than and one number less than the median, the median will not change since it will remain the very middle of the set.

On the PSAT Math Test, you will have a total of 8 grid-in questions: 4 on the calculator subsection and 4 on the noncalculator subsection. Here are some key things to know about these types of problems:

- It is possible that a question could have more than one correct answer. Enter just one correct answer.
- There are no negative answers.
- Long decimal answers can be rounded up or down but must fill the entire grid.
- You can also express a decimal answer as a fraction. For example, you can write $\frac{7}{9}$ as 7/9, as .777, or as .778.

➥ Example 4 (Grid-in)

What is the value of x if $(3x + 2) - (5x - 6) = -4$?

Solution

On a problem like this, the math is not too difficult. The challenge is to avoid making a careless error because of confusing a negative sign or incorrectly adding numbers. This is especially important on a grid-in question since you will not have four multiple choices to detect a major miscalculation. Avoid careless mistakes by writing out all of your steps. Start by writing the original equation:

$$(3x + 2) - (5x - 6) = -4$$

Remove the parentheses around $(3x + 2)$ and distribute the –1 through the $(5x - 6)$:

$$3x + 2 - 5x + 6 = -4$$

Check that you distributed the negative sign correctly. Then combine like terms:

$$-2x + 8 = -4$$

Subtract the 8 from both sides:

$$-2x = -12$$

Divide both sides by –2 to solve for x:

$$x = 6$$

You can check your work by plugging in 6 for x into the original equation:

$$(3x + 2) - (5x - 6) = -4$$
$$(3(6) + 2) - (5(6) - 6) = -4$$
$$18 + 2 - 30 + 6 = -4$$
$$-4 = -4$$

It checks out. So the final answer is 6, which you need to put onto the grid-in sheet.

HEART OF ALGEBRA PRACTICE

1. Which ordered pair (x, y) satisfies the pair of equations below?

$$3x + y = -3$$
$$x - 2y = -8$$

   (A) $(2, 4)$
   (B) $(-2, 3)$
   (C) $(-3, 2)$
   (D) $(1, -4)$

2. The United States primarily uses a 12-hour clock with 12-hour periods for the morning (A.M.) and the afternoon/evening (P.M.). Much of the rest of the world uses a 24-hour clock. Which of the following inequalities expresses the digits for hours, H, on a 24-hour clock that correspond to the business hours for a restaurant that is open from 7 P.M. until 11 P.M.?

   (A) $7 \leq H \leq 11$
   (B) $12 \leq H \leq 24$
   (C) $19 \leq H \leq 23$
   (D) $24 \leq H \leq 27$

3. A video arcade charges a set $5 charge to purchase a game card and then charges $0.50 for each video game played. What expression gives the relationship between the number of games played, G, and the total amount of dollars spent using the game card, T?

   (A) $T = 5G - 0.50$
   (B) $T = 4.5G + 5$
   (C) $T = 0.50G - 2.5$
   (D) $T = 0.50G + 5$

4. A cardiologist uses the following guidelines for maximum recommended heart rate (measured in beats per minute), which vary based on patient's age:

Age	Maximum Recommended Heart Rate
50	165
55	160
60	155
65	150

One of the cardiologist's patients, age 55, wants to start an exercise program. The cardiologist recommends that the patient maintain a heart rate greater than 50% and less than 85% of the maximum recommended heart rate while exercising. Which of the following expressions gives the range in which the patient's heart rate, H, should be during exercise?

(A) $50 < H < 85$

(B) $80 < H < 136$

(C) $85 < H < 160$

(D) $150 < H < 160$

5. Hannah has only nickels and dimes in her wallet. She has a total of $2.50, and a total of 30 coins. How many nickels does she have?

(A) 10

(B) 12

(C) 15

(D) 16

6. A two-digit number has a tens place, t, and a units place, u. The digits have the following relationships:

$$t + u = 8$$
$$t = 2 + u$$

What is the value of the two-digit number given by these two digits?

(A) 41

(B) 53

(C) 63

(D) 79

7. 18-karat gold has 18 parts gold for 24 total parts metal (the difference comes from the 6 parts that are metals other than gold). 24-karat gold is pure gold. In order to make a piece of jewelry that is 2.4 ounces in weight and is 20-karat gold, how many ounces of 18-karat gold, X, and of 24-karat gold, Y, are needed to make this piece of jewelry?

(A) $X = 0.4$, $Y = 0.6$

(B) $X = 0.9$, $Y = 1.7$

(C) $X = 1.2$, $Y = 1.1$

(D) $X = 1.6$, $Y = 0.8$

8. For the equation $3 + 4x - 2 = k + 6x - 2x$, what does the constant k need to equal in order for there to be multiple solutions for x?

(A) 1

(B) 2

(C) 3

(D) 4

9. What is the value of y in the system of equations below?

$$16x - 4y = 12$$
$$8x + 2y = 4$$

(A) 2

(B) $\dfrac{3}{2}$

(C) $-\dfrac{1}{2}$

(D) -4

10. What are the solutions for the equations below?

$$-\frac{3}{4}x + 2\left(y - \frac{1}{2}\right) = 3$$

$$\frac{2}{3}x = 6 - 2y$$

(A) $x = \dfrac{24}{17}$, $y = \dfrac{43}{17}$

(B) $x = \dfrac{2}{13}$, $y = \dfrac{14}{19}$

(C) $x = -3$, $y = \dfrac{7}{19}$

(D) $x = -\dfrac{4}{11}$, $y = \dfrac{18}{23}$

11. Electrical engineers use Ohm's law, $V = IR$, to give the relationship between voltage (V), current (I), and resistance (R). Which of the following statements is always true about the relationship among voltage, current, and resistance based on Ohm's law?

   I. If the current increases and the resistance remains the same, the voltage increases.

   II. If the voltage increases, the resistance must increase.

   III. If the resistance increases and the voltage remains the same, the current must decrease.

(A) I only

(B) II only

(C) I and III only

(D) II and III only

12. What is the graph of the following function?

$$3 + y = 2 + 3x$$

(A)

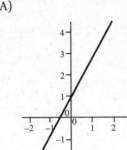

(C)

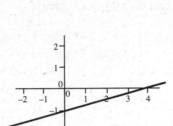

(B)

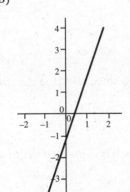

(D)

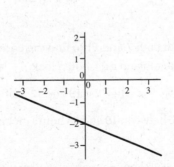

Heart of Algebra Solutions

ANSWERS EXPLAINED

1. **(B)** You can use substitution to solve, although elimination could also work.

$$3x + y = -3$$
$$x - 2y = -8$$

   Rearrange the second equation to be in terms of y:

$$x - 2y = -8 \rightarrow$$
$$x = 2y - 8$$

   Substitute into the first equation and solve for y:

$$3x + y = -3 \rightarrow$$
$$3(2y - 8) + y = -3 \rightarrow$$
$$6y - 24 + y = -3 \rightarrow$$
$$7y - 24 = -3 \rightarrow$$
$$7y = 21 \rightarrow y = 3$$

   Then plug in 3 for y into the first equation to solve for x:

$$3x + y = -3 \rightarrow$$
$$3x + 3 = -3 \rightarrow$$
$$3x = -6 \rightarrow$$
$$x = -2$$

2. **(C)** Simply add 12 to both 7 and 11 to find the correct range since all of the P.M. times are 12 hours less than the time on a 24-hour clock:

$$12 + 7 = 19 \text{ and } 12 + 11 = 23$$

   This makes the range between 19 and 23 hours inclusive, which is expressed as the inequality $19 \le H \le 23$.

3. **(D)** There will be a $5 charge no matter how many games are played. So the $5 should be represented as a constant. For each game played, there is an additional $0.50 fee. Since G represents the number of games played, the total cost is $0.50G + 5$ dollars. This can be expressed as $T = 0.50G + 5$. Alternatively, you could make up a number of games played and the total dollars spent. Then find which of the equations gives an identical result.

4. **(B)** Find the maximum recommended heart rate for a 55-year-old person—160 beats per minute—on the table. Then take 50% and 85% of 160 to determine the lower and upper bounds of the recommended heart rate:

$$50\% \text{ of } 160 = 0.50 \times 160 = 80$$
$$85\% \text{ of } 160 = 0.85 \times 160 = 136$$

So the range is between 80 and 136 beats per minute, which is expressed as the inequality $80 < H < 136$.

5. **(A)** Set up a series of two equations. Put everything in terms of cents for the sake of simplicity. Use N as the number of nickels and D as the number of dimes:

The total number of coins: $N + D = 30$
The total number of cents: $5N + 10D = 250$

Express D in terms of N based on the first equation:

$$N + D = 30 \rightarrow$$
$$D = 30 - N$$

Then substitute this for D in the second equation:

$$5N + 10\,D = 250 \rightarrow$$
$$5N + 10(30 - N) = 250 \rightarrow$$
$$5N + 300 - 10N = 250 \rightarrow$$
$$-5N = -50 \rightarrow$$
$$N = 10$$

Alternatively, you can solve this by working backward from the answers. Since the total number of cents must be 250, try the different possible values of nickels from the choices to see which one works. You can start with choices (B) or (C) since they are in the middle. Once you get to choice (A), you will find that if you have 10 nickels, you have 50 cents from nickels. That means there must be 200 cents from dimes, which also means there are 20 dimes. Since 20 dimes and 10 nickels add together to give 30 coins total, choice (A) is correct.

6. **(B)** Use substitution to solve for t and u:

$$t + u = 8$$
$$t = 2 + u$$

Plug in $2 + u$ for t into the first equation:

$$(2 + u) + u = 8 \rightarrow$$
$$2 + 2u = 8 \rightarrow$$
$$2u = 6 \rightarrow$$
$$u = 3$$

Plug in 3 for u into one of the original equations, and solve for t. This gives 5 in the tens place and 3 in the units place, making 53 the answer.

Alternatively, you can solve this using elimination.

$$t + u = 8$$
$$t = 2 + u$$

Rearrange the second equation:

$$t = 2 + u \rightarrow t - u = 2$$

Then you have this as the set of equations:

$$t + u = 8$$
$$t - u = 2$$

Add the two together to get:

$$2t = 10 \rightarrow$$
$$t = 5$$

Then substitute $t = 5$ into the first equation to solve for u:

$$t + u = 8 \rightarrow$$
$$5 + u = 8 \rightarrow$$
$$u = 3$$

The answer is still 53.

7. **(D)** Set up a system of two equations as follows:

One equation models the number of actual gold karats:

$$\frac{3}{4}X + Y = \frac{5}{6} \times 2.4$$

One equation models the weight of the jewelry: $X + Y = 2.4$

You can use either substitution or elimination to solve this system. However, using elimination is better since a Y-term in each equation will be easily canceled. Start by simplifying the first equation:

$$\frac{3}{4}X + Y = \frac{5}{6} \times 2.4 \rightarrow \frac{3}{4}X + Y = 2$$

Now subtract it from $X + Y = 2.4$:

$$X + Y = 2.4$$
$$-\left(\frac{3}{4}X + Y = 2 \right)$$
$$\overline{\frac{1}{4}X \quad = 0.4}$$

Then solve for X:

$$\frac{1}{4}X = 0.4 \rightarrow X = 4 \times 0.4 = 1.6$$

Now plug in 1.6 for X into one of the equations to solve for Y. Use $X + Y = 2.4$ since it is simpler:

$$X + Y = 2.4 \rightarrow$$
$$1.6 + Y = 2.4 \rightarrow$$
$$Y = 0.8$$

So the final answer is $X = 1.6$, $Y = 0.8$.

8. **(A)** Before proceeding too far, simplify the equation by grouping like terms:

$$3 + 4x - 2 = k + 6x - 2x \rightarrow$$
$$1 + 4x = k + 4x$$

So if $k = 1$, both sides of the equations are equivalent to one another. The equation reduces to $x = x$, which has an infinite number of solutions.

9. **(C)** Solve this using elimination by taking the first equation and multiplying it by $\frac{1}{2}$:

$$\begin{aligned} 16x - 4y &= 12 \\ 8x + 2y &= 4 \end{aligned} \rightarrow$$

$$\begin{aligned} 8x - 2y &= 6 \\ 8x + 2y &= 4 \end{aligned} \rightarrow$$

Subtract the two so we can easily find y:

$$\begin{aligned} 8x - 2y &= 6 \\ -(8x + 2y &= 4) \end{aligned} \rightarrow$$
$$-4y = 2$$

$$y = -\frac{1}{2}$$

10. **(A)** Start by simplifying both equations:

$$-\frac{3}{4}x + 2\left(y - \frac{1}{2}\right) = 3 \rightarrow -\frac{3}{4}x + 2y - 1 = 3 \rightarrow -\frac{3}{4}x + 2y = 4$$
$$\frac{2}{3}x = 6 - 2y \rightarrow \frac{2}{3}x + 2y = 6$$

Then use elimination to solve:

$$-\frac{3}{4}x + 2y = 4$$
$$-\left(\frac{2}{3}x + 2y = 6\right)$$
$$-\frac{3}{4}x - \frac{2}{3}x = -2 \rightarrow -\frac{9}{12}x - \frac{8}{12}x = -2 \rightarrow \frac{-17}{12}x = -2 \rightarrow$$
$$x = \frac{24}{17}$$

Since only choice (A) has x equal to $\frac{24}{17}$, you can save time by just picking it as the correct answer.

11. **(C)** Choice I is correct. Increasing current while keeping resistance constant increases the right side of the equation. This means the left side—the voltage—increases as well. Choice III is correct. If the voltage—the left side of the equation—remains the same while the resistance increases, the current must decrease in order for the value on the right side of the equation to remain the same. Choice II is NOT correct. The current could increase without the resistance increasing if the voltage increases.

12. **(B)** Put the equation in slope-intercept form:

$$3 + y = 2 + 3x \rightarrow y = 3x - 1$$

This line has a slope of 3 and a y-intercept of -1, which has the following graph:

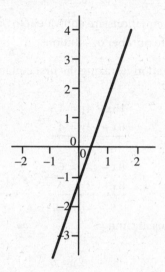

PROBLEM SOLVING AND DATA ANALYSIS PRACTICE

1. A subway map is drawn to scale so that 1 inch on the map corresponds to 2 miles of actual distance on the track. The subway train travels at a constant average rate of 30 miles per hour. How many minutes will a journey on the subway take if the track distance as portrayed on the map is 3 inches?

   (A) 6
   (B) 9
   (C) 12
   (D) 18

2. An electronic reader typically costs $100. However, the price is heavily discounted due to both a coupon and a sale that have the same percent off the regular price. If the price using both the coupon discount and the sale discount is $49, what is the percent off the regular price that the coupon and the sale each provide independently?

   (A) 25%
   (B) 30%
   (C) 35%
   (D) 40%

3. If n percent of 80 is 20, what is n percent of 220?

    (A) 42

    (B) 48

    (C) 55

    (D) 76

4. If 132 men and 168 women are living in a dormitory, what percent of the total dormitory residents are men?

    (A) 28%

    (B) 34%

    (C) 40%

    (D) 44%

5. If 1 Canadian dollar can be exchanged for 0.80 U.S. dollars and vice versa, how many Canadian dollars can a traveler receive in exchange for 120 U.S. dollars?

    (A) 60

    (B) 90

    (C) 150

    (D) 220

6. David is developing a fitness plan and wants to get his weight to a level that will be considered healthy in terms of the body mass index (BMI) calculation. The currently recommended BMI is between 18.6 and 24.9. To calculate BMI using inches and pounds, David takes his weight in pounds and divides it by the square of his height in inches. Then he multiplies the entire result by 703. David is 6 feet, 3 inches tall, and currently weighs 260 pounds. To the nearest whole pound, what is the least number of whole pounds he needs to lose in order for his BMI to be within the healthy range?

    (A) 61

    (B) 68

    (C) 75

    (D) 83

Questions 7–9 refer to the following information.

A marine biologist has conducted research into the population of blue whales over the past few decades. The estimated global blue whale population is plotted against the given year in the graph below:

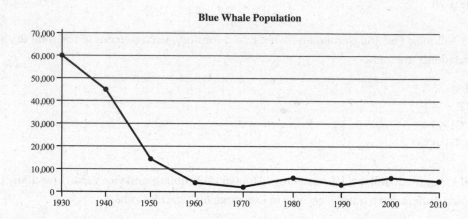

7. From 1940 until 1970, the best-fit equation for the values of the blue whale population has which general characteristic?

   (A) Linear decay
   (B) Linear growth
   (C) Exponential decay
   (D) Exponential growth

8. A worldwide treaty prohibiting commercial whaling (i.e., the hunting of whales) was passed at some point between 1930–2010. Based on the data, what is the year when this treaty most likely went into effect?

   (A) 1930
   (B) 1950
   (C) 1970
   (D) 2000

9. Another scientist is reviewing the results of the marine biologist's observations and assessing the impact of measurement error on such an ambitious project. The scientist is considering two possible sources of measurement error: (1) random error from any factor that would affect the scientist's measurements and (2) systematic error from a problem in the overall setup of the data-gathering project. Which of the following would be the best way that the marine biologist's measurement error could have been minimized?

   (A) Collecting whale population data from as many possible points from an even distribution throughout all the world's oceans
   (B) Comparing the blue whale data to data of other whales, such as the sperm whale, fin whale, and killer whale
   (C) Gathering data from a consistent single point in the Atlantic Ocean, doing so at the same day/time each year
   (D) Consistently taking a sample from a 100-square-mile range of the Pacific Ocean and electronically tagging each whale that is observed to ensure no whale is counted twice

Questions 10–11 refer to the following information.

The graph below gives the current GPA of every one of the 389 students at County High School.

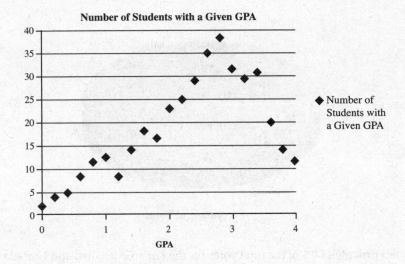

Number of Students with a Given GPA

◆ Number of Students with a Given GPA

GPA

10. Which of these values of the GPA for the students portrayed in the graph is between 2 and 3?

   I. Mean
  II. Median
 III. Mode

(A) I only
(B) II only
(C) I and II only
(D) I, II, and III

11. The school administrators have decided that too much grade inflation occurs at the school. They believe the average GPA is skewed too high by teachers giving too many A's and B's and by not enough students receiving C's, D's, and F's. If the administrators want to ensure that grade inflation is minimized, which of these quantities would be important to bring close to 2.0?

(A) Median only
(B) Mean only
(C) Both mean and median
(D) Neither mean nor median

In a recent election in a European country, the political parties divided the vote among the Social Democrats, the Christian Democrats, the Socialists, and the Green Party.

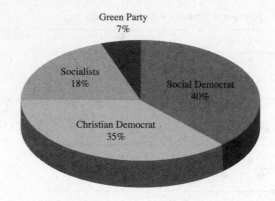

Percentage of Votes

12. If women provided 60% of the total votes for the Green, Socialist, and Christian Democrat parties and if males/females each represent 50% of the country's voters, what percent of the Social Democrat vote was from men?

    (A) 45%
    (B) 49%
    (C) 56%
    (D) 65%

13. The country's constitution states that in order for a party to come to power, it must have a majority of the votes. The constitution also states that the seats in the parliament are allocated proportionally to each party based on the percentage of votes each party received. So if no one political party receives a majority of the vote, a coalition party will have to be formed from 2 or more parties to give a governing majority. Which of the following combinations of political parties from this election would NOT result in a governing coalition?

    (A) Christian Democrat and Social Democrat
    (B) Green Party and Christian Democrat
    (C) Socialist and Social Democrat
    (D) Socialist and Christian Democrat

Questions 14–15 refer to the following information.

300 patients at a hospital were categorized based on whether they had high or low cholesterol and on whether they had high or low blood pressure. The results are tabulated below:

	High Cholesterol	Low Cholesterol	Total
High Blood Pressure	40	30	70
Low Blood Pressure	50	180	230
Total:	90	210	300

14. What is the probability that one of the 230 low blood pressure patients has high cholesterol?

    (A) $\dfrac{30}{230}$

    (B) $\dfrac{50}{230}$

    (C) $\dfrac{65}{230}$

    (D) $\dfrac{80}{230}$

15. What is the percent chance that one of the 300 patients will have at least one of the conditions—high cholesterol or high blood pressure?

    (A) 36%
    (B) 40%
    (C) 48%
    (D) 52%

Questions 16–17 refer to the following information.

A researcher surveyed several residents in a town about the types of vehicles the residents own. The results are shown in the table below.

	Car	Van	Truck/SUV	Total
Gas	104	31	43	178
Hybrid	10	1	m	n
Electric	6	3	0	9
Total	120	35	45	200

16. Jennifer and Bill were members of the group surveyed. They have a car and a van in their garage. What is the probability that both of the vehicles in their garage are hybrids?

(A) $\dfrac{1}{420}$

(B) $\dfrac{1}{380}$

(C) $\dfrac{1}{360}$

(D) $\dfrac{1}{240}$

17. What are the values of m and n in the table above?

(A) $m = 4$ and $n = 8$

(B) $m = 8$ and $n = 26$

(C) $m = 2$ and $n = 13$

(D) Cannot determine based on the given information.

Problem Solving and Data Analysis Solutions

ANSWER KEY

1. **C**	6. **A**	11. **C**	16. **A**
2. **B**	7. **C**	12. **D**	17. **C**
3. **C**	8. **C**	13. **B**	
4. **D**	9. **A**	14. **B**	
5. **C**	10. **D**	15. **B**	

ANSWERS EXPLAINED

1. **(C)** Since 1 inch on the map corresponds to 2 miles of actual distance, double the 3 inches shown on the map to determine that the subway has traveled 6 actual miles. Since the subway is traveling at 30 miles per hour, solve for the number of hours the subway has traveled:

$$\text{Distance} = \text{Rate} \times \text{Time}$$
$$6 = 30 \times \text{Time} \rightarrow$$
$$\text{Time} = \frac{1}{5} \text{ hours}$$

Then multiply $\frac{1}{5}$ by 60 minutes to determine how many minutes the train takes to travel the 6 miles:

$$\frac{1}{5} \times 60 = 12 \text{ minutes}$$

2. **(B)** Since both the coupon and the sale provide the same percent discount, you can set up an equation to determine what you must multiply $100 by in order to end up with a price of $49. Alternatively, you can simply multiply $100 by the same variable twice, which will indirectly let you determine the correct percentage:

$$x \cdot x \cdot 100 = 49 \rightarrow$$
$$x^2 = \frac{49}{100} = 0.49 \rightarrow$$
$$x = \sqrt{0.49} = 0.7$$

If x equals 0.7, subtract 0.7 from 1 to find the percent discount:

$$1 - 0.7 = 0.3 = 30\%$$

This means that a 30 percent discount has been applied to the original amount two times.

3. **(C)** Set this up as an equation to determine what n equals. Use the first bit of information in the question:

$$\frac{\text{Part}}{\text{Whole}} \times 100 = \text{Percent} \rightarrow$$
$$\frac{20}{80} \times 100 = n \rightarrow$$
$$n = 25\%$$

Then take 25% of 220:

$$0.25 \times 220 = 55$$

4. **(D)** Since $\frac{\text{Part}}{\text{Whole}} \times 100 = \text{Percent}$, take the number of men and divide it by the total number of residents to determine the percentage of just men:

$$\frac{132}{132+168} \times 100 = 44\%$$

5. **(C)** This is easiest to solve by using a simple proportion:

$$\frac{1\,\text{Canadian dollar}}{0.80\,\text{U.S. dollars}} = \frac{x}{120} \rightarrow$$

Cross multiply to get 150 Canadian dollars:

$$1\,\text{Canadian dollar} \times 120 = 0.80\,\text{U.S. dollars} \cdot x \rightarrow$$
$$x = \frac{120}{0.80} = 150\,\text{Canadian dollars}$$

6. **(A)** First solve for the weight that David must be in order to have a BMI of 24.9 given his height since this would put the BMI within the appropriate range. Use the wording in the question to set up an equation: "To calculate BMI using inches and pounds, David takes his weight in pounds and divides it by the square of his height in inches. Then he multiplies the entire result by 703." This gives the following BMI equation:

$$\frac{\text{Weight}}{\text{Height}^2} \times 703 = \text{BMI}$$

Since David is 6 feet, 3 inches tall, his height is $(12 \times 6) + 3 = 75$ inches. Plug in 24.9 for the BMI and 75 for the height into the equation, and solve for the weight:

$$\frac{\text{Weight}}{75^2} \times 703 = 24.9 \rightarrow \text{Weight} = \frac{24.9 \times 75^2}{703} \approx 199$$

Then subtract the desired weight from David's current weight to determine how many whole pounds he should lose:

$$260 - 199 = 61$$

7. **(C)** Between 1940 and 1970, the blue whale population is decreasing and the function has a substantial curve. So the graph shows exponential decay. Note that if the decay were linear, the graph would have gone down in a straight line.

8. **(C)** After the passage of a treaty banning whaling, it is most reasonable to expect that the population of blue whales would gradually increase. 1970 is the only choice after which there is an increase in the global blue whale population.

9. **(A)** This arrangement would ensure the most random gathering of data from as large a sample as possible, thereby minimizing random and systematic error. The other options focus on irrelevant or extremely narrow samples. Choice (B) has a major systematic error since it does not focus on gathering whale data. Instead, this choice focuses on comparing data. Choice (C) minimizes random error for this particular data point due to its consistent measurement. However, this choice has the systematic issue of not gathering a wide enough sample of data. Although choice (D) is superior to choices (B) and (C), it falls short of choice (A). Choice (D) limits the sample to a relatively small part of one ocean instead of considering whales all over the world.

10. **(D)** Since there is a large cluster of students with GPAs between 2 and 3, it is possible to estimate that the mean and median will fall in that range. The most frequent value, the mode, will also be in that range since the greatest number of students with a particular GPA is between 2 and 3.

11. **(C)** The median would be the middle value of all the GPAs, and if the middle value were much above 2.0, it would be a strong indication that there was grade inflation. The mean is the arithmetic average of the GPAs, so if it were much above 2.0, it would also indicate grade inflation. So, both the median and mean should be close to 2.0 in order to minimize grade inflation.

12. **(D)** Women provided 60% of the vote for the 60% of the total votes for the Green, Socialist, and Christian Democrat parties. That means that women provided 0.6 × 0.6 × Total votes = 36% of the Total votes, not including the Social Democrat votes. Since women make up 50% of the country's voters, 14% of the country's total voters are women who voted for the Social Democrats since 50 – 36 = 14. That means that 26% of the total population of the country are males who voted for the Social Democrats. To determine the percentage of Social Democrat votes from males, take 26 and divide it by the total percentage of 40 and then convert that value to a percent:

$$\frac{26}{40} \times 100 = 65\%$$

13. **(B)** The Green Party and Christian Democrat Party together would represent 7 + 35 = 42 percent of the entire vote. Since 42% is less than the 50% majority needed for a

governing coalition, these two parties would not be able to form a governing coalition on their own. All of the other options give combinations that add to at least 50% and could therefore form a majority governing coalition.

14. **(B)** There are 50 low blood pressure patients who have high cholesterol. So simply divide 50 by the 230 total patients:

$$\frac{50}{230}$$

15. **(B)** There are 40 patients with both conditions, 50 who have only high cholesterol, and 30 who have only high blood pressure:

$$40 + 50 + 30 = 120$$

Divide 120 by the 300 total to find the percent:

$$\frac{120}{300} \times 100 = 40\%$$

16. **(A)** Multiply the probability that the car is a hybrid, $\frac{10}{120}$, by the probability that the van is a hybrid, $\frac{1}{35}$:

$$\frac{10}{120} \times \frac{1}{35} = \frac{1}{420}$$

17. **(C)** The value of m must be 2. All of the trucks and SUVs must add up to a total of 45, and there are 43 of the other truck/SUV types: $43 + 2 = 45$. The value of n must be 13. The total of all the different types of vehicles must add up to 200. The numbers in the last column show a total of $178 + 9 = 187$ and $187 + 13 = 200$.

PASSPORT TO ADVANCED MATH PRACTICE

1. Mercedez wants to design a floor that will have a length and width that add up to 30 feet. She also wants the area of the floor to be 216 square feet. What will the dimensions of the floor need to be?

(A) 10 feet by 20 feet
(B) 12 feet by 18 feet
(C) 14 feet by 16 feet
(D) 17 feet by 17 feet

2. $\left(\dfrac{n^2-n^3}{n^4}\right)^{-2}$ is equivalent to which of the following?

(A) $\dfrac{n^4}{1-2n+n^2}$

(B) $\dfrac{n}{n^8}$

(C) $\dfrac{1-2n+n^2}{n^2}$

(D) $\dfrac{n^2}{1+4n-n^2}$

3. For the real integers x and y, what must $\dfrac{2x+2y}{4}$ equal?

(A) The mode of x and y
(B) $x^2 + y^2$
(C) The arithmetic mean of x and y
(D) The median of $2x$ and $2y$

4. Factor: $16a^2 - 9b^2$

(A) $(2a + b)(a - b)$
(B) $(3a + 2b)(6a - 3b)$
(C) $(4a + 3b)(4a - 3b)$
(D) $(8a + 3b)(2a - 3b)$

5. What are the two solutions for x in the equation $4x^2 + 8x - 4 = 0$?

(A) $x = 3\sqrt{2}$ and $x = -4$
(B) $x = 2\sqrt{3}$ and $x = \sqrt{11} + 13$
(C) $x = -\sqrt{7}$ and $x = -5$
(D) $x = -1 - \sqrt{2}$ and $x = \sqrt{2} - 1$

6. Simplify: $x^4y^2 + x^3y^5 + xy^6 + 2x^3y^5$

(A) $xy(x^4 + 3x^2y^3 + y^6)$

(B) $y^2(x^4 + 4x^3y^4 + y^3)$

(C) $xy^2(x^3 + 3x^2y^3 + y^4)$

(D) $x(x^3y^2 + x^2y^5 + y^6 + 2x^4y^4)$

7. $\dfrac{x}{2} = \dfrac{2(n^0)}{2} - \dfrac{1}{2x}$

What is the value of x?

(A) 0
(B) 1
(C) 2
(D) 3

8. What is the sum of $3x^3 + 5x - 3$ and $2x^2 - 4x + 6$?

(A) $x^2 - 9x + 9$
(B) $2x^3 + 4x^2 - x$
(C) $3x^3 - x^2 + 2x + 3$
(D) $3x^3 + 2x^2 + x + 3$

9. $(25a^4 + 40a^2b^4 + 16b^8) \div (5a^2 + 4b^4) = ?$

(A) $5b^4 + 40a^2b^4 + 5a^2$
(B) $4b^4 + 5a^2$
(C) $25a^4 + 8a^2b^4 + 4a^2$
(D) 1

10. The formula used by the National Weather Service to calculate wind chill in degrees Fahrenheit is:

$$35.74 + 0.6215 \times T - 35.75 \times \left(V^{(0.16)}\right) + 0.4275 \times T \times \left(V^{(0.16)}\right)$$

T represents the air temperature in degrees Fahrenheit, and V represents the wind velocity in miles per hour. Which of these is an accurate statement about the relationship between wind chill and temperature?

I. The relative impact on wind chill of a particular increase in wind speed is more significant at lower wind speeds than at higher wind speeds.

II. Wind chill has an impact on the relative temperature feeling only at temperatures greater than or equal to 35.75 degrees Fahrenheit.

III. Wind chill and temperature are inversely related to one another.

(A) I only
(B) II only
(C) I and II only
(D) II and IIII only

11. Consider the function below.

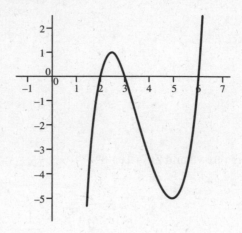

If the function is written as $f(x) = (x - 2) \times A \times (x - 3)$, what is the value of A?

(A) x

(B) $(x + 2)$

(C) $(x - 6)$

(D) $(x - 14)$

12. The function $y = 6x^3 + 19x^2 - 24x + c$ has zeros at the values of $-\frac{1}{2}$, $\frac{4}{3}$, and -4. What is the value of the constant c in this function?

(A) -16

(B) -9

(C) 2

(D) 14

13. The graph of the function below is given by which equation?

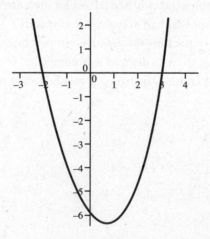

(A) $f(x) = 2x^2 - 2x - 4$

(B) $f(x) = 3x^2 - 6x - 7$

(C) $f(x) = x^2 + x - 3$

(D) $f(x) = x^2 - x - 6$

14. What will happen to the graph of $y = x^2$ in the x-y coordinate plane if it is changed to

$$y = (x + 8)^2 + 4?$$

(A) It will shift to the left eight units and shift up four units.
(B) It will shift to the right eight units and shift up four units.
(C) It will shift to the left eight units and shift down four units.
(D) It will shift to the right eight units and shift down four units.

15. Calculating the total cost C, including the sales tax (and no other fees), of a good with an untaxed price of P is given by the expression $C = 1.07P$. How could you calculate the cost of only the sales tax on the good?

(A) P
(B) $0.07P$
(C) $0.13P$
(D) $0.17P$

Passport to Advanced Math Solutions

ANSWER KEY

1. **B**	5. **D**	9. **B**	13. **D**
2. **A**	6. **C**	10. **A**	14. **A**
3. **C**	7. **B**	11. **C**	15. **B**
4. **C**	8. **D**	12. **A**	

ANSWERS EXPLAINED

1. **(B)** This is easiest to solve if you work your way backward from the answer choices. The only answer that multiplies to give an area of 216 is choice (B):

$$12 \times 18 = 216$$

If you wanted to solve this algebraically, the solution would be much more complicated. This question demonstrates that you should be open to plugging in answers when you anticipate a lengthy calculation. Set up two equations, one equation for the sum of the length and width and one equation for the area:

$$L + W = 30$$
$$L \times W = 216$$

Use substitution to solve:

$$L + W = 30 \rightarrow L = 30 - W$$

Substitute this in for L in the other equation:

$$L \times W = 216 \rightarrow$$
$$(30 - W) \times W = 216 \rightarrow$$
$$-W^2 + 30W - 216 = 0$$

This looks rather challenging to solve by factoring, so use the quadratic formula:

$$\frac{-b \pm \sqrt{b^2 - 4ac}}{2a} \rightarrow$$

$$\frac{-30 \pm \sqrt{30^2 - 4 \cdot (-1) \cdot (-216)}}{2(-1)} \rightarrow$$

$$\frac{-30 \pm 6}{-2} \rightarrow 15 \pm 3 \rightarrow 12, 18$$

If you plug in 12 as the width, you get 18 as the length. If we plug in 18 as the width, you get 12 as the length:

$$L \times W = 216 \rightarrow L \times 12 = 216 \rightarrow L = 18$$
$$L \times W = 216 \rightarrow L \times 18 = 216 \rightarrow L = 12$$

So the dimensions are 12 feet by 18 feet, regardless of what you call the length and width.

2. **(A)** Simplify the expression:

$$\left(\frac{n^2 - n^3}{n^4} \right)^{-2} \rightarrow$$

$$\left(\frac{n^2}{n^2} \left(\frac{1-n}{n^2} \right) \right)^{-2} \rightarrow \text{Cancel the } n^2 \text{ terms on the outside:}$$

$$\left(\frac{1-n}{n^2} \right)^{-2} \rightarrow \text{Flip it so it is to a positive power:}$$

$$\left(\frac{n^2}{1-n} \right)^{2} \rightarrow \text{Square both the top and bottom:}$$

$$\left(\frac{(n^2)^2}{(1-n)^2} \right) \rightarrow \left(\frac{n^4}{(1-n)(1-n)} \right) \rightarrow$$

$$\frac{n^4}{1 - 2n + n^2}$$

3. **(C)** $\frac{2x + 2y}{4} = \frac{x+y}{2}$, which is the arithmetic mean (simple average) of x and y.

4. **(C)** Both the first term and the second term of the expression are squared terms. So the expression can be restated as the difference of squares, the general form of which is $x^2 - y^2 = (x + y)(x - y)$:

$$16a^2 - 9b^2 = (4a)^2 - (3b)^2 = (4a + 3b)(4a - 3b)$$

5. **(D)** Solve by simplifying and completing the square:

$$4x^2 + 8x - 4 = 0 \rightarrow$$
$$x^2 + 2x - 1 = 0 \rightarrow$$
$$x^2 + 2x = 1$$

Then complete the square by adding 1 to both sides:

$$x^2 + 2x + 1 = 2$$

Then factor the left-hand side:

$$(x + 1)^2 = 2$$

Then take the square root of both sides, remembering to include positive and negative values on the right:

$$x + 1 = \sqrt{2} \text{ and } x + 1 = -\sqrt{2}$$

Solve for x to find the solutions:

$$x = \sqrt{2} - 1 \text{ and } x = -1 - \sqrt{2}$$

Alternatively, you could solve this using the quadratic equation. Start by dividing by 4 to simplify:

$$4x^2 + 8x - 4 = 0 \rightarrow$$
$$x^2 + 2x - 1 = 0$$

$$\frac{-b \pm \sqrt{b^2 - 4ac}}{2a} \rightarrow$$
$$\frac{-2 \pm \sqrt{2^2 - 4 \cdot 1 \cdot (-1)}}{2 \cdot 1} \rightarrow$$
$$\frac{-2 \pm \sqrt{8}}{2} \rightarrow \frac{-2 \pm 2\sqrt{2}}{2} = \frac{-1 \pm \sqrt{2}}{1} = -1 \pm \sqrt{2}$$

This is equivalent to the answers $x = -1 - \sqrt{2}$ and $x = \sqrt{2} - 1$.

6. **(C)** Combine like terms, and then factor out what is common to all of the terms:

$$x^4 y^2 + x^3 y^5 + xy^6 + 2x^3 y^5 \rightarrow$$
$$x^4 y^2 + 3x^3 y^5 + xy^6 \rightarrow$$
$$xy^2(x^3 + 3x^2 y^3 + y^4)$$

7. **(B)** This is probably easiest to solve by plugging in the answer choices. Start with choices (B) or (C) as your first attempt since the answers are in order from smallest to largest. If you plug in 1 for x, the equation works.

$$\frac{x}{2} = \frac{2(n^0)}{2} - \frac{1}{2x} \rightarrow$$

Note that $n^0 = 1$, since anything to the zero power is $1 \rightarrow$

$$\frac{1}{2} = \frac{2(1)}{2} - \frac{1}{2(1)} \rightarrow$$

$$\frac{1}{2} = 1 - \frac{1}{2} \text{ which is true.}$$

You can also solve for x algebraically, but doing so may take more time:

$$\frac{x}{2} = \frac{2(n^0)}{2} - \frac{1}{2x} \rightarrow$$

$$x = 2(n^0) - \frac{1}{x} \rightarrow$$

$$x = 2 - \frac{1}{x} \rightarrow$$

Multiply everything by $x \rightarrow$

$$x^2 = 2x - 1 \rightarrow$$

$$x^2 - 2x + 1 = 0 \rightarrow$$

$$(x-1)(x-1) = 0 \rightarrow$$

$$(x-1)^2 = 0 \rightarrow$$

$$x = 1$$

8. **(D)** Combine like terms to find the sum:

$$\begin{array}{r} 3x^3 + \qquad 5x - 3 \\ + \qquad 2x^2 - 4x + 6 \\ \hline 3x^3 + 2x^2 + \ x + 3 \end{array}$$

9. **(B)**

$$(25a^4 + 40a^2b^4 + 16b^8) \div (5a^2 + 4b^4) \rightarrow$$

$$\frac{25a^4 + 40a^2b^4 + 16b^8}{5a^2 + 4b^4} \rightarrow$$

$$\frac{(5a^2 + 4b^4)(5a^2 + 4b^4)}{5a^2 + 4b^4} = 5a^2 + 4b^4 = 4b^4 + 5a^2$$

10. **(A)** Choice I is correct. Since the velocity is raised to a fractional exponent, the impact of a certain amount of wind speed increase will be more significant at lower wind speeds than at higher wind speeds. Choice II is not correct. Wind chill still has an impact when the temperature is less than 35.75 degrees Fahrenheit since this number is a constant, not a minimal temperature. Choice III is not correct. As temperature increases, the perceived temperature due to wind chill will also increase.

11. **(C)** The function intersects the x-axis at $x = 6$, making 6 a zero of the function. Therefore, A can be expressed as $(x - 6)$.

12. **(A)** Plug in one of the zeros for x and plug in the number 0 for y since a zero intersects the x-axis. Remember that the y-value must be 0 for an x-intercept since that indicates where the function intersects the x-axis. Use this to solve for the constant c. Use –4 as that x-value so that you do not have to calculate with fractions:

$$y = 6x^3 + 19x^2 - 24x + c \rightarrow$$

$$0 = 6(-4)^3 + 19(-4)^2 - 24(-4) + c \rightarrow$$

$$-16 = c$$

13. **(D)** Since the parabola has zeros at 3 and –2, it can be written in this way:

$$f(x) = (x - 3)(x + 2)$$

Use FOIL:

$$f(x) = x^2 - x - 6$$

Alternatively, you can set $x = 0$. Then see which of the choices results in a y-value of –6 since that is the y-intercept of the parabola based on the graph. Only choice (D) works:

$$f(x) = x^2 - x - 6 \rightarrow$$
$$f(0) = 0^2 - 0 - 6 = -6$$

14. **(A)** When you add numbers to the x-value itself, the function shifts to the left by that number of places. When you add numbers to the function as a whole, the function shifts upward by that number of places. Since 8 is added to the x-value itself and 4 is added to the function as a whole, the function shifts to the left eight units and shifts up four units.

15. **(B)** The cost of the sales tax on the good is found by subtracting the untaxed price from the total cost:

$$1.07P - P = 0.07P$$

You can also visualize this by plugging in a sample value for the price of the good. A helpful sample value to use with percentages is 100 since it gives easily understood results. If, for example, you suppose that the price of the good is $100, the cost with the sales tax included is $1.07 \times \$100 = \$107$. So the sales tax on the good is $107 – $100 = $7. This is equivalent to $0.07 \times 100 = \$7$.

ADDITIONAL TOPICS IN MATH PRACTICE

1. If Alaina wants to paint all six faces of a rectangular box that has dimensions in feet of $8 \times 4 \times 6$, how many square feet of paint does she need?

(A) 124
(B) 168
(C) 208
(D) 256

2. If a circle has a radius of 3 units, what is the length in units of the arc on the circle that measures $\frac{\pi}{2}$ radians?

(A) π

(B) $\frac{3}{2}\pi$

(C) $\frac{5}{2}\pi$

(D) 7π

3. If x represents the diameter of a circle, what is the area of a 60-degree sector of the circle?

(A) πx^2

(B) $\dfrac{\pi x^2}{24}$

(C) $\dfrac{\pi x^2}{6}$

(D) $\dfrac{\pi x^2}{36}$

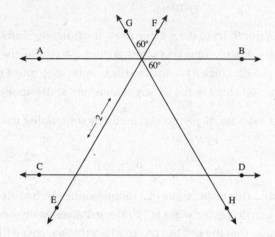

4. In the above drawing, lines AB and CD are parallel. Lines EF and GH intersect line AB at the same point and with the angle measures as indicated. What is the perimeter of the triangle formed by lines CD, EF, and GH between lines AB and CD?

(A) 2
(B) 4
(C) 6
(D) 8

Additional Topics in Math Solutions

ANSWER KEY

1. **C**   2. **B**   3. **B**   4. **C**

ANSWERS EXPLAINED

1. **(C)** The box is drawn below:

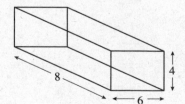

Add up all of the surface areas of the six faces of the box. Since there are 2 of each face dimension, you can set up your equation as follows:

$$2((8 \times 4) + (4 \times 6) + (8 \times 6)) = 208$$

2. **(B)** A measure of $\frac{\pi}{2}$ radians corresponds to $\frac{1}{4}$ of the distance around the circle since 2π radians is the entire distance around the circle.

First find the circumference of a circle with a radius of 3:

$$2\pi r = 2\pi 3 = 6\pi$$

Then calculate $\frac{1}{4}$ of the circumference:

$$\frac{1}{4} \text{ of } 6\pi = \frac{3}{2}\pi$$

3. **(B)** A 60-degree sector of the circle is $\frac{60}{360} = \frac{1}{6}$ of the total circle's area since there are 360 degrees in a circle.

The area of a circle is calculated using πr^2. Since the diameter of the circle is x, the radius of the circle is half of x: $\frac{x}{2}$.

So the area of this circle equals:

$$\pi r^2 = \pi \left(\frac{x}{2}\right)^2 = \frac{\pi x^2}{4}$$

Multiply the area of the circle by $\frac{1}{6}$ to find the area of the sector:

$$\frac{1}{6} \times \frac{\pi x^2}{4} = \frac{\pi x^2}{24}$$

4. **(C)** Perimeter is the sum of the side measures of the triangle. The internal angles of the triangle in question are all 60 degrees. Since the angles are all congruent, the sides of the triangle are all congruent as well. Thus the perimeter of the triangle is $2 + 2 + 2 = 6$ units. You can see this more clearly in the diagram below:

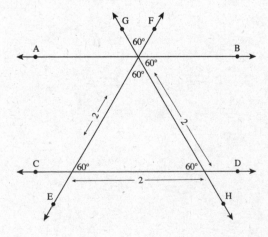

Practice
Tests

ANSWER SHEET
Practice Test 1

Reading Test

1. Ⓐ Ⓑ Ⓒ Ⓓ	13. Ⓐ Ⓑ Ⓒ Ⓓ	25. Ⓐ Ⓑ Ⓒ Ⓓ	37. Ⓐ Ⓑ Ⓒ Ⓓ
2. Ⓐ Ⓑ Ⓒ Ⓓ	14. Ⓐ Ⓑ Ⓒ Ⓓ	26. Ⓐ Ⓑ Ⓒ Ⓓ	38. Ⓐ Ⓑ Ⓒ Ⓓ
3. Ⓐ Ⓑ Ⓒ Ⓓ	15. Ⓐ Ⓑ Ⓒ Ⓓ	27. Ⓐ Ⓑ Ⓒ Ⓓ	39. Ⓐ Ⓑ Ⓒ Ⓓ
4. Ⓐ Ⓑ Ⓒ Ⓓ	16. Ⓐ Ⓑ Ⓒ Ⓓ	28. Ⓐ Ⓑ Ⓒ Ⓓ	40. Ⓐ Ⓑ Ⓒ Ⓓ
5. Ⓐ Ⓑ Ⓒ Ⓓ	17. Ⓐ Ⓑ Ⓒ Ⓓ	29. Ⓐ Ⓑ Ⓒ Ⓓ	41. Ⓐ Ⓑ Ⓒ Ⓓ
6. Ⓐ Ⓑ Ⓒ Ⓓ	18. Ⓐ Ⓑ Ⓒ Ⓓ	30. Ⓐ Ⓑ Ⓒ Ⓓ	42. Ⓐ Ⓑ Ⓒ Ⓓ
7. Ⓐ Ⓑ Ⓒ Ⓓ	19. Ⓐ Ⓑ Ⓒ Ⓓ	31. Ⓐ Ⓑ Ⓒ Ⓓ	43. Ⓐ Ⓑ Ⓒ Ⓓ
8. Ⓐ Ⓑ Ⓒ Ⓓ	20. Ⓐ Ⓑ Ⓒ Ⓓ	32. Ⓐ Ⓑ Ⓒ Ⓓ	44. Ⓐ Ⓑ Ⓒ Ⓓ
9. Ⓐ Ⓑ Ⓒ Ⓓ	21. Ⓐ Ⓑ Ⓒ Ⓓ	33. Ⓐ Ⓑ Ⓒ Ⓓ	45. Ⓐ Ⓑ Ⓒ Ⓓ
10. Ⓐ Ⓑ Ⓒ Ⓓ	22. Ⓐ Ⓑ Ⓒ Ⓓ	34. Ⓐ Ⓑ Ⓒ Ⓓ	46. Ⓐ Ⓑ Ⓒ Ⓓ
11. Ⓐ Ⓑ Ⓒ Ⓓ	23. Ⓐ Ⓑ Ⓒ Ⓓ	35. Ⓐ Ⓑ Ⓒ Ⓓ	47. Ⓐ Ⓑ Ⓒ Ⓓ
12. Ⓐ Ⓑ Ⓒ Ⓓ	24. Ⓐ Ⓑ Ⓒ Ⓓ	36. Ⓐ Ⓑ Ⓒ Ⓓ	

Writing and Language Test

1. Ⓐ Ⓑ Ⓒ Ⓓ	12. Ⓐ Ⓑ Ⓒ Ⓓ	23. Ⓐ Ⓑ Ⓒ Ⓓ	34. Ⓐ Ⓑ Ⓒ Ⓓ
2. Ⓐ Ⓑ Ⓒ Ⓓ	13. Ⓐ Ⓑ Ⓒ Ⓓ	24. Ⓐ Ⓑ Ⓒ Ⓓ	35. Ⓐ Ⓑ Ⓒ Ⓓ
3. Ⓐ Ⓑ Ⓒ Ⓓ	14. Ⓐ Ⓑ Ⓒ Ⓓ	25. Ⓐ Ⓑ Ⓒ Ⓓ	36. Ⓐ Ⓑ Ⓒ Ⓓ
4. Ⓐ Ⓑ Ⓒ Ⓓ	15. Ⓐ Ⓑ Ⓒ Ⓓ	26. Ⓐ Ⓑ Ⓒ Ⓓ	37. Ⓐ Ⓑ Ⓒ Ⓓ
5. Ⓐ Ⓑ Ⓒ Ⓓ	16. Ⓐ Ⓑ Ⓒ Ⓓ	27. Ⓐ Ⓑ Ⓒ Ⓓ	38. Ⓐ Ⓑ Ⓒ Ⓓ
6. Ⓐ Ⓑ Ⓒ Ⓓ	17. Ⓐ Ⓑ Ⓒ Ⓓ	28. Ⓐ Ⓑ Ⓒ Ⓓ	39. Ⓐ Ⓑ Ⓒ Ⓓ
7. Ⓐ Ⓑ Ⓒ Ⓓ	18. Ⓐ Ⓑ Ⓒ Ⓓ	29. Ⓐ Ⓑ Ⓒ Ⓓ	40. Ⓐ Ⓑ Ⓒ Ⓓ
8. Ⓐ Ⓑ Ⓒ Ⓓ	19. Ⓐ Ⓑ Ⓒ Ⓓ	30. Ⓐ Ⓑ Ⓒ Ⓓ	41. Ⓐ Ⓑ Ⓒ Ⓓ
9. Ⓐ Ⓑ Ⓒ Ⓓ	20. Ⓐ Ⓑ Ⓒ Ⓓ	31. Ⓐ Ⓑ Ⓒ Ⓓ	42. Ⓐ Ⓑ Ⓒ Ⓓ
10. Ⓐ Ⓑ Ⓒ Ⓓ	21. Ⓐ Ⓑ Ⓒ Ⓓ	32. Ⓐ Ⓑ Ⓒ Ⓓ	43. Ⓐ Ⓑ Ⓒ Ⓓ
11. Ⓐ Ⓑ Ⓒ Ⓓ	22. Ⓐ Ⓑ Ⓒ Ⓓ	33. Ⓐ Ⓑ Ⓒ Ⓓ	44. Ⓐ Ⓑ Ⓒ Ⓓ

ANSWER SHEET
Practice Test 1

Math Test (No Calculator)

1. Ⓐ Ⓑ Ⓒ Ⓓ   5. Ⓐ Ⓑ Ⓒ Ⓓ   9. Ⓐ Ⓑ Ⓒ Ⓓ   13. Ⓐ Ⓑ Ⓒ Ⓓ
2. Ⓐ Ⓑ Ⓒ Ⓓ   6. Ⓐ Ⓑ Ⓒ Ⓓ   10. Ⓐ Ⓑ Ⓒ Ⓓ
3. Ⓐ Ⓑ Ⓒ Ⓓ   7. Ⓐ Ⓑ Ⓒ Ⓓ   11. Ⓐ Ⓑ Ⓒ Ⓓ
4. Ⓐ Ⓑ Ⓒ Ⓓ   8. Ⓐ Ⓑ Ⓒ Ⓓ   12. Ⓐ Ⓑ Ⓒ Ⓓ

14.   15.   16.   17.

[Grid-in answer bubbles for questions 14–17]

Math Test (With Calculator)

1. Ⓐ Ⓑ Ⓒ Ⓓ   8. Ⓐ Ⓑ Ⓒ Ⓓ   15. Ⓐ Ⓑ Ⓒ Ⓓ   22. Ⓐ Ⓑ Ⓒ Ⓓ
2. Ⓐ Ⓑ Ⓒ Ⓓ   9. Ⓐ Ⓑ Ⓒ Ⓓ   16. Ⓐ Ⓑ Ⓒ Ⓓ   23. Ⓐ Ⓑ Ⓒ Ⓓ
3. Ⓐ Ⓑ Ⓒ Ⓓ   10. Ⓐ Ⓑ Ⓒ Ⓓ   17. Ⓐ Ⓑ Ⓒ Ⓓ   24. Ⓐ Ⓑ Ⓒ Ⓓ
4. Ⓐ Ⓑ Ⓒ Ⓓ   11. Ⓐ Ⓑ Ⓒ Ⓓ   18. Ⓐ Ⓑ Ⓒ Ⓓ   25. Ⓐ Ⓑ Ⓒ Ⓓ
5. Ⓐ Ⓑ Ⓒ Ⓓ   12. Ⓐ Ⓑ Ⓒ Ⓓ   19. Ⓐ Ⓑ Ⓒ Ⓓ   26. Ⓐ Ⓑ Ⓒ Ⓓ
6. Ⓐ Ⓑ Ⓒ Ⓓ   13. Ⓐ Ⓑ Ⓒ Ⓓ   20. Ⓐ Ⓑ Ⓒ Ⓓ   27. Ⓐ Ⓑ Ⓒ Ⓓ
7. Ⓐ Ⓑ Ⓒ Ⓓ   14. Ⓐ Ⓑ Ⓒ Ⓓ   21. Ⓐ Ⓑ Ⓒ Ⓓ

28.   29.   30.   31.

[Grid-in answer bubbles for questions 28–31]

Practice Test 1

READING TEST

60 MINUTES, 47 QUESTIONS

> **Directions:** Each passage or pair of passages is accompanied by several questions. After reading the passage(s), choose the best answer to each question based on what is indicated explicitly or implicitly in the passage(s) or in the associated graphics.

Questions 1–9 are based on the following excerpt.

The following passage is an excerpt from the 1912 French novel "The Gods Will Have Blood." Citizen Brotteaux, an elderly humanist, is visiting Citizeness Gamelin, a widowed artist, for lunch. They are briefly interrupted by Gamelin's son, Évariste, a young artist and recently appointed magistrate in the French Revolution.

That morning, very early, the Citizen
Brotteaux had made the Citizeness Gamelin
the magnificent gift of a capon.* It would
Line have been imprudent on his part to say how
(5) he had come by it: for he had been given
it by a certain lady of the market at Pointe
Eustache, whose letters he occasionally wrote
for her, and it was well known that the ladies
of the market cherished Royalist sympathies
(10) and were in touch by correspondence with
the émigrés. The Citizeness Gamelin had
accepted the capon with deep gratitude. Such
things were scarcely ever seen now; food of all
kinds became more expensive every day. The
(15) people feared a famine: everybody said that
that was what the aristocrats wanted, and that
the food-grabbers were preparing for it.

Invited to eat his share of the capon at
the midday meal, the Citizen Brotteaux duly
(20) appeared and congratulated his hostess on
the rich aroma of her cooking. For indeed
the artist's studio was filled with the smell of
savory meat soup.

"You are a true gentleman, monsieur,"
(25) replied the good lady. "As an appetizer for
your capon, I've made some vegetable soup
with a slice of bacon and a big beef bone.
There's nothing gives soup a flavor better
than a marrow bone."

(30) "A praiseworthy maxim, Citizeness,"
replied old Brotteaux. "And you will do
wisely, if tomorrow, and the next day, and
all the rest of the week, you put this pre-
cious bone back into the pot, so that it will
(35) continue to flavor it. The wise woman of
Panzoust used to do that: she made a soup of
green cabbages with a rind of bacon and an
old *savorados*. That is what they call the tasty
and succulent medullary bone in her coun-
(40) try, which is also my country."

"This lady you speak of, monsieur," the
Citizeness Gamelin put in, "wasn't she a little
on the careful side, making the same bone
last so long?"

(45)   "She did not live on a grand scale," Brotteaux replied. "She was poor, even though she was a prophetess."

        At that moment Évariste Gamelin came in, still deeply affected by the confession he had
(50) just heard and promising himself he would discover the identity of Élodie's seducer, so that he might wreak on him the vengeance of the Republic and of himself.

        After the usual politenesses, the Citizen
(55) Brotteaux resumed the thread of his discourse:

        "Those who make a trade out of foretelling the future rarely grow rich. Their attempts to deceive are too easily found out and arouse
(60) detestation. And yet it would be necessary to detest them much, much more if they foretold the future correctly. For a man's life would become intolerable, if he knew what was going to happen to him. He would be
(65) made aware of future evils, and would suffer their agonies in advance, while he would get no joy of present blessings since he would know how they would end. Ignorance is the necessary condition of human happiness,
(70) and it has to be admitted that on the whole mankind observes that condition well. We are almost entirely ignorant of ourselves; absolutely of others. In ignorance, we find our bliss; in illusions, our happiness."

(75)   The Citizeness Gamelin put the soup on the table, said the *Benedicite*, seated her son and her guest, and began to eat standing up, declining the chair which Brotteaux offered her next to him, since, she said, she knew
(80) what courtesy required of her.

        *A *capon* is a domesticated rooster.

1. The passage is best representative of what genre of world literature?

    (A) Magical realism
    (B) Short story
    (C) Historical fiction
    (D) Fantasy

2. The characters in the passage use the terms "citizen" and "citizeness" to distinguish between

    (A) different genders.
    (B) different social classes.
    (C) different ages.
    (D) different ethnicities.

3. It can reasonably be inferred that the "people" believe the "aristocrats" and "food-grabbers" in lines 14–17 are likely planning to

    (A) poison the food of the peasants.
    (B) save food to give away to the needy.
    (C) hoard food to profit at a later time.
    (D) develop better agricultural technology.

4. Which choice provides the best evidence for the answer to the previous question?

    (A) Lines 1–3 ("That morning . . . capon.")
    (B) Lines 5–8 ("for he . . . for her")
    (C) Lines 8–11 ("it was . . . émigrés.")
    (D) Lines 12–14 ("Such . . . every day.")

5. As used in line 45, "grand" most nearly means

    (A) vast.
    (B) imposing.
    (C) lavish.
    (D) prime.

6. We can reasonably infer from the passage that Évariste's approach to the treatment of lawbreakers is

    (A) tolerant and patient.
    (B) unforgiving and relentless.
    (C) ignorant and illusory.
    (D) generous and gentlemanly.

7. Which choice provides the best evidence for the answer to the previous question?

   (A) Lines 48–53 ("At that . . . himself.")
   (B) Lines 62–68 ("For a . . . would end.")
   (C) Lines 71–74 ("We . . . happiness.")
   (D) Lines 75–80 ("The Citizeness . . . of her.")

8. The main idea conveyed in Brotteaux's monologue in lines 57–74 can best be summarized as

   (A) let bygones be bygones.
   (B) the truth will set you free.
   (C) focus on the moment.
   (D) do unto others as you would have them do unto you.

9. As used in line 78, "declining" most nearly means

   (A) repulsing.
   (B) decreasing.
   (C) turning down.
   (D) plummeting.

Questions 10–19 are based on the following passage and the table below.

This passage is adapted from a 2014 article about Canada and the War of 1812.

Spanning a distance of more than 1,500 miles, the border between Canada and the United States has been called the longest
Line undefended international boundary in the
(5) world. This is true to some extent in that neither the U.S. nor Canada maintains a military presence at the border. But as anyone who has crossed from one side of Niagara Falls to the other knows, civilian law enforcement is
(10) present and accounted for at checkpoints on both sides of the boundary, where entrants are monitored and customs laws administered. Partly because of our cultural similarities and partly because of the remarkable
(15) amiability of our diplomatic relations over the past 150 years, it can sometimes seem almost as though the distinction between Canada and the United States is more one of policy than one of practice. But this has not
(20) always been the case. There was a time when the kinship between these two nations was far more dubious, particularly in the years prior to 1867, when Canada was granted its dominion status and thus its independence
(25) from the British parliament.

In 1812, U.S. president James Madison declared war on the British Empire. There were a variety of reasons for the declaration: British-U.S. relations were strained by
(30) England's attempts to thwart international trade between the U.S. and France—with whom the British were already at war—and on several occasions, the Royal Navy had endeavored to conscript American sailors
(35) by force. However, perhaps no cause for war was more compelling in the U.S. than the desire to expand the nation into the northern territories of modern-day Ontario and modern-day Quebec, which were still British
(40) colonies at the time.

With the United States paralyzed by partisan infighting and confused about its federal military policies, and Canada's meager militias practically unaided by the British
(45) army—which was largely embroiled in fighting against Napoleon's forces in Spain—neither side was well-prepared for a war. Nonetheless, in July of that year, Congress launched its untrained 35,000-man army
(50) into the first stage of a four-pronged offensive starting at Detroit, then Niagara, then Kingston, and finally at Montreal. Madison—who anticipated the conflict's resolution in a matter of weeks—had as grossly overesti-
(55) mated the efficacy of the American military as he had underestimated the tenacity of New England Federalists' opposition to the war. By adopting a cautious, defensive strategy, Native-American and Canadian militias
(60) led by British officers successfully rebuffed the invaders and eventually—following the surrender of General William Hull to British Major General Isaac Brock and Shawnee

Leader Tecumseh—captured not only Detroit
(65) but most of the Michigan territory as well.

The war dragged on for two years with
little progress on either side. By concentrat-
ing their defenses in Ontario, the Canadians
left Quebec vulnerable to invasion along the
(70) St. Lawrence River. Consequently, the U.S.
seized portions of Upper Canada but because
of a combination of poor military leadership,
logistical obstacles, and inadequate funding, never managed to take the key posi-
(75) tions of Montreal or Quebec City. By April
of 1814, Napoleon was defeated in Europe
and a greater brunt of the British military fell
upon the United States. The primary theaters
of war, in turn, shifted from the Canadian
(80) frontier to coastal American cities such
as Baltimore, Washington D.C., and New
Orleans. Canada's role in the conflict was by
that time essentially at an end, though fighting continued intermittently in the North
(85) until the signing of the Treaty of Ghent in
December of that year.

Since the War of 1812, Canada and the
U.S. have maintained a warm and neigh-
borly diplomatic relationship; the two
(90) nations fought as allies in both World Wars and
collaborated closely throughout the
Cold War with NORAD. More recently, the
Canada-United States Free Trade Agreement
implemented at the beginning of 1988 ushered
(95) in a tremendous increase in commerce and
business between the two. A shared British
colonial heritage and the English language
have provided all the common ground necessary to make our two neighboring nations
(100) fast friends, but the now-antique batteries
and ramparts that still line the St. Lawrence
River stand as testament to a time when our
international intercourse was far less friendly
than it is today.

Canadian-American Trade

Year*	Total Annual Exports from the U.S. to Canada (Billions of U.S. Dollars)	Total Annual Imports from Canada to the U.S. (Billions of U.S. Dollars)
1986	45.3	68.3
1987	59.8	71.0
1988	71.6	81.4
1989	78.8	87.9
1990	83.7	91.4
1991	85.1	91.0
1992	90.6	98.6

*Data obtained from *https://www.census.gov/foreign-trade/
balance/c1220.html#1985*

10. It can be inferred from the passage as a
whole that the author believes that many
present-day readers of this piece are

(A) knowledgeable about the history of the
major battles in the different military
theaters in the War of 1812.
(B) well-informed about the difficult early
relations that the U.S. and Canada had in
the early 1800s.
(C) eager to use the information in this
reading to advocate the increased
militarization of the undefended
U.S.-Canada border.
(D) generally unaware of the past hostility
between the U.S. and Canada given the
present-day friendliness between the
two countries.

11. Which of the following does the author argue
was the most significant motivation for
U.S. citizens who wanted to go to war with
Canada in the early 1800s?

(A) Vengeance toward the British
(B) Territorial ambitions
(C) The continued capture of American sailors
(D) Defense against Native-American
incursions

12. Which choice provides the best evidence for the answer to the previous question?

    (A) Lines 20–25 ("There was . . . parliament.")
    (B) Lines 33–35 ("on several . . . force.")
    (C) Lines 35–40 ("However . . . the time.")
    (D) Lines 59–64 ("Native-American . . . Tecumseh")

13. As it is used in line 22, "dubious" most nearly means

    (A) congenial.
    (B) suspect.
    (C) familial.
    (D) loathsome.

14. As it is used in line 56, "tenacity" most nearly means

    (A) determination.
    (B) anger.
    (C) existence.
    (D) function.

15. Based on the fourth paragraph, lines 66–86, which of the following was NOT an obstacle to a lasting U.S. victory in Quebec?

    (A) The quality of the U.S. generals
    (B) The lack of good transportation and supplies
    (C) A lack of funding
    (D) A strong Canadian defense

16. According to the passage, the North American battles in the War of 1812 gradually shifted from

    (A) being fought and led by great generals to being fought and led by elected representatives.
    (B) decisive victories by the British to decisive victories by the United States.
    (C) being fought in the wilderness to being fought in urban areas.
    (D) French to British military involvement.

17. Which choice provides the best evidence for the answer to the previous question?

    (A) Lines 61–64 ("following . . . Tecumseh")
    (B) Lines 75–78 ("By April . . . States.")
    (C) Lines 78–82 ("The primary . . . Orleans.")
    (D) Lines 83–86 ("fighting . . . year.")

18. The table after the passage is most helpful when quantifying the qualitative description given by which word in the passage?

    (A) "Collaborated," line 91
    (B) "Tremendous," line 95
    (C) "Neighboring," line 99
    (D) "Intercourse," line 103

19. According to lines 92–96, a free trade agreement between the U.S. and Canada was implemented in 1988. Based on the data provided in the table, what type of business can we reasonably conclude would most likely have had the greatest immediate benefit in the first year of the treaty becoming law?

    (A) A company that manufactures cars in the United States and sells them to Canadians
    (B) A company that purchases raw materials from Canada to manufacture products in its U.S. factories
    (C) A Canadian company that manufactures products exclusively for the Canadian government
    (D) A U.S. company that provides retail services to customers in the continental United States

Questions 20–28 are based on the following passage.

This passage is adapted from the article "Woman Suffrage Must Be Non-Partisan," by Susan B. Anthony, August 1896.

The different woman suffrage committees
of Southern California, it is understood, are
planning to do some very effective campaign
Line work on behalf of the eleventh amendment
(5)   by forming allied women's clubs to the old
parties. The plan, it is argued, will be perfectly
consistent, owing to the fact that the
Republicans, Populists and Prohibitionists
all put a woman-suffrage plank in their State
(10) platforms, and that while the Democracy
refused this, many of the delegates from this
end of the State favored it and are staunch
supporters of the movement. It is considered
"good politics" to work in connection with
(15) instead of independent of the present organized political parties.

The plan of action proposed in the above
item from Los Angeles in yesterday's Call
would be most disastrous to the woman's
(20) suffrage amendment. Every one must see
that for a part of the suffrage women to thus
ally themselves with the Republican party,
another portion with the Democratic party,
another with the Populist, another with the
(25) Prohibition, another with the Nationalist,
and yet another with the Socialist Labor
party, would be to divide and distract public
thought from women as suffragists to women
as Republicans, Populists, etc. To do this may
(30) be "good politics," for the different political parties, but it would surely be very "bad
politics" for amendment No. XI. It doesn't need
a prophet to see that "allied clubs to the old
parties" will turn the thought of the women
(35) themselves to proselyting for members to their
respective political party clubs instead of each
and every one holding herself non-partisan, or
better all-partisan, pleading with every man of
every party to stamp "yes" at amendment No.
(40) XI, not for the purpose of insuring success to
his party at the coming election, or to win the

good will of the women of the State for future
partisan ends, but instead, pleading with every
one to thus vote that he may help to secure
(45) to all the women of California who can "read
the constitution in the English language" their
citizen's right to vote to help the political party
of their choice in all elections in the good times
to come.

(50) Of course each of the political parties, old
and new, would be glad of the help of the
women throughout this fall campaign, but
who can fail to see that the women who should
join one alliance would thereby lose their
(55) influence with the men of each of the other
parties. They would at once be adjudged
partisans, working for the interest of the
party with which or to which they were allied.
Women of California, you cannot keep the
(60) good will and win the good votes of all the
good men of all the good parties of the State
by allying yourselves with one or the other or
all of them! You must stand as disfranchised
citizens—outlaws—shut out of "the body
(65) politic," humble supplicants, veriest beggars
at the feet of all men of all parties alike.

The vote of the humblest man of the
humblest party is of equal value to that of the
proudest millionaire of the largest party. And
(70) every woman must see that if a vast majority
of the women of the State should, under the
Los Angeles plan, ally themselves to either
one of the parties, the men of all the others
might well take alarm lest their party's chances
(75) of success would be vastly lessened if women
were allowed to vote and so from mere party
interest, be influenced to stamp "no" at
amendment No. XI.

It is very clear to every student of politics
(80) that what is "good politics" for political parties
is "mighty poor politics" for a reform measure
dependent upon the votes of the members
of all parties. It will be time enough for the
women of California to enroll themselves as
(85) Republicans, Democrats, Populists, etc., after
they have the right to vote secured to them by
the elimination of the word "male" from the
suffrage clause of the constitution. And to work

most efficiently to get the right to become a
(90) voting member of one or another of the parties
of the State women must now hold themselves
aloof from affiliation with each and all of them.

20. The primary purpose of this passage is to

    (A) confront a geographical region.
    (B) dispute a historical recollection.
    (C) attack a gender identity.
    (D) make a tactical argument.

21. In order to ratify the eleventh amendment, the
    author most directly encourages women to
    focus on winning over which group of men?

    (A) Leaders of major political parties
    (B) Men who are less fortunate
    (C) Literate, educated men
    (D) Men from all walks of life

22. Which option gives the best evidence for the
    answer to the previous question?

    (A) Lines 1–6 ("The different . . . parties.")
    (B) Lines 17–20 ("The plan . . . amendment.")
    (C) Lines 45–49 ("all the . . . come.")
    (D) Lines 63–66 ("You must . . . alike.")

23. The author most strongly suggests that the
    interests of the political parties and of women
    are

    (A) aligned.
    (B) uniform.
    (C) divergent.
    (D) belligerent.

24. Which option gives the best evidence for the
    answer to the previous question?

    (A) Lines 6–10 ("The plan . . . platforms")
    (B) Lines 13–16 ("It is . . . parties.")
    (C) Lines 29–32 ("To do . . . XI.")
    (D) Lines 67–69 ("The vote . . . party.")

25. As used in line 12, "staunch" most closely
    means

    (A) strong.
    (B) democratic.
    (C) disloyal.
    (D) mistaken.

26. The author uses quotation marks around
    the phrase "good politics" in line 14
    primarily to

    (A) properly cite her past writings.
    (B) distance herself from a point of view.
    (C) predict a likely course of events.
    (D) explain a controversial position.

27. As used in line 43, "ends" most closely
    means

    (A) completions.
    (B) objectives.
    (C) sorrows.
    (D) casualties.

28. The sentence in lines 83–88 ("It will be . . .
    constitution.") serves mainly to

    (A) encourage women to be patient in
        fighting for their ultimate political
        goal.
    (B) underscore the importance of identifying
        oneself with a political party.
    (C) demonstrate how a historical precedent
        applies to a modern situation.
    (D) explain how women will achieve elected
        positions.

Questions 29–38 are based on the following passages and table.

The passages are adapted from 2013 articles about microwaves.

Passage 1

It's a common fixture in household kitchens all across the United States, but remarkably few of us who use them have any
Line real idea of how our microwave ovens work.
(5) Contrary to most other food-heating appliances—the toaster, the convection oven, and the stove for instance—the microwave itself has no internal heating element: flame, coil, or otherwise. Instead, the microwave oven
(10) uses the principle of dipole rotation to generate heat from the molecules within the food itself.

Polar molecules, like a bar magnet, possess an electrical dipole moment, and, when
(15) introduced to a strong enough electromagnetic field, will align their positive and negative ends appropriately. The microwave oven produces a strong electromagnetic field, but this is not enough to generate heat from
(20) within the food.

As anyone who has watched a bag of instant popcorn expand knows, the tray inside of a microwave oven rotates as the food cooks. This rotation has the interesting
(25) effect of increasing the kinetic energy of the food's polar molecules as they too must constantly rotate in order to remain aligned with the field. As they do so, these molecules rub and grind against their neighbors, converting
(30) their kinetic energy into intermolecular friction, thus evolving heat. In fact, the motion of molecules is so directly related to internal heat that one can actually calculate a material's exact temperature by averaging the
(35) kinetic energy of the atoms and molecules that comprise it.

Passage 2

It is probable that humans have been cooking since not long after our ancestors harnessed the power of fire some several
(40) hundred thousand years ago. Since that time, the sophistication of our technology has increased more or less exponentially, and the technology of cooking is no exception. Insofar as it pertains to heat, the nature
(45) of culinary innovation has fallen primarily into one of two categories common to many technology arcs: speed and precision.

The first great breakthrough in cooking had to be the division of fires into their
(50) component functions. That is, a campfire used to produce light or to heat a large area is not typically the ideal fire for cooking. Once a fire ring was designated specifically for the preparation of food, the earliest
(55) earthen stoves almost certainly began to evolve shortly afterward and would have significantly increased the degree to which primitive cooks could distribute heat evenly. Discovered in the Ukraine, the oldest known
(60) stoves appear to date from about 30,000 years ago and were used primarily to bake mammoth meat.

The stove and the oven remain to this day our most commonly used cooking tech-
(65) nologies. Innovations in the field of heating elements have frequently ameliorated the mechanism without much change to the principle design. The commercialization of natural gas in late 17th-century England
(70) eventually gave cooks the ability to manipulate their cooking flame precisely as well as the convenience of instantaneous ignition. To this day, gas ranges are preferred by many professional chefs.

(75) The electric oven is an anomaly in the cooking technology arc, as it developed nearly one hundred years after the gas oven but is markedly slower and often less precise. Nonetheless, advancements in conductive

(80) materials, convection technology, and electromagnetic induction have tremendously improved on the efficacy of the original resistive-coil ranges.

(85) Electricity in the kitchen, of course, ushered in a new age of powered cooking appliances. Perhaps none is more curious, clever, and common than the microwave oven. The epitome of speed cooking, the microwave uses a wholly different approach to heating

(90) food than any of its predecessors—however, its remarkable swiftness comes at the expense of precision, particularly when dealing with physically dense foodstuffs. In consequence, the microwave is a fantastic device for thawing

(95) stored vegetables but should hardly be relied upon to properly prepare, say, a Thanksgiving turkey or perhaps a mammoth steak.

Polar Substances	Nonpolar Substances
Ethanol	Methane
Water	Carbon dioxide
Glucose	Ethylene
Ethyl alcohol	Gasoline
Acetic acid	Hexane

29. It is reasonable to infer that the primary scholarly fields of the two authors of Passage 1 and Passage 2 are respectively

(A) cooking and history.
(B) physics and paleontology.
(C) science and anthropology.
(D) chemistry and biology.

30. Unlike Passage 1, Passage 2 discusses what about the microwave?

(A) Its popularity
(B) Its shortcomings
(C) Its methodology
(D) Its possible applications

31. As it is used in line 31, "evolving" most nearly means

(A) advancing.
(B) reproducing.
(C) selecting.
(D) generating.

32. According to Passage 1, what is the aspect of microwaves that most distinguishes it from other types of cooking devices?

(A) Its capacity to increase the kinetic energy of food
(B) The precision with which it can cook food
(C) Its lack of an internal heating element
(D) The presence of intermolecular friction in its cooking process

33. Which choice provides the best evidence for the answer to the previous question?

(A) Lines 6–8 ("the . . . element")
(B) Lines 13–17 ("Polar . . . appropriately.")
(C) Lines 24–28 ("This . . . field.")
(D) Lines 31–36 ("In . . . it.")

34. What is the overall structure of Passage 2?

(A) A persuasive argument in favor of the use of older cooking methods
(B) A technical explanation of the workings of cooking devices
(C) A survey of the gradual developments in cooking technology
(D) An evaluation of which cooking technology is most effective in the modern kitchen

35. As it is used in line 47, "arcs" most nearly means

(A) discharges of energy.
(B) curvatures of machinery.
(C) portions of circles.
(D) lines of development.

36. Which of the following does the author of Passage 2 state is a step backward in the progression of cooking technology?

(A) The electric oven
(B) The microwave
(C) The Ukrainian earthen stove
(D) The gas oven

37. A scientist states that microwaves have increasing difficulty penetrating materials of gradually increasing layers since many of the microwaves are reflected out of the material as they encounter molecules. If this scientist is correct, it would best explain which of these excerpts from the passages?

(A) Lines 9-12 ("Instead . . . itself.")
(B) Lines 28-31 ("As they . . . heat.")
(C) Lines 79-83 ("Nonetheless . . . ranges.")
(D) Lines 93-97 ("In consequence . . . steak.")

38. Based on the information in the passages and the table, which combination of substances can it reasonably be inferred would be most likely to be heated by a microwave oven?

(A) Ethylene and acetic acid
(B) Glucose and water
(C) Carbon dioxide and methane
(D) Ethyl alcohol and gasoline

Questions 39–47 are based on the following passage.

This passage is adapted from a 2013 article about Halley's Comet

Much like Old Faithful at Yellowstone National Park—by far the most well-known of the American geysers—Halley's Comet
Line is neither the most visually brilliant nor the
(5) largest of its kind; its renown derives from the dependable frequency with which it can be observed. Halley's falls into a category called Great Comets, which are those that become bright enough during their passage
(10) near Earth to be observed by the naked eye. Predicting whether or not a comet will be

"great" has proven to be a treacherous task even for the most talented of astronomers and astrophysicists. The comet must pass
(15) through a relatively small expanse of space near enough to the Sun to reflect a large amount of light but remain close enough to Earth for the light to reach and penetrate our atmosphere. Moreover, it is thought
(20) that a Great Comet must possess a large and active nucleus, though the exact physics of comet nuclei—which consist of dust, ice, and perhaps particulate minerals—are still poorly understood. Even so, comets meeting these
(25) criteria have on occasion failed to achieve "greatness." To date, the most recent Great Comet was C/2006 P1, which appeared in January 2007 and was the brightest in more than 40 years.
(30) The intrinsic difficulty of predicting a comet's greatness makes the consistency of Halley's visibility all the more remarkable. Most Great Comets will pass near Earth only once every several thousand years,
(35) while Halley's does so on a cycle of about 75 years—making it the only Great Comet with the potential to appear twice in a human lifetime. With an eccentricity of 0.967, the orbit of Halley's Comet is extremely elliptical; at
(40) one end of its major axis, Halley's is roughly the same distance from the Sun as Pluto. At the other end, it passes between the orbits of Mercury and Venus. The highly elliptic character of Halley's orbit means that, apart
(45) from having one of the highest velocities of any body in our solar system, it passes near Earth both during its approach and its return from the Sun. Though becoming visible during only one of these passes, the two near
(50) points of the orbit make Halley's the parent body of two annual meteor showers: the Eta Aquariids in early May and Orionids of late October.
Though humans have likely marveled at
(55) the spectacle of Halley's Comet for thousands of years (the Talmudic astronomers of the 1st century describe a star that appears once every 70 years to wreak havoc on nauti-

cal navigation), it was little more than 300
(60) years ago that Edmond Halley—a friend of Sir
Isaac Newton's—used Newton's newly conceived laws of gravity to explain the motion
and predict the periodicity of comets. By
using these equations in tandem with histori-
(65) cal records, Halley surmised that the comets observed in 1531 by German Humanist
Petrus Apianus, in 1607 by Johannes Kepler,
and by himself and Newton in 1683 were one
and the same. Moreover, he predicted its
(70) return in 1758. Halley passed away in January
1742 at the age of 85, nearly 16 years to the
day short of seeing his prediction confirmed
firsthand. Yet, in an almost poetic cyclicity,
Halley's Comet—the periodicity of which
(75) Halley had derived from the observations of
two German astronomers—was observed
and documented by German farmer and
amateur astronomer Johann Palitzsch on
Christmas Day, 1758. The confirmation of
(80) Halley's theory constituted the first occasion
in which Western science had proven that
any bodies apart from planets orbit the Sun.
Halley's Comet has been visible in our sky
just three times since Palistzch's observation,
(85) but it will return again sometime in the summer of 2061.

39. The overall tone of the passage is best
characterized as one of

(A) solemn pessimism.
(B) playful whimsy.
(C) analytical curiosity.
(D) religious fervor.

40. As it is used in line 4, "brilliant" most nearly
means

(A) luminous.
(B) showy.
(C) intellectual.
(D) august.

41. It can reasonably be inferred that "Old Faithful"
(line 1) and Halley's Comet share what aspect
that primarily contributes to their fame?

(A) Presence of water
(B) High eccentricity
(C) Nuclear particulates
(D) Periodic observability

42. Which choice provides the best evidence for the
answer to the previous question?

(A) Lines 5–7 ("its . . . observed.")
(B) Lines 14–19 ("The . . . atmosphere.")
(C) Lines 20–23 ("large . . . minerals")
(D) Lines 38–39 ("With . . . elliptical")

43. According to the passage, which characteristic
of a comet is most essential to its being
categorized as a "Great Comet"?

(A) Whether it has a significant proportion of
dust and ice in its core
(B) Whether it has an orbital eccentricity
greater than zero
(C) Whether humans can observe it without a
telescope
(D) Whether it contributes to meteor activity
visible by astronomers

44. Which choice provides the best evidence for the
answer to the previous question?

(A) Lines 7–10 ("Halley's . . . eye.")
(B) Lines 21–23 ("though . . . minerals")
(C) Lines 38–39 ("With . . . elliptical")
(D) Lines 48–53 ("Though . . . October.")

45. The primary purpose of the second paragraph (lines 30–53) in the passage as a whole is to

   (A) discuss the physical definition of elliptical eccentricity.
   (B) provide scientific justification for the rarity of Halley's predictable visibility.
   (C) give historical evidence of human observation of Halley's velocity.
   (D) differentiate Halley from other celestial bodies, such as planets and meteors.

46. As used in line 65, "surmised" most nearly means

   (A) fancied.
   (B) conjectured.
   (C) knew.
   (D) foretold.

47. The scientist Halley's relationship to the ideas of Newton most resembles the relationship between

   (A) a musician who uses music theory to enable creative compositions.
   (B) a politician who uses philosophical maxims to predict societal outcomes.
   (C) a mathematician who uses scientific data to justify algebraic theories.
   (D) an engineer who uses the laws of physics to build long-lasting constructions.

35 MINUTES, 44 QUESTIONS

> **Directions:** The passages below are each accompanied by several questions, some of which refer to an underlined portion in the passage and some of which refer to the passage as a whole. For some questions, determine how the expression of ideas can be improved. For other questions, determine the best sentence structure, usage, or punctuation given the context. A passage or question may have an accompanying graphic that you will need to consider as you choose the best answer.
>
> Choose the best answer to each question, considering what will optimize the writing quality and make the writing follow the conventions of standard written English. Some questions have a "NO CHANGE" option that you can pick if you believe the best choice is to leave the underlined portion as is.

Questions 1–11 are based on the following passage and supplementary material.

Occupational Therapy

When a child with developmental delay ties his shoes independently, an adult recovering from stroke returns to driving, ❶ a teenager learns to use a power wheelchair following spinal cord injury, and an older adult stays in her home longer, an occupational therapist was part of ❷ our care.

Occupational therapy began in the United States in 1917 with the establishment of the Society for the Promotion of Occupational ❸ Therapy, now named, the American Occupational Therapy Association (AOTA). Historically, AOTA stood for restorative properties of everyday, meaningful

1. Which choice is most consistent with the listing pattern of the sentence as a whole?

   (A) NO CHANGE
   (B) a spinal cord injury is suffered by a teenager learning to use a power wheelchair,
   (C) a power wheelchair is used by a teenager after a spinal cord injury,
   (D) a spinal cord injury causes a teenager to suffer which a power wheelchair helps her overcome,

2. (A) NO CHANGE
   (B) his or her
   (C) their
   (D) her

3. (A) NO CHANGE
   (B) Therapy, now named the
   (C) Therapy now name the
   (D) Therapy now named, the

activity and occupational therapy ❹ today is one of the fastest growing occupational categories in the United States.

Today, occupational therapy has grown into a science-driven and evidence-based practice that serves people across the lifespan. According to AOTA, occupation refers to the activities that people, populations, and organizations engage in, not necessarily a job. The areas of ❺ occupations—or categories of ways people use their time—that an occupational therapist considers when working with clients include activities of daily living, instrumental activities of daily living, rest and sleep, education, work, play, leisure, and social participation.

Newly licensed occupational therapists have a minimum of a four-year undergraduate degree and a two-year master's degree. ❻ Many occupational therapists also have a doctorate. Occupational therapy assistants have a two-year associate's degree and work under the supervision of an occupational therapist. Occupational therapists and occupational therapy assistants work in a wide variety of settings, like hospitals, skilled nursing facilities, schools, home health, outpatient clinics, sports medicine, and private practice ❼ alongside all types of healthcare practitioners.

In these settings, occupational therapists work with clients to help them better participate ❽ in all the any of the areas of occupation. For example, in a school, an occupational therapist may help children learn to write. In hospitals, occupational therapists may make splints to prevent contracture in patients with burns. At an outpatient clinic, an occupational therapist might work with families to develop better sleep habits for their children. In sports medicine, occupational therapists often help golfers return to the links after rotator cuff surgery. In skilled nursing facilities, occupational therapists ❾ taught older adults how to prevent falls and safely ambulate through their morning routines. If an activity occupies

4. Which choice maintains the focus of and appropriate ending to the paragraph?

   (A) NO CHANGE
   (B) will one day be recognized for its contributions to modern medical science.
   (C) has extensive requirements for the educational background of its practitioners.
   (D) was widely used in large mental health facilities and with veterans returning from World War I.

5. (A) NO CHANGE
   (B) occupations: categories
   (C) occupations; or categories
   (D) occupations, or categories

6. The writer is considering deleting the underlined sentence. Should the sentence be kept or deleted?

   (A) Kept, because it gives the first mention of the educational qualifications to become an occupational therapist.
   (B) Kept, because it further elaborates on the educational possibilities for occupational therapists.
   (C) Deleted, because it repeats information stated elsewhere in the passage.
   (D) Deleted, because it contradicts information found later in the paragraph.

7. (A) NO CHANGE
   (B) conjoined to
   (C) what with
   (D) in addition to

8. (A) NO CHANGE
   (B) in any all of
   (C) in any or all of
   (D) in all of and any of

9. (A) NO CHANGE
   (B) has taught
   (C) teached
   (D) teach

10 their clients' time, it's something an occupational therapist can treat.

Fortunately for students considering careers, the job prospects for both occupational therapists and occupational therapy assistants are excellent. In 2012, 113,200 people were employed as occupational therapists and 38,600 as occupational therapy assistants. **11** The Bureau of Labor Statistics estimates that the employment for occupational therapists will increase 43% between 2012 and 2022. The estimate for the increase in all jobs is 29%.

10. (A) NO CHANGE
    (B) they're clients
    (C) there client's
    (D) their clients

Percent Change in Employment, Projected 2012–2022

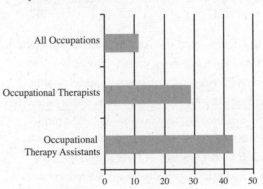

Adapted from the Bureau of Labor Statistics

11. Which choice offers an accurate interpretation of the data in the chart above?

    (A) NO CHANGE
    (B) The Bureau of Labor Statistics estimates that the employment for occupational therapists will increase 29% between 2012 and 2022. The estimate for the increase in all jobs is 11%.
    (C) The Bureau of Labor Statistics estimates that the employment for occupational therapists will increase 43% between 2012 and 2022. The estimate for the increase in all jobs is 11%.
    (D) The Bureau of Labor Statistics estimates that the employment for occupational therapists will increase 11% between 2012 and 2022. The estimate for the increase in all jobs is 29%.

Frick

[1]

Of all the legacies left behind by American industrialists of the 19th century, Henry Clay Frick's is perhaps the most ⓬ interesting. Frick is most remembered for his role in precipitating the violent outcome of the 1892 Homestead Steel labor strike.

[2]

In an effort to oust the Amalgamated Association of Iron and Steel Workers, or AA, from the Homestead Works in Pennsylvania, Frick—after ⓭ fortifying the factory with fences water cannons, barbed wire, and sniper towers—locked union workers out of the plant one day prior to the expiration of its contract. A renegotiation of the contract had failed recently when AA workers—citing a steady rise in the price of steel—requested an 8% wage increase and were met by Frick with a 22% decrease. ⓮ Incensed by Frick's actions, AA workers alongside townspeople and several other labor unions began picketing the factory two days after the lockout.

[3]

After about one week in which strikers successfully prevented new laborers and supervisors from entering the plant, Frick contracted 300 Pinkerton Detectives to break the strike by ⓯ working quite hard. Hoping to catch the picketers off guard, the Pinkertons—armed with Winchester rifles—boarded two shielded barges around 4 A.M. and were towed two miles upriver to the plant.

[4]

Conflicting testimonies exist as to ⓰ whom fired the first shot. The strikers, having been tipped off about the assault, ⓱ were laying in wait and prevented the barges from coming ashore. For more than twenty-four hours, the strikers and

12. Which of these words would be most consistent with the characterization of Frick that follows in the passage?

(A) NO CHANGE
(B) well-known.
(C) infamous.
(D) unusual.

13. (A) NO CHANGE
(B) fortifying the factory with fences, water, cannons barbed wire,
(C) fortifying, the factory with fences, water cannons, barbed wire,
(D) fortifying the factory with fences, water cannons, barbed wire,

14. (A) NO CHANGE
(B) Encouraged by
(C) Inspired by
(D) Dispirited by

15. Which choice would best express the firm determination of Frick to accomplish his goal?

(A) NO CHANGE
(B) using force only rarely.
(C) any means necessary.
(D) focusing energetically.

16. (A) NO CHANGE
(B) who
(C) what
(D) that

17. (A) NO CHANGE
(B) was lying
(C) was laying
(D) were lying

Pinkertons were embroiled in ⓲ an intermittent exchange of gunfire and makeshift incendiaries that left several dead and many wounded. At the earliest escalations of the situation, AA leaders sought to contact Frick in order that the skirmish might be quelled and further bloodshed avoided. Frick, however, refused to speak with the leaders. He realized that the more dangerous and lawless conditions grew, ⓳ the more likely it was that the strikers would eventually emerge victorious.

[5]

He was correct. Not long after the Pinkertons surrendered, Pennsylvania Governor Robert Pattison authorized the militia to advance and placed the town of Homestead under martial law. In the days that followed, steel production at the plant resumed with strikebreakers living on the ⓴ mills grounds: it was still too dangerous for them to cross the picket.

[6]

㉑ Initially, the events at Homestead galvanized sympathy and support for labor unions nation-wide, ㉒ and public fervor quickly dissipated following a failed attempt on Frick's life by the notorious anarchist Alexander Berkman. Though Frick survived the assassination attempt and ultimately won the conflict when it entered the courts, his relationship with Carnegie* was irrevocably blemished, and his reputation as "America's most hated man" was solidified for years to come.

*Carnegie refers to Andrew Carnegie, the American industrialist and philanthropist.

18. (A) NO CHANGE
(B) some rather intense combat that was rather harmful to the participants
(C) a rough fight
(D) a really deadly exchange

19. Which choice would give the most logical explanation for what comes earlier in the sentence while providing a good transition to the next paragraph?

(A) NO CHANGE
(B) the less likely it was his company would be in a position to negotiate a long-lasting end to the work stoppage.
(C) the more likely it became that the governor would call in the state militia and put the strike down for good.
(D) the less likely it was that Frick's end goal of securing high-paying positions for his workers would be accomplished.

20. (A) NO CHANGE
(B) mills' grounds—it was still
(C) mill's grounds, it was still
(D) mill's grounds; it was still

21. Where would paragraph 6 most logically be placed?

(A) Where it currently is.
(B) Before paragraph 1
(C) Before paragraph 3
(D) Before paragraph 4

22. (A) NO CHANGE
(B) consequently
(C) but
(D) in fact

Dali and Surrealism

㉓ The use of discrete symbolism is essential to the surrealist movement. One of the most highly regarded surrealist artists, Salvador Dali, often drew on symbols that he saw in his dreams and incorporated them into his paintings. Dali's formal art education began in 1921 at the School of Fine Arts in Madrid, where he studied for several years. However, Dali was expelled shortly before graduating because he claimed **㉔** for his teachers were insufficiently competent to examine him. In this same year, he painted *Basket of Bread,* which features four slices of buttered bread in a basket with one set off from the others and missing a bite. **㉕** Dali was recognized for the great skill that his uniquely crafted paintings demonstrated.

By 1931, Dali had officially joined the surrealist group in Paris and **㉖** completes perhaps his most famous work, *The Persistence of Memory,* which depicts several pocket watches melting away in an immense landscape that includes a mountain and seascape. **㉗** There are [1] several symbols [2] in this painting [3] that Dali used in many other paintings from the same [4] period—one of which is ants that cover the watch in the lower left of the piece. Dali used ants as a symbol for death in several of his other paintings. Supposedly, *The*

23. Which choice provides the best introduction to the paragraph?

(A) NO CHANGE
(B) Art has been appreciated by millions of museumgoers the world over.
(C) Salvador Dali was born in Spain in the city of Figueres.
(D) It is rare to find artistic works that have truly stood the test of time.

24. (A) NO CHANGE
(B) in
(C) on
(D) that

25. Which choice would most specifically support Dali's beliefs about his abilities?

(A) NO CHANGE
(B) The painting uses a dematerializing lighting technique that shows just how far Dali's skill had already developed when he was only 22.
(C) This work focuses on the outstanding by-products of Dali's culinary ingenuity— freshly baked, flawlessly crafted bread.
(D) Dali was publicly recognized for his revolutionary abilities, yet he retained a noteworthy internal modesty.

26. (A) NO CHANGE
(B) has completed
(C) completed
(D) have complete

27. What would be the most logical place to insert the word "present" in this sentence?

(A) [1]
(B) [2]
(C) [3]
(D) [4]

Persistence of Memory is partially **28** inspired by a dream sequence while sleeping that Dali experienced, where the clocks represented the passage of time as felt by the dreamer.

In 1940, Dali and his wife Gala moved to the United States, and he **29** reclaimed his Catholic faith. Following their return to Spain in the late 1940s, Dali began drawing inspiration from his faith for his work. During this period of Dali's life, he produced *La Gare de Perpignan,* which contains several religious symbols and references. **30** In contrast, there is the shadow of Christ on the cross bearing his thorny crown near the center of the painting. Additionally, there is a boat passing **31** to a calm sea, which is an ancient depiction symbolizing the passage of death to life and which strengthens the symbol of Christ in reference to the Resurrection.

Dali's interests weren't limited to painting; **32** he had an intense interest in great literary works. One of his most prominent sculptural pieces is the *Lobster Telephone,* also called the *Aphrodisiac Phone.* In his book *The Secret Life,* Dali inquired as to why in a restaurant when he requested a grilled lobster, he was never **33** brung a boiled telephone. The lobster phone is a prime example of surrealist sculpture since it evokes immense introspection.

28. (A) NO CHANGE
    (B) encouraged by a subconscious night time mental event
    (C) constructed from the brain that
    (D) based on a dream

29. (A) NO CHANGE
    (B) reproduced
    (C) rejected
    (D) redomesticated

30. (A) NO CHANGE
    (B) Surprisingly,
    (C) For instance,
    (D) As an example of what can be seen,

31. (A) NO CHANGE
    (B) over
    (C) and journeying throughout
    (D) sequencing

32. Which choice would best support and elaborate on the first part of the sentence?

    (A) NO CHANGE.
    (B) his artistic skill was well-regarded worldwide.
    (C) he also explored film, literature, and sculpture.
    (D) he was devoted to the mastery of sculptural techniques.

33. (A) NO CHANGE
    (B) brought
    (C) bring
    (D) brang

Unmanned Space Exploration

We must ask ourselves as a society, what is it that we most value? **34** Do we seek out knowledge and wisdom or are we only concerned with chest-thumping and braggadocio? If the former, we should shift away from an obsession with manned space flight and invest resources in robotic exploration. **35** One should be focused on what will enable us to learn the most about our universe in the most cost-effective manner.

Most people would cite Neil Armstrong's first steps on the Moon as the most exciting moment in space exploration. Seeing a human walk another heavenly body for the first time sends chills down your spine. **36** But why should it be this way? I would argue that the exploration of the *Voyager 2* unmanned spacecraft has given us far more momentous accomplishments. Among many discoveries, it **37** found that Io a moon of Jupiter has volcanic activity—the first time another astronomical body was found to have this Earthlike characteristic. *Voyager* gave us evidence that the Great Red Spot of Jupiter was an enormous storm,

34. Which choice would best connect the preceding and following sentences?

(A) NO CHANGE
(B) Are we interested in focusing on exploring the moon, nearby planets, and even faraway star systems?
(C) Do we want only to save money so that we can use it for domestic research programs to fight disease here on Earth?
(D) Are we focused on making the world a better place for our children, or do we want to leave them a legacy of environmental devastation?

35. (A) NO CHANGE
(B) They should have been focused
(C) He or she needs to focus
(D) We should focus

36. Should the underlined sentence be kept or removed?

(A) Kept, because it provides a key transition to the following sentence.
(B) Kept, because it provides details on the emotional reaction to space flight.
(C) Removed, because it provides irrelevant details.
(D) Removed, because it does not logically connect the preceding and following sentences.

37. (A) NO CHANGE
(B) found that Io, a moon of Jupiter has
(C) found that Io, a moon of Jupiter, has
(D) found that Io a moon, of Jupiter has

that distant planets have rings, and **38** which undiscovered moons are had by many outer planets. It also left the solar system and is now on an interstellar mission. If we had insisted that humans be a part of the *Voyager* craft, it wouldn't have been able to accomplish nearly as much.

Sure, there **39** isn't a made-for-television moment like disembarking a spacecraft onto the Moon's surface for the first time. However, **40** isn't it time we realize that space exploration needs to be a top priority of our country, instead of merely being given lip service?

One possible justification for involving humans in the actual exploration is that **41** they do increase interest in funding space exploration projects. Humans are naturally drawn to want to explore space vicariously by seeing astronauts do it on television. It is much like how humans would rather hear about someone's trip to a foreign country **42** then to look merely at photographs of the country on the Internet. An interesting approach is the one taken by the new Mars One project. In an effort to spur interest in exploration and minimize costs, the project managers

38. Which choice is most consistent with the structure of the previous part of the sentence?

(A) NO CHANGE
(B) outer planets have moons that are undiscovered.
(C) where we find the unprecedented discovery of the outer planet moons.
(D) that outer planets have many undiscovered moons.

39. (A) NO CHANGE
(B) isn't a television made
(C) isn't a television that is made for
(D) isn't a made-for-the-television

40. Which choice would provide a rhetorical question that provides a fitting conclusion to the paragraph?

(A) NO CHANGE
(B) are we more interested in the theater of science or the actuality of improving our understanding of the universe?
(C) why should we spend valuable money on advanced robotic space exploration when there are better Earth-bound investments we can make?
(D) who is to say what will have more of an impact a century from now—a man on the Moon or a manned mission to Mars?

41. (A) NO CHANGE
(B) it does
(C) one do
(D) OMIT the underlined portion

42. (A) NO CHANGE
(B) then to merely look
(C) than too look merely
(D) than merely look

have recruited volunteers who will be the first
43 to go to Mars, and won't be able to return
to Earth. If only we could be satisfied with
acquiring knowledge instead of treating space
exploration like some kind of competitive sport,
44 there would be no thought of people needing
to die on a foreign world in order to promote
interest in space.

43. (A) NO CHANGE
    (B) to go to Mars, however won't
    (C) to go to Mars but won't
    (D) to go to Mars, and, won't

44. Which choice most logically concludes the
    paragraph?

    (A) NO CHANGE
    (B) we should focus on space exploration
        using the most efficient means possible
        to maximize our understanding of the
        universe.
    (C) we wouldn't have to waste money on
        pointless projects like the Mars One
        mission.
    (D) there wouldn't be the slow, lonely death
        of astronauts on a distant world.

25 MINUTES, 17 QUESTIONS

Directions: For questions 1–13, solve each problem and choose the best answer from the given options. Fill in the corresponding oval on the answer sheet. For questions 14–17, solve the problem and fill in the answer on the answer sheet grid. Please use scrap paper to work out your answers.

Notes:
- You **CANNOT** use a calculator on this section.
- All variables and expressions represent real numbers unless indicated otherwise.
- All figures are drawn to scale unless indicated otherwise.
- All figures are in a plane unless indicated otherwise.
- Unless indicated otherwise, the domain of a given function is the set of all real numbers x for which the function has real values.

Radius of a circle = r
Area of a circle = πr^2
Circumference of a circle = $2\pi r$

Area of a rectangle = length × width = lw

Area of a triangle = $\dfrac{1}{2}$ × base × height = $\dfrac{1}{2} bh$

Pythagorean theorem: $a^2 + b^2 = c^2$

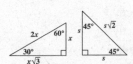

Special right triangles: 30-60-90 and 45-45-90

Volume of a box = length × width × height = lwh

Volume of a cylinder = $\pi r^2 h$

Volume of a sphere = $\dfrac{4}{3} \pi r^3$

Volume of a cone = $\dfrac{1}{3}\pi r^2 h$

Volume of a pyramid =
$\dfrac{1}{3}$ × length × width × height = $\dfrac{1}{3} lwh$

KEY FACTS:

- A circle has 360 degrees.
- There are 2π radians in a circle.
- There are 180 degrees in a triangle.

1. If $x^2 > y^2$ which statement must be correct?

   (A) $x > y$
   (B) $x < y$
   (C) $x \neq y$
   (D) $x^3 > y^3$

2. What values of y satisfy this system of equations?

$$x = y^2 - 3y + 1$$
$$2x = 10$$

   (A) -4 and 2
   (B) -1 and 4
   (C) 3 and 4
   (D) 6 and 10

3. Which of the following operations could be performed on both sides of the inequality $-2x > 4$ to require the direction of the inequality sign be changed while keeping x on the left-hand side of the inequality?

   (A) Add 4
   (B) Subtract 7
   (C) Divide by -2
   (D) Multiply by 12

4. What are the values of a in this equation?

$$3a^2 - 27a - 108 = 0$$

   (A) $-9, -3$
   (B) $6, -4$
   (C) $9, 6$
   (D) $12, -3$

5. When Andrew does his homework, he always takes 10 minutes to set up his desk and get totally ready to begin. Once he starts working, he is able to complete 1 homework problem every 5 minutes. Assuming that Andrew studies for over 10 minutes, which of the following represents the total number of homework problems, p, Andrew is able to complete in m minutes?

   (A) $p = 5m + 10$
   (B) $p = 5m - 1$
   (C) $p = \dfrac{1}{5}(m - 10)$
   (D) $p = \dfrac{1}{10}(m - 5)$

6. The variables x and y have a linear relationship; the table below contains several corresponding x-y values for the line:

x	y
-1	-6
1	2
5	18
7	26

   What is the equation of the line made up of x-y values?

   (A) $y = 4x - 2$
   (B) $y = 2x$
   (C) $y = -2x + 4$
   (D) $y = -4x + 2$

7. How many solutions does the equation below have?

$$3x - 4y = 73$$

   (A) None
   (B) Exactly 1
   (C) Exactly 2
   (D) Infinite

8. What is the product of xy given the system of equations below?

$$4 + y = 32x$$
$$y = 2x + 2$$

(A) $\dfrac{6}{25}$

(B) $\dfrac{12}{25}$

(C) 12

(D) 15

9. Maria currently has $10,000 in her retirement fund. She wants to see how much money she will have in her fund for several different years in the future, assuming that her portfolio has a steady annual growth rate of 10%. What function $f(n)$ would model the amount she should have in her portfolio in n years?

(A) $f(n) = 10{,}000^n$

(B) $f(n) = 10{,}000 \times 0.1^n$

(C) $f(n) = 10{,}000 \times 1.1^n$

(D) $f(n) = 10{,}000 \times 1.11^n$

10. The amount of money (A) in a bank account after a principal amount (P) is on deposit for t years at an annual interest rate r compounded n times per year is given by this equation:

$$A = P\left(1 + \frac{r}{n}\right)^{nt}$$

Suppose that a banker would like to determine how changes in these variables would cause the bank to pay *less* interest to its clients. Which of the variables— $P, r, n,$ and t—if minimized, would cause less interest paid to clients?

(A) P only

(B) r and t only

(C) n and t only

(D) $P, r, n,$ and t

11. Which of these equations, when combined into a set of equations with $4x = 2y - 6$, will result in no solutions to the set?

(A) $y = x - 4$

(B) $y = 2x + 10$

(C) $y = 4x - 1$

(D) $y = \dfrac{1}{4}x - 6$

12. A dry cleaner has a computer program to determine the price it will charge an individual customer to clean a bag full of shirts (S) and pants (P). The total cost in dollars (C) is given by the following expression:

$$C = 10S + 6P + 5$$

What does the constant 5 most likely represent in the above expression?

(A) A set fee the cleaner assesses to do any amount of cleaning

(B) The cost to clean a shirt

(C) The cost to clean a pair of pants

(D) The total minimum cost to clean either one shirt or one pair of pants

13. What will happen to the graph of the function $f(x) = 4x^2 - 18$ if it is transformed into the function $g(x) = 4(x - 2)^2 - 15$?

(A) It will shift down 2 units and shift to the left 3 units.

(B) It will shift up 3 units and shift to the right 2 units.

(C) It will shift up 2 units and shift to the left 3 units.

(D) It will shift down 3 units and shift to the right 2 units.

Grid-in Response Directions

In questions 14–17, first solve the problem, and then enter your answer on the grid provided on the answer sheet. The instructions for entering your answers follow.

- First, write your answer in the boxes at the top of the grid.
- Second, grid your answer in the columns below the boxes.
- Use the fraction bar in the first row or the decimal point in the second row to enter fractions and decimals.

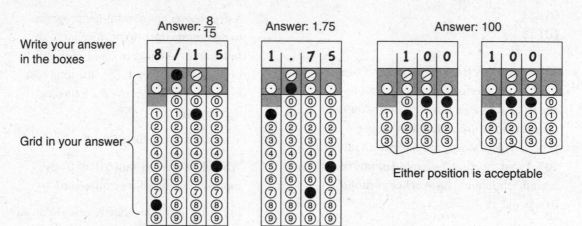

Write your answer in the boxes

Grid in your answer

Answer: $\frac{8}{15}$ Answer: 1.75   Answer: 100

Either position is acceptable

- Grid only one space in each column.
- Entering the answer in the boxes is recommended as an aid in gridding but is not required.
- The machine scoring your exam can read only what you grid, so you **must grid-in your answers correctly to get credit**.
- If a question has more than one correct answer, grid-in only one of them.
- The grid does not have a minus sign; so no answer can be negative.
- A mixed number *must* be converted to an improper fraction or a decimal before it is gridded.

  Enter $1\frac{1}{4}$ as $\frac{5}{4}$ or 1.25; the machine will interpret 11/4 as $\frac{11}{4}$ and mark it wrong.

- **All decimals must be entered as accurately as possible.** Here are three acceptable ways of gridding

$$\frac{3}{11} = 0.272727\ldots$$

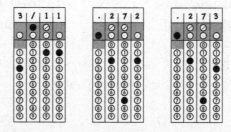

- Note that rounding to .273 is acceptable because you are using the full grid, but you would receive **no credit** for .3 or .27, because they are less accurate.

14. If $2x + 3 = 4$, what is the value of $6x + 9$?

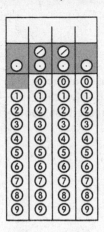

15. If $x > 0$ and $x^2 + 10x = 11$, what is the value of $x + 5$?

16. The function $f(x) = (x - 3)(x + 2)((x - 1)^2)$ will intersect the x-axis how many times?

17. In a certain right triangle, the sine of angle A is $\frac{5}{13}$ and the cosine of angle A is $\frac{12}{13}$.

What is the ratio of the smallest side of the triangle to the median side of the triangle?

45 MINUTES, 31 QUESTIONS

Directions: For questions 1–27, solve each problem and choose the best answer from the given options. Fill in the corresponding oval on the answer sheet. For questions 28–31, solve the problem and fill in the answer on the answer sheet grid. Please use any space in the test booklet to work out your answers.

Notes:

- You CAN use a calculator on this section.
- All variables and expressions represent real numbers unless indicated otherwise.
- All figures are drawn to scale unless indicated otherwise.
- All figures are in a plane unless indicated otherwise.
- Unless indicated otherwise, the domain of a given function is the set of all real numbers x for which the function has real values.

Radius of a circle = r

Area of a circle = πr^2

Circumference of a circle = $2\pi r$

Area of a rectangle = length × width = lw

Area of a triangle = $\frac{1}{2}$ × base × height = $\frac{1}{2} bh$

Pythagorean theorem: $a^2 + b^2 = c^2$

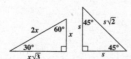

Special right triangles: 30-60-90 and 45-45-90

Volume of a box = length × width × height = lwh

Volume of a cylinder = $\pi r^2 h$

Volume of a sphere = $\frac{4}{3} \pi r^3$

Volume of a cone = $\frac{1}{3}\pi r^2 h$

Volume of a pyramid =

$\frac{1}{3}$ × length × width × height = $\frac{1}{3} lwh$

KEY FACTS:

- A circle has 360 degrees.
- There are 2π radians in a circle.
- There are 180 degrees in a triangle.

1. What is the difference between $7a^2 + 3ab - 8b$ and $-2a^2 + ab - 2b$?

   (A) $5a^2 + 4ab - 10b$
   (B) $9a^2 + 4ab - 8b$
   (C) $9a^2 + 2ab - 6b$
   (D) $7a + 3ab - 10$

2. $(2x^2 + 4xy + 2y^2) \times \dfrac{1}{2x+2y} =$

   (A) $y + x$
   (B) $\dfrac{2x+4y+2}{x+y}$
   (C) $2x + 4xy + 2y$
   (D) 2

3. A professor will cancel his sociology class if the number of students in attendance is less than or equal to 10. Which of the following expressions would give the possible values of students, S, necessary for the professor to conduct class, given that S is an integer?

   (A) $S < 10$
   (B) $S > 10$
   (C) $S \leq 10$
   (D) $S \geq 10$

4. What is a possible value for x in the expression below?

   $$-6 < \frac{8}{3}\, x < -\frac{1}{4}$$

   (A) 8
   (B) 1
   (C) –2
   (D) –5

Questions 5–7 refer to the following information and table.

The data are collected from a survey of 500 randomly selected people in the United States. The researcher asked participants their ages and what type of social media they use the most frequently: video sharing, photo sharing, text sharing, or none. The goal of the researcher was to determine the general characteristics of social media use by different age groups throughout the United States.

				No	
Age Group	Video Sharing	Photo Sharing	Text Sharing	Social Media	Total
12–18	40	32	20	2	94
19–30	31	51	43	6	131
31–45	20	20	40	24	104
46–60	9	8	36	35	88
61–up	2	3	29	49	83

Type of Social Media Use by Numbers of People in Different Age Groups

5. If one were to create a graph with age groupings (from younger to older) as the variable along the x-axis and percentage of group members who use video sharing (from smaller to larger) along the y-axis, what would be the relationship portrayed by the data?

   (A) Positive correlation
   (B) Negative correlation
   (C) Equivalence
   (D) Exponentially inverse

6. The researcher is going to pick two of his research subjects from this survey to speak anecdotally about their experiences with social media so that he may have qualitative data to supplement his quantitative data. The first person who will speak will be from the 12–18-year-old group. The second person will be from the 31–45-year-old group. What is the probability (to the nearest hundredth) that the first speaker will primarily use photo sharing and that the second speaker will primarily use text sharing?

(A) 0.02
(B) 0.06
(C) 0.11
(D) 0.13

7. The survey summary states that the researcher collected the data "randomly." Which of these methods of finding survey participants would likely provide the most accurate results given the researcher's goal?

(A) Ask for volunteer responses through television advertising and give a number for interested subjects to call in, ensuring a high level of motivation among survey participants
(B) Have a survey booth at a local shopping mall where only every 5th person is selected to share his or her individual thoughts about social media use, ensuring that each participant provides photo ID to verify his or her identity
(C) Post a survey advertisement on a variety of websites that appeal to a great number of demographic groupings, including income, gender, and ethnicity
(D) Call randomly selected phone numbers from across the country, both cellular and landlines, and ask for household members of a particular random age group to share their thoughts

8. A politician proposes a new federal tax bracket system for single tax payers with the following tax rates for the given ranges of income:

Taxable Income Range	Tax Rate
$0 up to $9,000	15%
Greater than $9,000 up to $50,000	20%
Greater than $50,000	30%

If Julian has $62,000 in taxable income, what is the total amount of federal tax he would pay under the proposed system?

(A) $9,300
(B) $12,400
(C) $13,150
(D) $15,000

9. If the line given by the equation $y = 4x + 7$ is reflected about the x-axis, what will be the graph of the resulting function?

(A)

(C)

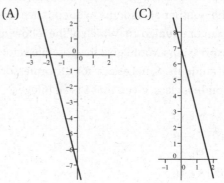

(B)

(D)

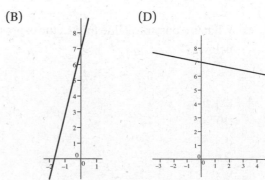

10. What is the solution(s) for x in this equation?

$$\frac{12}{\sqrt[3]{x}} = 4$$

(A) –3 and 81

(B) –27 and 27

(C) 9 only

(D) 27 only

Questions 11–12 refer to the following information and graph.

A new business uses a crowdfunding website to raise money for its expansion. The graph below plots the number of new investment pledges per week, collecting the data once at the end of each week after the crowdfunding has begun. For example, "Week 1" gives the total number of new pledges at the very end of Week 1.

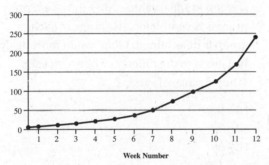

Number of New Investment Pledges Per Week

11. A marketing professional defines the point at which something goes "viral" as the point at which the item shifts from linear to exponential growth. During which week does the value of the new investment pledges become viral?

(A) 2

(B) 3

(C) 6

(D) 10

12. Given that the function increases at the same geometric rate as it does in weeks 9–12, what would most likely come closest to the number of new investment pledges in week 14?

(A) 450

(B) 650

(C) 800

(D) 1,000

13. How many solution(s) does this system of equations have?

$$m + 2n = 1$$
$$6n + 3m = 9$$

(A) None

(B) 1

(C) 2

(D) 3

14. A convenience store has a "change bowl" on its counter in which there can be 5-cent nickels and/or 1-cent pennies. The store manager insists that whenever there is a dollar (100 cents) or more in the bowl, some change must be removed. What expression gives range of P pennies and N nickels that could be in the change bowl at any given time without the cashier needing to remove any coins?

(A) $100P - N > 5$

(B) $6(P + N) < 100$

(C) $0.01P + 0.05N < 100$

(D) $P + 5N < 100$

Questions 15–18 refer to the following tables.

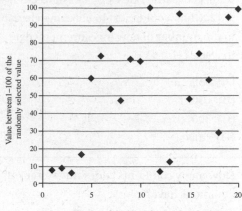

Number of the 20 randomly selected values

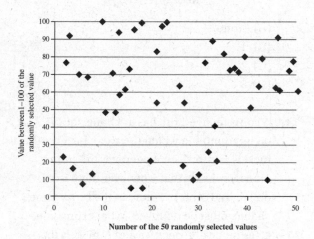

Number of the 50 randomly selected values

15. If a third graph of 1,000 randomly selected values were created, what would most likely be the average of the randomly selected values?

(A) 35
(B) 50
(C) 60
(D) 75

16. Out of the following options, what is the most unexpected result of the collection of the random sets of numbers?

(A) The values in both sets of data have a range of roughly between 1 and 100.
(B) The selection of 50 random numbers has a significantly higher percentage of values above 50 than does the selection of 20 random numbers.
(C) The selection of 20 random numbers has a much greater range among its values than does the selection of 50 random numbers.
(D) The sets of both data are portrayed as scatter plots rather than as best-fit lines.

17. Suppose that the random selection process of numbers between 1 and 100 was conducted for a group of 100 values and for a group of 1,000 values. After the selection process is completed, the range of each group is determined. What would most likely be closest to the difference between each group's range of values?

(A) 0
(B) 20
(C) 50
(D) 100

18. What would most likely be the average of the slopes of the best-fit lines of the data if the researcher collects and plots the 50 randomly selected values 100 times?

(A) –2
(B) 0
(C) 1
(D) 3.5

19. In the equation $y = 2x^n$, in which x is an integer greater than 1, what is a possible value of n that will ensure that the expression has exponential growth?

(A) 0
(B) 1
(C) 4
(D) Not sufficient information

20. Assume that a scientist is able to measure the average weight of lobsters within a 50-mile radius of an island with a confidence level of 90% by collecting data from 100 random spots around the island. If he wishes to increase the confidence level in his results to 95%, what would best help him achieve his goal?

(A) Compare the results to those from another island 300 miles away.
(B) Expand the radius of sampling to 100 miles and redistribute his 100 random spots within the larger range.
(C) Increase the number of data samples.
(D) Use a scale with 5% more accuracy.

21. How many more kilograms (to the nearest hundredth) will a 2 cubic meter balloon that is filled with air weigh than an identical balloon that is filled with helium, given that helium has a density of $0.179 \frac{\text{kg}}{\text{m}^3}$ and air has a density of $1.2 \frac{\text{kg}}{\text{m}^3}$?

(A) 0.21
(B) 1.02
(C) 1.38
(D) 2.04

22. If a set of 20 different numbers has its smallest and largest values removed, how will that affect the standard deviation of the set?

(A) The standard deviation will increase.
(B) The standard deviation will decrease.
(C) The standard deviation will remain the same.
(D) Not enough information is provided.

23. Jay is purchasing gifts for his four friends' high school graduation. He has a budget of at most $150. He is purchasing a restaurant gift card of $25 for one friend, a tool set that costs $40 for another friend, and a $35 college sweatshirt for a third friend. For his fourth friend, he wants to see how many $0.25 quarters ($Q$) he can give for the friend to use for laundry money. What expression gives the range of quarters Jay can acquire given his budgetary restrictions?

(A) $1 \le Q \le 300$
(B) $1 \le Q \le 200$
(C) $10 \le Q \le 120$
(D) $40 \le Q \le 60$

24. A pretzel stand has fixed costs for the facility and cooking supplies of $500. The cost for the labor and supplies to cook one pretzel after the pretzel stand has been set up is $2 per pretzel. What is the graph of the cost function $c(x)$ given x pretzels?

(A)
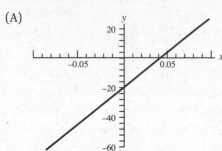

(B)
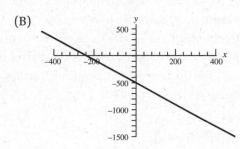

(C)
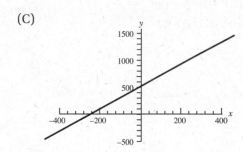

(D)
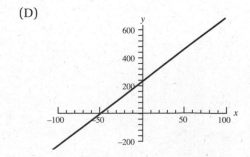

25. Which of the following could be a value of x in this equation?

$$8x^2 = -16x - 2$$

I. $-1 - \dfrac{\sqrt{3}}{2}$

II. $\dfrac{1}{2}\left(-2 - \sqrt{6}\right)$

III. $\dfrac{1}{2}(\sqrt{3} - 2)$

(A) I only
(B) II only
(C) I and III only
(D) II and III only

26. An interior designer is selling wood flooring to be used by his client for a new room. The client has already purchased a set length of trim, which goes between the edge of the wood flooring and the wall. The trim is straight and cannot be curved, yet it can be joined to make right angle corners. The client does not wish to purchase any more trim and would like to use all of the trim when building the new room. If the interior designer wants to maximize the amount of wood flooring that the client purchases while satisfying the client's requirements, what should be the relationship between the length (L) and width (W) of the room's dimensions?

(A) $L = W$
(B) $L = 2W$
(C) $W = L^2$
(D) $L = W^3$

27. Given that $i = \sqrt{-1}$, what is the value of $i^4 + i^{12}$?

(A) $\sqrt{-1}$
(B) -1
(C) 1
(D) 2

Grid-in Response Directions

In questions 28–31, first solve the problem, and then enter your answer on the grid provided on the answer sheet. The instructions for entering your answers follow.

- First, write your answer in the boxes at the top of the grid.
- Second, grid your answer in the columns below the boxes.
- Use the fraction bar in the first row or the decimal point in the second row to enter fractions and decimals.

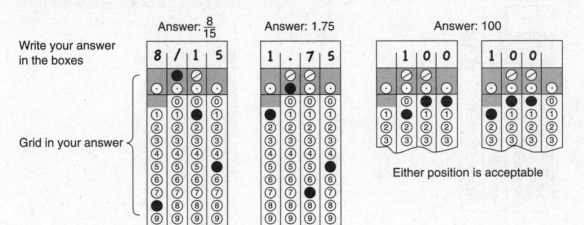

Answer: $\frac{8}{15}$ Answer: 1.75   Answer: 100

Write your answer in the boxes

Grid in your answer

Either position is acceptable

- Grid only one space in each column.
- Entering the answer in the boxes is recommended as an aid in gridding but is not required.
- The machine scoring your exam can read only what you grid, so you **must grid-in your answers correctly to get credit**.
- If a question has more than one correct answer, grid-in only one of them.
- The grid does not have a minus sign; so no answer can be negative.
- A mixed number *must* be converted to an improper fraction or a decimal before it is gridded.

  Enter $1\frac{1}{4}$ as $\frac{5}{4}$ or 1.25; the machine will interpret 11/4 as $\frac{11}{4}$ and mark it wrong.

- **All decimals must be entered as accurately as possible.** Here are three acceptable ways of gridding

$$\frac{3}{11} = 0.272727\ldots$$

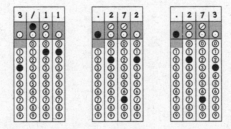

- Note that rounding to .273 is acceptable because you are using the full grid, but you would receive **no credit** for .3 or .27, because they are less accurate.

28. Eloise is told by her doctor that she should try to average 9 hours of sleep a night since that is what a typical teenager needs for optimal mental and physical health. If Eloise was awake for 126 hours in a given week, how many additional hours of sleep should she have had in order to follow her doctor's advice?

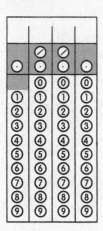

29. The variables m and n have a directly proportional relationship given by the equation $m = kn$, where k is a constant of proportionality. When $m = 10$, $n = 2$. What will be the value of n if m equals 38?

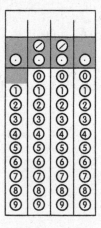

30. A botanist plants a small ivy plant and evaluates its growth function. She finds that 2 months after planting, the plant is 5 inches tall; at 4 months after planting, the plant is 8 inches tall. Additionally, the botanist has noticed that the plant has grown at a constant rate since its initial planting. Given this information, what was the plant's height in inches at the time it was planted?

31. The table below shows the number of applications and the number of admissions to a particular college at the end of each calendar year.

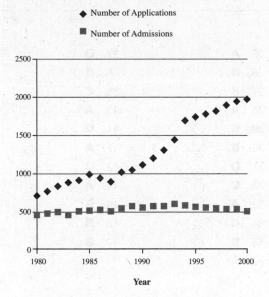

During one year between 1980 and 2000, the college started to accept the Common Application and also began offering early decision to its applicants. The Common Application allows students to use the same application to apply to multiple schools, making applying easier. Early decision gives students the opportunity to apply early for admission. If accepted, though, students must commit to go to the school. The college made these two changes to encourage more students to apply and to enable the school to admit only students who were really committed to attending, thus helping the college's application yield (i.e., the number of students admitted who actually attend). These factors resulted in an overall increase in the selectivity of the college. In what year did the college most likely first implement these policies?

ANSWER KEY
Practice Test 1

Reading Test

1.	C	13.	B	25.	A	37.	D
2.	A	14.	A	26.	B	38.	B
3.	C	15.	D	27.	B	39.	C
4.	D	16.	C	28.	A	40.	A
5.	C	17.	C	29.	C	41.	D
6.	B	18.	B	30.	B	42.	A
7.	A	19.	A	31.	D	43.	C
8.	C	20.	D	32.	C	44.	A
9.	C	21.	D	33.	A	45.	B
10.	D	22.	D	34.	C	46.	B
11.	B	23.	C	35.	D	47.	B
12.	C	24.	C	36.	A		

Writing and Language Test

1.	A	12.	C	23.	A	34.	A
2.	C	13.	D	24.	D	35.	D
3.	B	14.	A	25.	B	36.	A
4.	D	15.	C	26.	C	37.	C
5.	A	16.	B	27.	B	38.	D
6.	B	17.	D	28.	D	39.	A
7.	A	18.	A	29.	A	40.	B
8.	C	19.	C	30.	C	41.	B
9.	D	20.	D	31.	B	42.	D
10.	A	21.	A	32.	C	43.	C
11.	B	22.	C	33.	B	44.	A

Math Test (No Calculator)

1.	C	6.	A	11.	B	16.	3
2.	B	7.	D	12.	A	17.	5/12 or .416
3.	C	8.	B	13.	B		or .417
4.	D	9.	C	14.	12		
5.	C	10.	D	15.	6		

Math Test (With Calculator)

1. C
2. A
3. B
4. C
5. B
6. D
7. D
8. C
9. A
10. D
11. C
12. A
13. A
14. D
15. B
16. B
17. A
18. B
19. C
20. C
21. D
22. B
23. B
24. C
25. C
26. A
27. D
28. 21
29. 7.6 or 38/5
30. 2
31. 1994

Note: This table represents our *best estimate* of how many questions you will need to answer correctly to achieve a certain score on the PSAT.

PSAT Section Score	PSAT Math (48 Total Questions)	PSAT Evidence-Based Reading and Writing (91 Total Questions)	PSAT Section Score
760	48	91	760
710	45	86	710
660	43	79	660
610	38	71	610
560	34	63	560
510	28	53	510
460	24	43	460
410	18	30	410
360	13	19	360
310	8	12	310
260	4	6	260
210	2	3	210
160	0	0	160

Reading Test

1. **(C)** As indicated by the introduction, this excerpt is from a novel about the French Revolution. Further, the descriptions of events in the story are realistic. Thus, this passage is best characterized as historical fiction. Magical realism and fantasy would involve more fantastic elements. A short story would be self-contained, while this is an excerpt.

2. **(A)** "Citizen" is consistently used to refer to Brotteaux, who is a man; "citizeness" is consistently used to refer to Gamelin, a woman. There is no clear indication that Gamelin and Brotteaux are of different social classes, age groupings, or ethnicities. After all, they both refer to the aristocracy with an outside perspective. In addition, they are both elderly. Finally, they are both most likely French.

3. **(C)** The sentence before the one in lines 14–17 refers to how the food is becoming more expensive every day. This gives a logical justification to the motives of the food-grabbers. If the food became more expensive, the food-grabbers would profit more from selling it to needy consumers. Choice (A) would be too grotesquely negative. Choices (B) and (D) are the opposite of the purported aristocratic goal of starving and controlling the lower classes.

4. **(D)** Lines 12–14 give evidence in support of the answer to the previous question because they state that food was becoming increasingly expensive, making it more likely that people would want to hoard food. The other options provide no such evidence.

5. **(C)** The sentence that follows indicates that she was "poor." Therefore, it makes the most sense that she did not live in a luxurious or "lavish" way. "Vast" relates to size, "imposing" relates to intimidation, and "prime" relates to high quality but not necessarily luxury.

6. **(B)** Lines 48–53 give evidence of Évariste Gamelin being unforgiving and relentless. He resolved to discover the identity of Élodie's seducer and further resolved to seek out vengeance on the person. None of the adjectives in the other choices are applicable to his treatment of lawbreakers.

7. **(A)** Lines 48–53 give the most direct evidence about Évariste's unforgiving and relentless attitude. Choices (B) and (C) support an attitude of ignorance, and choice (D) supports a polite attitude.

8. **(C)** Brotteaux discusses the futility of spending time trying to predict the future. Additionally, he discusses how knowing the future would take away one's enjoyment in the present. Hence, he would advise people to "focus on the moment." Choice (A) means to be forgiving, choice (B) advocates seeking knowledge, and choice (D) advocates reciprocal kindness.

9. **(C)** Gamelin politely refuses to sit in the chair that is offered to her, so she is best described as "turning down" the chair. "Repulsing" is too negative, and "decreasing" and "plummeting" generally relate to amounts of things.

10. **(D)** This is best seen from the first paragraph, in which the author thoroughly acknowledges how surprising it must be to modern readers that hostility once existed between the U.S. and Canada. The first paragraph contradicts the supposed knowledge described in

choices (A) and (B). The passage does support the notion that people are eager to militarize the U.S.-Canada border as mentioned in choice (C).

11. **(B)** Lines 35–38 provide the evidence for this answer, saying that "no cause for war was more compelling in the U.S. than the desire to expand the nation into the northern territories." Although the other options would motivate U.S. citizens to fight against the British, they do not represent the "most significant" motivation to do so.

12. **(C)** Lines 35–40 state that the most compelling cause for war with Canada was the desire to expand the boundaries of the United States. The other line selections do not provide direct evidence in support of the answer to the previous question.

13. **(B)** Based on the surrounding context, the relations between the U.S. and Canada were not very positive in the past. So it would be appropriate to say that these relations were "suspect," which means "mistrustful." "Congenial" means "friendly," "familial" means "family-like," and "loathsome" means "repulsive," which is too negative in this context.

14. **(A)** "Tenacity" refers to the attitude held by the New England Federalists who were strongly determined not to enter the war. Although their attitude was likely angry, existed, and had a function, these words do not best capture the overall attitude.

15. **(D)** A strong Canadian defense was NOT an obstacle to U.S. victory in Quebec. Line 69 indicates that the Canadians left "Quebec vulnerable to invasion" by moving their defenses elsewhere. The other choices give reported obstacles to a lasting U.S. victory. Be sure you did not miss the "not" in the question.

16. **(C)** Lines 78–82 discuss how the "theaters of war," i.e., the places where the battles were fought, shifted from the frontier to cities. The passage does not mention a shift to elected representatives leading the armies as described in choice (A). The war was not marked by decisive victories by either side as listed in choice (B). The British were involved throughout the war in contrast to choice (D).

17. **(C)** Lines 78–82 best demonstrate that the battles shifted from being fought in the wilderness to being fought in urban areas. Choice (A) focuses on a singular event in the war. Choice (B) focuses on foreign affairs. Choice (D) focuses on the end of the war.

18. **(B)** Line 95 discusses how a free trade agreement in 1988 caused a "tremendous" increase in trade between the U.S. and Canada. The data in this table show just how large that increase in trade was between the countries. The other options do not focus on quantitative changes but just on the overall relations between the two countries.

19. **(A)** A significant increase in exports from the U.S. to Canada occurred after the treaty's passage, so a U.S. company that manufactures cars to be sold in Canada benefited most from the free trade agreement. The answer is not choice (B), because there is not as significant an increase in imports from Canada to the U.S. No information is provided about how this treaty impacted commerce within each country, making choices (C) and (D) incorrect.

20. **(D)** Susan B. Anthony is arguing that the major goal of passing women's suffrage would more likely be accomplished if women maintain a united front and avoid attaching themselves to individual political parties. Hence, the primary purpose of the passage is to make a tactical argument, i.e., to explain how this goal can best be attained. The other options refer to much more specific elements of the passage, and all misinterpret the general meaning of the passage.

21. **(D)** This can most clearly be seen in lines 63–66, in which Anthony states, "you must stand as disfranchised citizens—outlaws—shut out of 'the body politic,' humble supplicants, veriest beggars at the feet of all men of all parties alike." The phrase "all walks of life" refers to people from all sorts of backgrounds. Therefore, choice (D) is correct. There is no evidence that Anthony is directly encouraging women to win over the other groups of men mentioned.

22. **(D)** Lines 63–66 give the best evidence in support of the idea that Anthony encouraged women to focus on winning the support of men from all different backgrounds. The other line selections do not give such evidence.

23. **(C)** This can be seen most directly in lines 29–32, in which Anthony argues that dividing women into political parties is in the interest of the political parties but not in the interest of women's ultimate political goal, which is passage of women's suffrage. Since the interests of the political parties and of women differ, they can be described as "divergent." Choices (A) and (B) express the opposite of the intended meaning, and choice (D) is too extreme since there is no evidence in the essay that political parties and women will violently fight with one another.

24. **(C)** Lines 29-32 give the best evidence that Anthony believed the goals of political parties and of women diverged. The other lines do not provide direct evidence in support of the answer to the previous question.

25. **(A)** The first paragraph of the essay presents the viewpoint with which Anthony disagrees, namely that it is a good idea to have women identify with political parties rather than maintain a united front. The word "staunch" means "strong" in this context because the delegates are strongly supporting dividing female political efforts among different political parties. The other options fail to capture the intended meaning of the word and do not use commonly understood definitions of the word "staunch."

26. **(B)** Based on the passage as a whole, Anthony disagrees with the main idea presented in the first paragraph—she believes that women should remain united in their quest for voting rights and avoid dividing themselves by declaring loyalty for individual political parties. Putting quotation marks around a phrase is a common stylistic device that one can use to express distance from a point of view. Choice (A) is incorrect because there is no evidence that she said any such thing. Choice (C) is incorrect because she is not making a prediction. Choice (D) is incorrect because such a short phrase cannot offer much in the way of an explanation.

27. **(B)** Based on the context of the sentence, Anthony is referring to future goals of the political party, which could be expressed as "objectives." Choice (A) mistakenly uses an alternative meaning of "ends," and choices (C) and (D) skew the meaning in an overly negative direction.

28. **(A)** For this question, be sure to focus on the primary function of the sentence. Anthony uses this sentence to express that there will be plenty of time to focus on other political goals once the major goal of earning the right to vote is achieved. Choice (B) expresses the opposite of the intended purpose. Choices (C) and (D) do not relate to the intended purpose of this sentence.

29. **(C)** The first passage focuses on the scientific aspects of microwave cooking, such as the microwave's use of electromagnetic properties to heat food. The second passage discusses changes to the human practice of cooking over time, which fits under the umbrella of anthropology, which is the holistic study of humans and their ancestors. Choice (A) is incorrect because although history might be correct for Passage 2, the technical analysis in Passage 1 is beyond what would be needed to study cooking. Choice (B) is incorrect since paleontology involves the excavation of ancient remains. Choice (D) is incorrect because Passage 2 does not focus on biology.

30. **(B)** Passage 1 does not discuss problems with the microwave. In contrast, Passage 2 does mention how the speed of microwave cooking comes at the expense of precision (lines 90–93). Both passages mention the widespread popularity, cooking methodology, and possible cooking applications of the microwave.

31. **(D)** "Evolving" is used to describe the process by which molecules gradually give off heat in the microwave, so "generating" best captures this meaning. Although the other options do give possible definitions of "evolving," they do not reflect the process of giving off heat.

32. **(C)** The first paragraph gives evidence of this, stating that other types of cooking devices have internal heating elements while the microwave uses dipole rotation to heat food. Choices (A) and (D) are incorrect because all types of cooking increase the kinetic energy and intermolecular friction of food molecules, albeit by different methods. Choice (B) is not correct because this is a focus of Passage 2, not Passage 1.

33. **(A)** Lines 6–8 give the most direct support to the fact that microwaves lack an internal heating element. Choices (B), (C), and (D) give technical explanations of dipole rotation but do not clarify how the microwave is distinct from other forms of cooking.

34. **(C)** A "survey" best represents the structure of this passage since the author gives general facts and analysis about human cooking techniques over time. Choice (A) is not correct because the author is not attempting to persuade readers in favor of using older cooking methods. Choice (B) is incorrect because Passage 2 is more of a historical survey than a technical explanation, as found in Passage 1. Choice (D) is incorrect because the author does not take sides as to what type of cooking method is best overall.

35. **(D)** "Lines of development" is correct because in the context of the first paragraph of Passage 2, the "arcs" are referring to gradual trends in cooking innovation. The other options provide valid definitions of "arc" but not appropriate definitions in this context.

36. **(A)** Lines 75–83 discuss how the electric oven is an anomaly in the development of cooking. Even though the electric oven developed later, the electric oven is technologically inferior to the technology that preceded it. The other options are presented chronologically and demonstrate the gradual improvement in cooking technology.

37. **(D)** Lines 93–97 best support the scientist's statement since the author writes that microwaves are good for cooking less thick items but have much more difficulty with extremely thick foods like turkeys or a large steak. Choice (A) is incorrect because the scientist's statement does not directly relate to the dipole rotation discussed in lines 9–12. Choice (B) is not correct because lines 28–31 do not refer to the thickness of what is cooked. Choice (C) is incorrect as lines 79–83 do not even focus on microwave cooking.

38. **(B)** The second and third paragraphs of Passage 1 discuss how microwaves use the rotation of the polar molecules within food to heat up the food. Therefore, glucose and water would be heated within a microwave because they are both polar molecules according to the table. The other options each include at least one nonpolar substance.

39. **(C)** The author gives an in-depth analysis of the history and science of Halley's Comet, using words like "remarkable" and "poetic." The tone of the passage is best described as "analytical curiosity," because the author is clearly interested in understanding Halley's comet. Choice (A) is not correct because it is too negative. Choice (B) is incorrect because the passage gives quite a bit of scientific detail and stays focused on the topic. Choice (D) is wrong because although the author is clearly interested in Halley's Comet, he does not worship the comet.

40. **(A)** The first paragraph discusses the fact that Halley's Comet is a rare "Great Comet," i.e., one that is bright enough for humans on Earth to see without the aid of a telescope. Therefore, the brilliance referred to in line 4 describes the light-giving aspect of the comet, which is luminance. The other options are meanings of "brilliant" but are not correct in this context.

41. **(D)** Lines 1–7 assert that Halley's Comet and Old Faithful are renowned because of the dependable frequency with which they can be observed. Other ways of phrasing this idea are to say "periodic observability" or regular observability. Both the comet and the geyser contain water and nuclear particulates as listed in choices (A) and (C), but these factors do not contribute to their fame because water and nuclear particulates are relatively commonplace. Choice (B) is not correct because high eccentricity applies only to the comet, not to the geyser.

42. **(A)** Lines 5–7 most directly support the idea that Halley's Comet and Old Faithful are famous because of the regularity with which they can be seen. The other choices focus on aspects of the comet only.

43. **(C)** Lines 8–10 define a Great Comet as one that is bright enough to be observed by people on Earth with the naked eye. Although the other options may be attributes of a Great Comet, they are not, by definition, necessarily attributes.

44. **(A)** Lines 7–10 provide the best evidence for the idea that a Great Comet is one that can be observed without a telescope. The other options do not provide a definition of this term.

45. **(B)** The author uses this paragraph to give scientific reasons, such as Halley's unusually elliptical orbit, as to why Halley's Comet is a uniquely observable comet. The other options do not give the "primary" purpose of the paragraph, just minor things that are mentioned.

46. **(B)** The astronomer Halley used Newtonian theories and the historical records of previous observations to hypothesize about when this large comet, later named "Halley's Comet," would again be seen. To "conjecture" is the same as to hypothesize. "Fancied" means "wished," and "knew" or "foretold" indicate more certainty.

47. **(B)** Newton's theories gave Halley a general structure he could use to make better predictions about the behavior of comets. Out of the options, this is most similar to a politician who uses philosophical maxims to predict societal outcomes since the philosophical maxims give the theoretical structure that the politician would use to predict what would come next. Choice (A) is incorrect because the musician is not making predictions. Choice (C)

is wrong because the mathematician is using the data to create theories, while Halley was using the theory to make experimental predictions as to what the data would be. Choice (D) is not correct because the engineer is not focused on making predictions about data but, instead, on using established laws of physics for construction.

Writing and Language Test

1. **(A)** The other parts of the sentence list things by placing the subject followed by the verb and by using the active voice. This is the only choice that maintains parallelism with the rest of the sentence.

2. **(C)** The pronoun is referring to the "child," "adult," and "teenager," and so needs to be "their" in order to be plural. The other options do not match with a third-person plural subject.

3. **(B)** One comma is necessary to separate the independent clause that comes before "now" and the dependent clause that begins with the "now." Choice (A) is too choppy, choice (C) lacks any pauses, and choice (D) puts the pause in the incorrect place.

4. **(D)** The paragraph is focused on the origins and early history of occupational therapy. Choice (D) is the only answer that focuses on the profession's past. Although the other choices do discuss topics related to occupational therapy, they do not connect to the paragraph's focus on this history of occupational therapy.

5. **(A)** A dash is needed to set off the parenthetical phrase in the same way the parenthetical phrase is ended, namely with another dash. Choices (B) and (C) are incorrect because a complete sentence must come before a semicolon or a colon. Choice (D) would start the parenthetical phrase with a comma even though it ends with a dash. This would be fine if the phrase instead ended with a comma.

6. **(B)** The previous sentence discusses some of the educational degree possibilities for occupational therapists, and the underlined sentence continues that focus. The underlined sentence is not redundant. It provides information that is helpful in understanding the full range of educational options for occupational therapists. So the underlined sentence should be left as is.

7. **(A)** Occupational therapists work "along with" doctors, nurses, and other health professionals. So "alongside" is the best option. Choice (B) means more of a literal, physical joining. Choices (C) and (D) give illogical and disconnected transitions.

8. **(C)** This answer works because the occupational therapist could potentially help with "any" of the areas or with "all" of the areas. Choices (A) and (B) do not use prepositions correctly. Choice (D) uses "and," which would not make sense because it links "all of" and "any of."

9. **(D)** This is the only choice consistent with the present tense used elsewhere in the nearby context of the paragraph. Choice (A) is in the past tense, choice (B) is in the present perfect, and choice (C) is not a proper form of the verb.

10. **(A)** "Their" shows possession by the occupational therapists, and "clients'" shows that the time belongs to the plural clients. "They're" is the same as "they are," and "there" refers to a place.

11. **(B)** Based on the first bar at the top of the graph, all occupations will experience an 11% increase from 2012–2022. Based on the middle bar of the graph, occupational therapists will experience a 29% increase in employment in the same time period. The other options give incorrect information based on the graph.

12. **(C)** Frick is described as helping bring about violence during a labor strike, which would be generally considered an "infamous" accomplishment. "Infamous" means "famous for doing something bad." The other options could be applicable. However, they are far too vague to give the most consistent characterization of Frick.

13. **(D)** This is the only option that clearly separates all of the unique items listed. Choice (A) does not include commas to separate "fences" and "water cannons." Choice (B) puts a comma between "water" and "cannons," changing the intended meaning since a water cannon is a type of crowd-control device. Choice (C) breaks up the complete expression "fortifying the factory."

14. **(A)** Based on the context, the union workers would have been angered by Frick's actions—"incensed" means to anger greatly. Choices (B) and (C) are too positive. Choice (D) implies a lack of energy, although the workers were actually quite energetic in their response.

15. **(C)** "Firm determination" involves not letting anything get in one's way of accomplishing a goal. Saying that one will use "any means necessary" best conveys this desire to do what one wants, no matter the consequences. The other options do not express the strength of will that choice (C) does.

16. **(B)** The clause that matters is "who/whom fired the first shot." What occurs beforehand does not affect the choice between who and whom. In the phrase "he fired the first shot," the "he" is acting as a subject. Therefore, the relative pronoun comes in the place of the subject and should be "who." Choices (C) and (D) are incorrect because these refer to non-persons.

17. **(D)** The phrase "were lying" correctly uses the past progressive plural form of "to lie," indicating what the plural strikers were doing over an extended period in the past. The appropriate form of "lie" should be used since it means "being still," while "lay" means "put something down." The strikers were being still as they awaited the barges.

18. **(A)** This choice provides the most vivid details about the events while maintaining the more scholarly tone of the essay. The other options are too vague and informal.

19. **(C)** After considering the paragraph that immediately follows, you can see that it is logical to connect Frick's fears about the consequences of these events to the fact that he was correct in his prediction. Choices (A) and (B) connect to what happens in the next paragraph but are too vague to be solid explanations. Choice (D) contradicts Frick's goals.

20. **(D)** The mill is singular, and it possesses the grounds. Also, the two complete sentences need clear separation, which the semicolon, but not a comma, can provide. Choice (A) provides no possession, choice (B) is correct for plural mills, and choice (C) causes a comma splice.

21. **(A)** The paragraph should stay where it currently is. It concludes the essay, and generally refers to events that come later than the events discussed in the paragraphs beforehand. The other placements would change the chronology of the essay and interrupt the essay's narrative flow.

22. **(C)** The word "but" correctly indicates the logical contrast between the first and second halves of the sentence. The other options do not indicate contrast.

23. **(A)** This sentence begins the paragraph with a general introduction to the subject that is specifically elaborated upon in the next sentence. Choices (B) and (D) are too broad. Choice (C) is too specific.

24. **(D)** In this context, the word "claimed" should be followed by the word "that" in order to fit the common idiomatic phrasing, "claimed that." The other options do not use the proper idiomatic phrasing.

25. **(B)** This choice gives by far the most specific support for Dali's beliefs about his highly-developed abilities by mentioning the "dematerializing lighting technique." The other choices are too vague.

26. **(C)** "Completed" uses the correct singular past tense in reference to Dali's actions in the past. Choice (A) is present tense, choice (B) is present perfect, and choice (D) uses an improper form of the verb.

27. **(B)** It is most logical to state that there are "several symbols present in this painting," since this means that several symbols can be found in the painting.

28. **(D)** This choice maintains the original meaning while eliminating unnecessary wording. Choices (A) and (B) are too wordy. The meaning of choice (C) is unclear.

29. **(A)** "Reclaimed" is the only wording given that would be appropriately applied to a renewal of one's religion, which is what happened based on Dali's actions in the following sentences, making "rejected" incorrect. A person does not "reproduce" or "redomesticate" his or her religion.

30. **(C)** "For instance" provides a connection between the general statement made about the artwork in the previous sentence and the specific example given in the current sentence. Choices (A) and (B) do not provide this sort of transition. Choice (D) is too wordy.

31. **(B)** A boat is best described as passing "over" the sea since it travels along the sea's surface. A boat does not pass "to" or "sequence" over the sea, making choices (B) and (D) incorrect. Choice (C) is too wordy.

32. **(C)** The first part of the sentence mentions that Dali had a wide range of interests. This choice elaborates on what those specific interests were. In addition, the next several sentences describe Dali as creating sculptural pieces and writing a book.

33. **(B)** "Brought" is the correctly used tense of "to bring" in this context.

34. **(A)** The following sentence particularly clarifies which choice makes the most sense. The "former" would be referring to "knowledge and wisdom"—a sensible rationale for changing to robotic exploration since such exploration would increase our knowledge but wouldn't give humans bragging rights as the first to land on another planet. Choices (B) and (C) each

present only one option instead of two. Choice (D) does not give an option that is the focus of the context that follows.

35. **(D)** This is consistent with the use of "we" elsewhere in the paragraph.

36. **(A)** Without this sentence, there would be no logical transition from the discussion of human exploration to the discussion of what the author considers to be a better, robotic alternative. Choice (B) is not correct because it does not provide any details.

37. **(C)** The commas correctly surround the clarification of what Io is. This grammatical construction is known as an "appositive," which is when an interchangeable name for what comes before is surrounded with commas. For example, "My oldest daughter, the Prime Minister, is well respected." The other options do not provide sufficient pauses.

38. **(D)** Each of the previous phrases in the sentence start with "that." Choice (D) is the only answer that continues this parallel structure.

39. **(A)** "Made-for-television" is an appropriate idiomatic expression that indicates that something was done with the intent of turning it into a television program. The other choices are nonsensical.

40. **(B)** This choice is the only one that focuses on the key argument of the passage, that it is time to move from human-centered to robot-centered exploration. The other choices present pairings that are not both discussed in the passage.

41. **(B)** The "it" refers to the act of involving humans in exploration, which is singular. "Does" is the correct form of the verb "to do" when coupled with a singular subject. Choice (D) could potentially work if instead of "that," the sentence used "the" immediately before the underlined phrase and if instead of "increase," it used "increased" immediately following the underlined phrase.

42. **(D)** The word "than" is used when comparing. While "to" is used in conjunction with a verb like "to run" and "too" in comparisons like "too much," neither of these is needed because (D) is the only choice that is parallel to the earlier phrasing in the sentence, "would rather hear."

43. **(C)** This is the only choice that does not have an unnecessary comma between the first and second contrasting parts of the sentence. This section of the sentence has only one subject—"volunteers." With only one subject, the two contrasting sections must be linked and therefore not be separated by a comma. Choice (A) is illogical, choice (B) includes an unnecessary pause, and choice (D) has two unnecessary commas.

44. **(A)** The paragraph discusses how strong public motivation to explore space will increase interest in it, citing the Mars One project as a good example. Choice (A) is the only option that correctly connects to the general theme of the paragraph to the specific example of Mars One.

Math Test (No Calculator)

1. **(C)** x and y could both be either negative or positive to make this true. Therefore, the only thing you can safely assume is that x and y are different. You can try this with sample values that make this expression true:

x	y	$x^2 > y^2$
–5	4	$25 > 16$
6	–1	$36 > 1$
3	0	$9 > 0$

2. **(B)** The easiest method is to substitute x into the first equation.

$$2x = 10 \rightarrow x = 5$$

   Substitute 5 into the first equation:

$$5 = y^2 - 3y + 1 \rightarrow y^2 - 3y - 4 = 0 \rightarrow$$

   Factor it: $(y + 1)(y - 4) = 0$

   Therefore, the solutions are –1 and 4.

3. **(C)** Multiplying or dividing an inequality by a negative number requires that the direction of the inequality sign be reversed. The other operations mentioned do not do so. Here is how the inequality can be solved when dividing by –2:

$$-2x > 4 \rightarrow \frac{-2x}{-2} < \frac{4}{-2} \rightarrow x < -2$$

   If you try some sample values that work for x, such as –3 or –5, you will see that the inequality is true.

4. **(D)** You could work backward from the choices if you are so inclined. Algebraically, divide the expression by 3 to simplify:

$$3a^2 - 27a - 108 = 0 \rightarrow a^2 - 9a - 36 = 0 \rightarrow$$

   Factor it: $(a - 12)(a + 3) = 0$

   If $a = 12$, the whole left-hand side equals 0. Similarly, if $a = -3$, the whole left-hand side equals 0.

   Therefore, the solutions are 12, –3.

5. **(C)** Whenever Andrew starts a problem, he always takes the 10 minutes of time to set up. Then he completes 1 problem every 5 minutes of actual study. So the number of minutes he takes to do p problems is $10 + 5p$. If you set up the equation for this, it is $m = 10 + 5p$. Solving for p gives the correct answer:

$$m = 10 + 5p \rightarrow m - 10 = 5p \rightarrow \frac{(m-10)}{5} = p \rightarrow p = \frac{1}{5}(m-10)$$

6. **(A)** Take the slope of the line using relatively simple points from the table, like (1, 2) and (5, 18):

$$\text{Slope} = \frac{Rise}{Run} = \frac{y_2 - y_1}{x_2 - x_1} = \frac{18 - 2}{5 - 1} = \frac{16}{4} = 4$$

   The only choice with a slope of 4 is (A).

7. **(D)** Since this is one equation with two variables, it has infinite solutions. If you knew another line with which this equation intersected, the two equations would have a single solution. To see how this equation has more than two solutions, substitute some sample values for x and y into the equation:

$$3x - 4y = 73$$

If x is 1, y is -17.5.

If x is 2, y is -16.75.

If x is 3, y is -16.

You can keep on going, and you will find endless possibilities for x and y.

8. **(B)** Solve for x and y by using substitution:

$$4 + y = 32x \text{ and } y = 2x + 2 \rightarrow$$

$$4 + (2x + 2) = 32x \rightarrow 6 = 30x \rightarrow x = \frac{1}{5} \rightarrow$$

Substitute $\frac{1}{5}$ for x to solve for y: $y = (2 \times \frac{1}{5}) + 2 = \frac{12}{5}$

Then multiply x and y to solve for their product: $\frac{1}{5} \times \frac{12}{5} = \frac{12}{25}$

9. **(C)** For each year she has the portfolio, its value increases 10%. Therefore, the amount after one year of growth over the original amount at the beginning of that year will be 1.1 times the original amount. This process will repeat for each year Maria has the portfolio growing at this rate, making $f(n) = 10,000 \times 1.1^n$.

You can also see this using concrete numbers. If Maria starts with \$10,000, after 1 year, she will have 10% interest added to the original amount:

$$10\% \text{ of } 10,000 = 0.1 \times 10,000 = 1,000$$

Then you can add 1,000 to the original 10,000 to have \$11,000 after the first year. To see how much money Maria will have after two years, find 10% of this new total:

$$10\% \text{ of } 11,000 = 0.1 \times 11,000 = 1,100$$

Then add this to the original 11,000 to find how much she will have in her account at the end of year 2:

$$11,000 + 1,100 = 12,100$$

The only option that fits these concrete numbers is choice (C).

10. **(D)** Minimizing all of the variables will decrease the amount of money in the account after a given period of time. You could plug in a variety of sample values and test the impact of changing each variable on the overall amount of money in the account. However, determining the answer is easier simply by using common sense. If you start off with less money, have a lower interest rate, and have less frequent compounding of interest, less money will be in the account.

11. **(B)** Begin by determining the slope of the line in the given equation by putting it in slope-intercept form ($y = mx + b$):

$$4x = 2y - 6 \rightarrow 2y = 4x + 6 \rightarrow y = 2x + 3$$

The line portrayed in choice (B), $y = 2x + 10$, is the only option that has the same slope as the line in the problem. This means that the two lines will never intersect and will have no common solutions since they are parallel to one another. Be mindful that this will be true only as long as the y-intercepts of the lines are different. If the y-intercepts are the same, the lines will overlap, resulting in an infinite number of solutions.

12. **(A)** No matter how many shirts or pants are cleaned, the cleaner charges a $5 fee. The only logical explanation out of the given choices is that this is some kind of set fee. The cost to clean a shirt is $10 since the shirt variable is multiplied by 10. The cost to clean a pair of pants is $6 since the pants variable is multiplied by 6. The total minimum cost to clean either one shirt or one pair of pants is $11:

$$C = 10S + 6P + 5 \rightarrow C = (10 \times 0) + (6 \times 1) + 5 = 11$$

13. **(B)** When you add a positive number to the y-value of a function, the function shifts up. When you subtract a number from the x-value of a function, the function shifts to the right. This function has had 2 subtracted from its x-value, so the function shifts to the right 2 units. This function has had 3 added to its y-value, so the function shifts up 3 units.

GRID-IN QUESTIONS

14.

12 Triple the given equation $2x + 3 = 4$ to give you the equation $6x + 9 = 12$:

$$2x + 3 = 4 \rightarrow 3 \cdot 2x + 3 \cdot 3 = 3 \cdot 4 \rightarrow 6x + 9 = 12$$

15.

6 Look for a way to seamlessly make the original expression a variation of $x + 5$. Add 25 to both sides of the equation $x^2 + 10x = 11$ to form $x^2 + 10x + 25 = 36$. The result can be expressed as $(x + 5)^2 = 36$. Therefore, $x + 5 = 6$.

Alternatively, you could determine the value of x using the quadratic formula, $\dfrac{-b \pm \sqrt{b^2 - 4ac}}{2a}$. However, this will be more labor intensive than if you use the shortcut.

16.

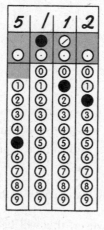

3 There are 3 values of the function where it will intersect the *x*-axis. You can see this by looking at the graph of the equation below:

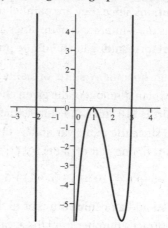

The values of 3, –2, and 1 are all zeros of the function.

You can perhaps more easily determine the zeros of the function if you recognize that the function is already factored:

$$f(x) = (x - 3)(x + 2)((x - 1)^2)$$

All you need to do is look at the values of *x* that would make the entire expression equal to zero. If $(x - 3) = 0$, if $(x + 2) = 0$, or if $(x - 1) = 0$, the entire expression is equal to zero. Since $(x - 1)$ is squared, the $(x - 1)$ term repeats. So you will have only three zeros even though this equation is actually to the 4th power.

17.

$\dfrac{5}{12}$ The triangle as described looks like this:

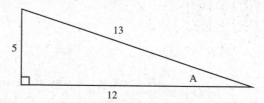

Given this sine and cosine, the triangle will be a multiple of the special right triangle 5-12-13. The smallest side is 5, and the median side is 12. So the ratio of the smallest side of the triangle to the median side of the triangle is $\dfrac{5}{12}$.

Another way to think about the answer is to realize that the question is asking for the tangent of angle *A*. The tangent is the opposite side over the adjacent side, which is $\dfrac{5}{12}$.

Math Test (With Calculator)

1. **(C)** The "difference" between two terms is the result when you subtract one term from another. Subtract one term from another. This is easiest to do if you place one term over the other so you can easily match up common terms and carefully apply the negative sign:

$$\begin{array}{r} (7a^2 + 3ab - 8b) \\ - (-2a^2 + ab - 2b) \\ \hline 9a^2 + 2ab - 6b \end{array}$$

2. **(A)**

$$\left(2x^2 + 4xy + 2y^2\right) \times \frac{1}{2x+2y} = \frac{2x^2 + 4xy + 2y^2}{2x+2y} \rightarrow$$

$$\frac{x^2 + 2xy + y^2}{x+y} = \frac{(x+y)(x+y)}{(x+y)} = x + y = y + x$$

3. **(B)** The professor will cancel if there are 10 or fewer students in the class. So more than 10 students must be present for the professor to conduct the class. Therefore, the answer is $S > 10$.

4. **(C)** What is a possible value for x in the expression below?

   Take the original expression: $-6 < \frac{8}{3}x < -\frac{1}{4}$

   Multiply everything by $\frac{3}{8}$ in order to get x by itself:

   $$-\frac{9}{4} < x < -\frac{3}{32}$$

   Make solving the inequality easier by converting each fraction to a decimal. Then determine what numbers fall within this range. The fractions would convert to the following range when expressed as decimals:

   $$-2.25 < x < -0.09375$$

   -2 is the only choice within this range.

5. **(B)** As the age groups gradually increase in value (from 12 through 61+), the number of group members using video sharing steadily decreases (from 40 to 2). A negative correlation is defined as the relationship between two variables such that when one variable increases, the other variable decreases. So the relationship between age groups and percentage of group members using video sharing can best be described as a negative correlation. A positive correlation is when the variables increase with one another. Equivalence simply means the variables are equal. An exponentially inverse relationship means that as one variable increases, the other decreases at an exponential rate. The decrease in video sharing is relatively steady, so the terms cannot be described as having an exponentially inverse relationship.

6. **(D)** Take the fractions of the portion of each group who uses that type of social media and divide by the total of each group; then multiply:

$$\frac{12-18\text{-year-olds who photo share}}{\text{Total number of } 12-18\text{-year-olds}} \times \frac{31-45\text{-year-olds who text share}}{\text{Total number of } 31-45\text{-year-olds}} = \frac{32}{94} \times \frac{40}{104} \approx 0.13$$

7. **(D)** Calling people from as large a group as possible from as many phone types and age groups as possible will ensure that the results are highly accurate. The other choices limit the samples to groups who do particular types of activities. The other choices would give results accurate for that sample but not for the population as a whole.

8. **(C)** Take how much money from the $62,000 total falls in each tax bracket, and calculate the amount of tax applied to it:

First $9,000 at 15% = $9,000 × 0.15 = $1,350

Next $41,000 at 20% = $41,000 × 0.20 = $8,200

Next $12,000 at 30% = $12,000 × 0.30 = $3,600

$1,350 + $8,200 + $3,600 = $13,150 total

As an alternative solution or as a way of checking your math, you could estimate. The answer must fall somewhere within the range of 15% to 30% of $62,000 since all of the tax brackets are within this range. Most of the money is taxed at 20%, so the answer should be close to 20%. Since more money is taxed at 30% and since 30% is twice as far away from 20% as is 15%, the amount of tax should be a bit more than 20% of the total. 20% of $62,000 is $12,400, and the answer is a bit greater than this.

9. **(A)** Multiply both the slope and the y-intercept of the given line by –1 to get the reflection of the line. For $y = 4x + 7$, this is the equation $y = -4x - 7$.

The general rule to find the reflection of a function $f(x)$ across the x-axis is that the reflection is $-f(x)$.

10. **(D)** Solve for x as follows:

$$\frac{12}{\sqrt[3]{x}} = 4 \rightarrow 12 = 4\sqrt[3]{x} \rightarrow 3 = \sqrt[3]{x} \rightarrow \text{Cube both sides} \rightarrow 27 = x$$

11. **(C)** The slope of the function is steady and linear until around week 6, at which point it starts curving upward exponentially. An exponential function is one that goes up at a rapidly increasing rate or goes down at a rapidly decreasing rate, as opposed to a steady, linear rate.

12. **(A)** "Geometric" is synonymous with "exponential." Estimate the approximate increase given the rate of exponential growth and starting point at week 12. Fortunately, the answers are far enough apart that 450 is the only reasonable option. The other options all represent far too large an increase.

13. **(A)** $m + 2n = 1$ and $6n + 3m = 9$ are parallel lines that will not intersect since they have the same slopes and different y-intercepts. Since they never intersect, they have no common solutions.

14. **(D)** Each penny is worth 1 cent, and each nickel is worth 5 cents. So the total number of cents given by the total coins in the change bowl is $P + 5N$. This needs to be less than 1 dollar total, i.e., 100 cents. So the inequality $P + 5N < 100$ is the solution.

15. **(B)** Since the data set would be far larger than either of the data sets portrayed and since the values are selected at random, it is most reasonable to conclude that the average (mean) of the set of 1,000 randomly selected values would be 50. Generally speaking, the larger your data sample, the more likely your actual mean will approach your estimated mean.

16. **(B)** Since the values are selected at random, such a high proportion of values greater than 50 in the selection of 50 random numbers is most surprising. With a larger data set, the values would be expected to average closer to the mean than those in the set of 20 random numbers. Since values are taken between 1 and 100, both sets of data should have a range between 1–100, which explains why choice (A) is incorrect. Choice (C) is incorrect because the ranges of the data sets are similar even though the means of the sets are different. Choice (D) is not correct because portraying these random values in a scatter plot is logical. You can impose a best-fit line on top of the scattered data if you would like to determine a trend.

17. **(A)** The range is the difference between the maximum and minimum values in the set. With such large data sets, it is highly likely that both sets would have a wide range of large and small values, with both almost certainly having a value close to or at 1 and a value close to or at 100. So the range for both sets would be about 100. The difference between the ranges is calculated by subtracting one range from the other: $100 - 100 = 0$.

18. **(B)** A best-fit line is a line on the graph that shows the overall direction the points seem to be going. The best-fit lines of both of these sets would most likely be a horizontal line with a y-intercept of approximately 50. Horizontal lines have a slope of 0, so the average of the slopes of both of these lines would most likely be 0 as well.

19. **(C)** A value of 4 for n will ensure that the expression has exponential growth since any power of 2 or greater will ensure exponential growth in the function. Anything raised to the 0 power simply equals 1. Anything raised to an exponent of 1 is simply itself. So choices (A) and (B) result in lines, not exponential functions.

20. **(C)** The best way to increase a confidence level is to increase the amount of relevant sample data. A more accurate scale could be of minor help but not as much as increasing the overall data samples. Choices (A) and (B) would provide irrelevant and less accurate data, respectively.

21. **(D)** The weight of the balloon itself is irrelevant since the balloon is identical in both situations.

    $1.2 - 0.179 = 1.021$ is the difference in density between the two balloons. Since you have a 2 cubic meter balloon, simply multiply 1.021×2 to give approximately 2.04.

22. **(B)** The smaller the range of values in a data set, the lower the standard deviation will be. If the smallest and largest values are removed, the range of values will decrease, thereby decreasing the standard deviation.

    To be more precise, you can calculate standard deviation using this formula:

    $$\text{Standard deviation} = \sqrt{\text{Average of the squared distances of the data points from their mean}}$$

    For example, the standard deviation of the set $\{1, 5, 6, 7, 10\}$ is approximately 3.3. The standard deviation of the same set with the highest and lowest values removed $\{5, 6, 7\}$ is 1. By using this example, you can see that removing the smallest and largest values from the set decreases the standard deviation of the set.

23. **(B)** After purchasing gifts for his other friends, Jay has $50 left. Since 200 quarters equals $50, the range of what Jay can give his friend is between 1 and 200 quarters, inclusive. This is expressed as $1 \leq Q \leq 200$.

24. **(C)** The fixed costs for the pretzel stand are $500, and the variable costs are $2 per pretzel. So the cost function $c(x)$ given x pretzels is $c(x) = 2x + 500$. The graph of this function has a y-intercept of 500 and a slope of 2:

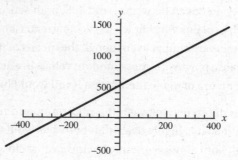

25. **(C)** Since this is a 2nd-degree equation, it should have two solutions.

$$8x^2 = -16x - 2$$
$$8x^2 + 16x = -2$$
$$x^2 + 2x = -\frac{1}{4}$$

Complete the square:

$$(x+1)^2 = \frac{3}{4} \rightarrow x^2 + 2x + 1 = \frac{3}{4} \rightarrow x^2 + 2x + \frac{1}{4} = 0$$

Use the quadratic equation to find the answers:

$$\frac{-b \pm \sqrt{b^2 - 4ac}}{2a} \rightarrow \frac{-2 \pm \sqrt{2^2 - 4 \cdot 1 \cdot \frac{1}{4}}}{2 \cdot 1} = \frac{-2 \pm \sqrt{3}}{2 \cdot 1} = -1 \pm \frac{\sqrt{3}}{2}$$

Then simplify the two solutions to see what they equal:

$$-1 + \frac{\sqrt{3}}{2} = \frac{-2}{2} + \frac{\sqrt{3}}{2} = \frac{1}{2}(\sqrt{3} - 2)$$

and

$$-1 - \frac{\sqrt{3}}{2} = \frac{-2}{2} - \frac{\sqrt{3}}{2} = -1 - \frac{\sqrt{3}}{2}$$

26. **(A)** In order to maximize the area of flooring while minimizing the floor's perimeter, a square floor would be the best choice. A square always has at least as much and typically more area for a particular perimeter than a rectangle of the same perimeter. Therefore, the length and width should be equivalent.

To see this, try using concrete numbers. If you have a square and a rectangle, each with a perimeter of 20 units, the length of each side for the square must be 5 and the lengths of the sides of the rectangle could be a wide range of possibilities, such as 2, 8, 2, 8. The area of the square with a side of 5 is $5^2 = 25$. The area of the rectangle is $2 \times 8 = 16$, which is much less than the area of the square. You can try this with other sample values for the rectangle's sides. However, you will consistently find that having the sides equivalent will lead to the greatest possible area.

27. **(D)** $i^4 + i^{12} = 1 + 1 = 2$. Know that the powers of i repeat in a cycle of four:

$$i^1 = i, \, i^2 = -1, \, i^3 = -i, \, i^4 = 1, \, i^5 = i, \ldots$$

That way, you can look at the value of the exponent and know what the value of i^x will be without having to do any long calculations.

28.

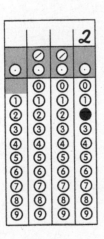

21 In a typical week, Eloise should get $9 \times 7 = 63$ hours of sleep. To see how many hours she has actually slept, subtract the total hours she has been awake from the total hours in a week:

$$(24 \times 7) - 126 = 42$$

Then calculate the additional hours of sleep she should get by subtracting how many hours she *actually* got (42) from the amount of sleep she *should have* gotten (63):

Eloise should get an additional $63 - 42 = 21$ hours of sleep.

29.

7.6 Plug in the given values for m and n to determine what the value of the constant k is:

$$m = kn$$
$$10 = k \times 2$$
$$5 = k$$

Now plug in 38 for m and 5 for k to get the value of n:

$$38 = 5n$$
$$7.6 = n$$

30.

2 The plant increases 3 inches in height every 2 months. Simply backtrack 2 months from the time when it is 5 inches tall in order to see how tall it was when it was planted:

$$5 - 3 = 2 \text{ inches}$$

31.

1994 1994 is the year during which the college had the largest spike in applications. Moreover, the number of admissions began to decrease at that time. This decrease most likely occurred because the college knew that, since it could secure a large number of students from early decision (since students admitted early were committed to going), it could fill all of its student spots without having to offer as many admissions. Having more applications and fewer admissions results in greater selectivity because being accepted to the college is more difficult for the majority of students applying.

ANSWER SHEET
Practice Test 2

Reading Test

1. Ⓐ Ⓑ Ⓒ Ⓓ
2. Ⓐ Ⓑ Ⓒ Ⓓ
3. Ⓐ Ⓑ Ⓒ Ⓓ
4. Ⓐ Ⓑ Ⓒ Ⓓ
5. Ⓐ Ⓑ Ⓒ Ⓓ
6. Ⓐ Ⓑ Ⓒ Ⓓ
7. Ⓐ Ⓑ Ⓒ Ⓓ
8. Ⓐ Ⓑ Ⓒ Ⓓ
9. Ⓐ Ⓑ Ⓒ Ⓓ
10. Ⓐ Ⓑ Ⓒ Ⓓ
11. Ⓐ Ⓑ Ⓒ Ⓓ
12. Ⓐ Ⓑ Ⓒ Ⓓ

13. Ⓐ Ⓑ Ⓒ Ⓓ
14. Ⓐ Ⓑ Ⓒ Ⓓ
15. Ⓐ Ⓑ Ⓒ Ⓓ
16. Ⓐ Ⓑ Ⓒ Ⓓ
17. Ⓐ Ⓑ Ⓒ Ⓓ
18. Ⓐ Ⓑ Ⓒ Ⓓ
19. Ⓐ Ⓑ Ⓒ Ⓓ
20. Ⓐ Ⓑ Ⓒ Ⓓ
21. Ⓐ Ⓑ Ⓒ Ⓓ
22. Ⓐ Ⓑ Ⓒ Ⓓ
23. Ⓐ Ⓑ Ⓒ Ⓓ
24. Ⓐ Ⓑ Ⓒ Ⓓ

25. Ⓐ Ⓑ Ⓒ Ⓓ
26. Ⓐ Ⓑ Ⓒ Ⓓ
27. Ⓐ Ⓑ Ⓒ Ⓓ
28. Ⓐ Ⓑ Ⓒ Ⓓ
29. Ⓐ Ⓑ Ⓒ Ⓓ
30. Ⓐ Ⓑ Ⓒ Ⓓ
31. Ⓐ Ⓑ Ⓒ Ⓓ
32. Ⓐ Ⓑ Ⓒ Ⓓ
33. Ⓐ Ⓑ Ⓒ Ⓓ
34. Ⓐ Ⓑ Ⓒ Ⓓ
35. Ⓐ Ⓑ Ⓒ Ⓓ
36. Ⓐ Ⓑ Ⓒ Ⓓ

37. Ⓐ Ⓑ Ⓒ Ⓓ
38. Ⓐ Ⓑ Ⓒ Ⓓ
39. Ⓐ Ⓑ Ⓒ Ⓓ
40. Ⓐ Ⓑ Ⓒ Ⓓ
41. Ⓐ Ⓑ Ⓒ Ⓓ
42. Ⓐ Ⓑ Ⓒ Ⓓ
43. Ⓐ Ⓑ Ⓒ Ⓓ
44. Ⓐ Ⓑ Ⓒ Ⓓ
45. Ⓐ Ⓑ Ⓒ Ⓓ
46. Ⓐ Ⓑ Ⓒ Ⓓ
47. Ⓐ Ⓑ Ⓒ Ⓓ

Writing and Language Test

1. Ⓐ Ⓑ Ⓒ Ⓓ
2. Ⓐ Ⓑ Ⓒ Ⓓ
3. Ⓐ Ⓑ Ⓒ Ⓓ
4. Ⓐ Ⓑ Ⓒ Ⓓ
5. Ⓐ Ⓑ Ⓒ Ⓓ
6. Ⓐ Ⓑ Ⓒ Ⓓ
7. Ⓐ Ⓑ Ⓒ Ⓓ
8. Ⓐ Ⓑ Ⓒ Ⓓ
9. Ⓐ Ⓑ Ⓒ Ⓓ
10. Ⓐ Ⓑ Ⓒ Ⓓ
11. Ⓐ Ⓑ Ⓒ Ⓓ

12. Ⓐ Ⓑ Ⓒ Ⓓ
13. Ⓐ Ⓑ Ⓒ Ⓓ
14. Ⓐ Ⓑ Ⓒ Ⓓ
15. Ⓐ Ⓑ Ⓒ Ⓓ
16. Ⓐ Ⓑ Ⓒ Ⓓ
17. Ⓐ Ⓑ Ⓒ Ⓓ
18. Ⓐ Ⓑ Ⓒ Ⓓ
19. Ⓐ Ⓑ Ⓒ Ⓓ
20. Ⓐ Ⓑ Ⓒ Ⓓ
21. Ⓐ Ⓑ Ⓒ Ⓓ
22. Ⓐ Ⓑ Ⓒ Ⓓ

23. Ⓐ Ⓑ Ⓒ Ⓓ
24. Ⓐ Ⓑ Ⓒ Ⓓ
25. Ⓐ Ⓑ Ⓒ Ⓓ
26. Ⓐ Ⓑ Ⓒ Ⓓ
27. Ⓐ Ⓑ Ⓒ Ⓓ
28. Ⓐ Ⓑ Ⓒ Ⓓ
29. Ⓐ Ⓑ Ⓒ Ⓓ
30. Ⓐ Ⓑ Ⓒ Ⓓ
31. Ⓐ Ⓑ Ⓒ Ⓓ
32. Ⓐ Ⓑ Ⓒ Ⓓ
33. Ⓐ Ⓑ Ⓒ Ⓓ

34. Ⓐ Ⓑ Ⓒ Ⓓ
35. Ⓐ Ⓑ Ⓒ Ⓓ
36. Ⓐ Ⓑ Ⓒ Ⓓ
37. Ⓐ Ⓑ Ⓒ Ⓓ
38. Ⓐ Ⓑ Ⓒ Ⓓ
39. Ⓐ Ⓑ Ⓒ Ⓓ
40. Ⓐ Ⓑ Ⓒ Ⓓ
41. Ⓐ Ⓑ Ⓒ Ⓓ
42. Ⓐ Ⓑ Ⓒ Ⓓ
43. Ⓐ Ⓑ Ⓒ Ⓓ
44. Ⓐ Ⓑ Ⓒ Ⓓ

ANSWER SHEET
Practice Test 2

Math Test (No Calculator)

1. Ⓐ Ⓑ Ⓒ Ⓓ   5. Ⓐ Ⓑ Ⓒ Ⓓ   9. Ⓐ Ⓑ Ⓒ Ⓓ   13. Ⓐ Ⓑ Ⓒ Ⓓ
2. Ⓐ Ⓑ Ⓒ Ⓓ   6. Ⓐ Ⓑ Ⓒ Ⓓ   10. Ⓐ Ⓑ Ⓒ Ⓓ
3. Ⓐ Ⓑ Ⓒ Ⓓ   7. Ⓐ Ⓑ Ⓒ Ⓓ   11. Ⓐ Ⓑ Ⓒ Ⓓ
4. Ⓐ Ⓑ Ⓒ Ⓓ   8. Ⓐ Ⓑ Ⓒ Ⓓ   12. Ⓐ Ⓑ Ⓒ Ⓓ

14.   15.   16.   17.

Math Test (With Calculator)

1. Ⓐ Ⓑ Ⓒ Ⓓ   8. Ⓐ Ⓑ Ⓒ Ⓓ   15. Ⓐ Ⓑ Ⓒ Ⓓ   22. Ⓐ Ⓑ Ⓒ Ⓓ
2. Ⓐ Ⓑ Ⓒ Ⓓ   9. Ⓐ Ⓑ Ⓒ Ⓓ   16. Ⓐ Ⓑ Ⓒ Ⓓ   23. Ⓐ Ⓑ Ⓒ Ⓓ
3. Ⓐ Ⓑ Ⓒ Ⓓ   10. Ⓐ Ⓑ Ⓒ Ⓓ   17. Ⓐ Ⓑ Ⓒ Ⓓ   24. Ⓐ Ⓑ Ⓒ Ⓓ
4. Ⓐ Ⓑ Ⓒ Ⓓ   11. Ⓐ Ⓑ Ⓒ Ⓓ   18. Ⓐ Ⓑ Ⓒ Ⓓ   25. Ⓐ Ⓑ Ⓒ Ⓓ
5. Ⓐ Ⓑ Ⓒ Ⓓ   12. Ⓐ Ⓑ Ⓒ Ⓓ   19. Ⓐ Ⓑ Ⓒ Ⓓ   26. Ⓐ Ⓑ Ⓒ Ⓓ
6. Ⓐ Ⓑ Ⓒ Ⓓ   13. Ⓐ Ⓑ Ⓒ Ⓓ   20. Ⓐ Ⓑ Ⓒ Ⓓ   27. Ⓐ Ⓑ Ⓒ Ⓓ
7. Ⓐ Ⓑ Ⓒ Ⓓ   14. Ⓐ Ⓑ Ⓒ Ⓓ   21. Ⓐ Ⓑ Ⓒ Ⓓ

28.   29.   30.   31.

Practice Test 2

READING TEST

60 MINUTES, 47 QUESTIONS

Directions: Each passage or pair of passages is accompanied by several questions. After reading the passage(s), choose the best answer to each question based on what is indicated explicitly or implicitly in the passage(s) or in the associated graphics.

Questions 1–10 are based on the following excerpt.

The following passage is taken from the 1852 novel, *The Blithedale Romance*. Mr. Coverdale, an idealistic young man, who has recently moved onto a utopian communal farm, is recovering from a fever. He is attended first by Hollingsworth, a philanthropist, and second by Zenobia, a beautiful wealthy resident of the farm.

Happy the man that has such a man
beside him when he comes to die! And unless
a friend like Hollingsworth be at hand—as
Line most probably there will not—he had better
(5) make up his mind to die alone. How many
men, I wonder, does one meet with, in a lifetime, whom he would choose for his death-
bed companion? At the crisis of my fever, I
besought Hollingsworth to let nobody else
(10) enter the room, but continually to make me
sensible of his own presence, by a grasp of
the hand, a word, a prayer, if he thought good
to utter it; and that then he should be the witness to how courageously I would encounter
(15) the worst. It still impresses me as almost a

matter of regret, that I did not die then, when
I had tolerably made up my mind to do it;
for Hollingsworth would have gone with me
to the hither verge of life, and have sent his
(20) friendly and hopeful accents far over on the
other side, while I should be treading the
unknown path. Now, were I to send for him,
he would hardly come to my besdside, nor
should I depart the easier for his presence.
(25) "You are not going to die, this time," said
he, gravely smiling. "You know nothing about
sickness, and think your case a great deal
more desperate than it is."
"Death should take me while I am in the
(30) mood," replied I, with a little of my custom-
ary levity.
"Have you nothing to do in life," asked
Hollingsworth, "that you fancy yourself so
ready to leave it?"
(35) "Nothing," answer I; "nothing, that I know
of, unless to make pretty verses, and play a
part, with Zenobia and the rest of the ama-
teurs, in our pastoral. It seems but an unsub-
stantial sort of business, as viewed through a
(40) mist of fever. But, dear Hollingsworth, your
own vocation is evidently to be a priest, and

to spend your days and nights in helping
your fellow-creatures to draw peaceful dying
breaths."

(45)   "And by which of my qualities, " inquired
he, "can you suppose me fitted for this awful
ministry?"

        "By your tenderness," I said. "It seems to
me the reflection of God's own love."

(50)   "And you call me tender!" repeated
Hollingsworth, thoughtfully. "I should rather
say that the most marked trait in my character is an inflexible severity of purpose. Mortal
man has no right to be so inflexible as it is my
(55) nature and necessity to be."

        "I do not believe it," I replied.

        But, in due time, I remembered what he
said.

        Probably, as Hollingsworth suggested,
(60) my disorder was never so serious as, in my
ignorance of such matters, I was inclined to
consider it. After so much tragical preparation, it was positively rather mortifying to
find myself on the mending hand.

(65)   All other members of the Community
showed me kindness according to the full
measure of their capacity. Zenobia brought
me my gruel, every day, made by her own
hands; and whenever I seemed inclined to
(70) converse, would sit by my bed-side, and
talk with so much vivacity as to add several
gratuitous throbs to my pulse. Her poor little
stories and tracts never half did justice to her
intellect. It was only the lack of a fitter ave-
(75) nue that drove her to seek development in
literature. She was made (among a thousand
other things that she might have been) for a
stump-oratress. I recognized no severe culture in Zenobia; her mind was full of weeds.
(80) It startled me, sometimes, in my state of
moral as well as bodily faint-heartedness, to
observe the hardihood of her philosophy. She
made no scruple of oversetting all human
institutions, and scattering them as with a
(85) breeze from her fan. A female reformer, in
her attacks upon society, has an instinctive
sense of where the life lies, and is inclined to
aim directly at that spot. Especially the rela-

tion between the sexes is naturally among
(90) the earliest to attract her notice. Zenobia was
truly a magnificent woman.

1. The point of view from which the passage is
    told is

    (A) first person.
    (B) third person.
    (C) objective.
    (D) omniscient.

2. Based on the passage as a whole, the narrator
    can best be characterized as

    (A) calmly resolute.
    (B) completely morbid.
    (C) overly dramatic.
    (D) patiently optimistic.

3. Which choice provides the best evidence
    for the answer to the previous question?

    (A) Lines 25–28 ("You are . . . it is.")
    (B) Lines 45–47 ("And by . . . ministry?")
    (C) Lines 65–67 ("All other . . . capacity.")
    (D) Lines 74–76 ("It was . . . literature.")

4. As used in line 43, "draw" most nearly
    means

    (A) inhale.
    (B) provoke.
    (C) infer.
    (D) sketch.

5. What best describes the figure of speech
    used by the narrator in lines 62–64
    ("After . . . hand")?

    (A) Metaphor
    (B) Understatement
    (C) Personification
    (D) Irony

6. What is the most likely reason that the author has capitalized the word "Community" in line 65?

    (A) To be consistent with common cultural practices in the writing of the 1800s

    (B) To label it as a formal proper noun since it likely refers to an idealistic commune

    (C) To demonstrate the narrator's unusual passion for large urban developments

    (D) To distinguish it from other municipalities discussed earlier in the passage

7. In the narrator's view, what was the major factor that drove Zenobia into her primary intellectual pursuit?

    (A) Significant natural talent

    (B) Her desire to shock her contemporaries

    (C) Religious zeal

    (D) A scarcity of opportunities

8. Which choice provides the best evidence for the answer to the previous question?

    (A) Lines 67–69 ("Zenobia . . . hands")

    (B) Lines 74–76 ("It was . . . literature.")

    (C) Lines 80–82 ("It . . . philosophy.")

    (D) Lines 82–85 ("She . . . fan.")

9. As used in line 78, "severe" most nearly means

    (A) dangerous.

    (B) intense.

    (C) uncomfortable.

    (D) fertile.

10. Based on lines 82–90, what aspect of society is Zenobia most eager to reform?

    (A) Xenophobic universities

    (B) Widespread economic corruption

    (C) Antiquated gender roles

    (D) Environmental negligence

Questions 11–19 are based on the following passage.

The following passage is adapted from a speech delivered on June 26, 1963 by President John F. Kennedy. The speech was given in the Western-controlled part of Berlin in Germany during the Cold War between the United States and the Soviet Union.

    I am proud to come to this city as the guest of your distinguished Mayor, who has symbolized throughout the world the fighting
Line spirit of West Berlin. And I am proud to visit
(5) the Federal Republic with your distinguished Chancellor who for so many years has committed Germany to democracy and freedom and progress, and to come here in the company of my fellow American, General
(10) Clay, who has been in this city during its great moments of crisis and will come again if ever needed.

    Two thousand years ago the proudest boast was "civis Romanus sum." ("I am a
(15) citizen of Rome.") Today, in the world of freedom, the proudest boast is "Ich bin ein Berliner." ("I am a citizen of Berlin.")

    I appreciate my interpreter translating my German!
(20)   There are many people in the world who really don't understand, or say they don't, what is the great issue between the free world and the Communist world. Let them come to Berlin. There are some who say that
(25) communism is the wave of the future. Let them come to Berlin. And there are some who say in Europe and elsewhere we can work with the Communists. Let them come to Berlin. And there are even a few who say that it is true that
(30) communism is an evil system, but it permits us to make economic progress. Lass' sie nach Berlin kommen. Let them come to Berlin.

    Freedom has many difficulties and democracy is not perfect, but we have never
(35) had to put a wall up to keep our people in, to prevent them from leaving us. I want to say, on behalf of my countrymen, who live many miles

away on the other side of the Atlantic, who are
far distant from you, that they take the greatest
(40) pride that they have been able to share with
you, even from a distance, the story of the last
18 years. I know of no town, no city, that has
been besieged for 18 years that still lives with
the vitality and the force, and the hope and
(45) the determination of the city of West Berlin.
While the wall is the most obvious and
vivid demonstration of the failures of the
Communist system, for all the world to see,
we take no satisfaction in it, for it is, as your
(50) Mayor has said, an offense not only against
history but an offense against humanity,
separating families, dividing husbands and
wives and brothers and sisters, and dividing a
people who wish to be joined together.
(55)   What is true of this city is true of Germany—
real, lasting peace in Europe can never be
assured as long as one German out of four
is denied the elementary right of free men,
and that is to make a free choice. In 18 years
(60) of peace and good faith, this generation of
Germans has earned the right to be free,
including the right to unite their families and
their nation in lasting peace, with good will to
all people. You live in a defended island of free-
(65) dom, but your life is part of the main. So let me
ask you as I close, to lift your eyes beyond the
dangers of today, to the hopes of tomorrow,
beyond the freedom merely of this city of
Berlin, or your country of Germany, to the
(70) advance of freedom everywhere, beyond the
wall to the day of peace with justice, beyond
yourselves and ourselves to all mankind.
     Freedom is indivisible, and when one man
is enslaved, all are not free. When all are free,
(75) then we can look forward to that day when this
city will be joined as one and this country and
this great Continent of Europe in a peaceful
and hopeful globe. When that day finally
comes, as it will, the people of West Berlin can
(80) take sober satisfaction in the fact that they
were in the front lines for almost two decades.
     All free men, wherever they may live, are
citizens of Berlin, and, therefore, as a free man,
I take pride in the words "Ich bin ein Berliner."

11. The primary purpose of the passage is to

(A) express hostility.
(B) recount history.
(C) demonstrate solidarity.
(D) explain policy specifics.

12. As used in lines 8–9, the phrase "in the
company of" most closely means

(A) joined by.
(B) in a business venture.
(C) under the orders of.
(D) at the request of.

13. The fourth paragraph, lines 20–32, can best
be described as

(A) considering historical objections to a
modern way of thinking.
(B) predicting the future course of events
with specific observational evidence.
(C) encouraging the mass immigration of
foreigners into a major city.
(D) addressing different thoughts about an
idea with a common solution.

14. It can be reasonably inferred that President
Kennedy considers the people of West Berlin
to be best described as

(A) admirably resolute.
(B) security-conscious.
(C) emotionally distant.
(D) unusually anxious.

15. Which option gives the best evidence for the
answer to the previous question?

(A) Lines 28–31 ("And there . . . progress.")
(B) Lines 33–36 ("Freedom . . . leaving us.")
(C) Lines 36–41 ("I want . . . distance")
(D) Lines 42–45 ("I know . . . Berlin.")

16. President Kennedy suggests that the people of East and West Berlin are most likely interested in which of the following?

   (A) Initial interaction
   (B) Visiting military allies
   (C) Reunification
   (D) Emulating ancient empires

17. Which option gives the best evidence for the answer to the previous question?

   (A) Lines 13–17 ("Two . . . Berlin.")
   (B) Lines 36–42 ("I want to . . . years.")
   (C) Lines 49–54 ("for it is . . . together.")
   (D) Lines 78–81 ("When that . . . decades.")

18. As used in line 66, the word "close" most closely means

   (A) shut.
   (B) finish.
   (C) clasp.
   (D) approach.

19. An unstated assumption of the paragraph in lines 73–81 is that

   (A) if one person is enslaved, no one is free.
   (B) financial independence is a key to true freedom.
   (C) free people are inherently interested in peace.
   (D) Berliners will continue to take the preeminent role in expanding freedom worldwide.

Questions 20–28 are based on the following passage.

This passage is adapted from a 2012 article on Blackletter.

The familiar, somewhat calligraphic anachronism that today we often refer to as "Old English" did not emerge until the 12th
Line century, around the time of the extinction of
(5) the Old English language. The Old English script or, more accurately, blackletter, is in reality not even English but evolved in medieval universities along the Franco-German border as an efficient alternative to both the
(10) highly variable "insular" scripts of England and Ireland, and the consistent though cumbersome Carolingian minuscule of Christian monasteries.

In 1454, Johannes Gutenberg carved an
(15) unusually ornamental blackletter script called "textualis" for his much-celebrated movable type printing press and a year later used the font to print his 42-line Bible. Compared with their Carolingian anteced-
(20) ents, the letters of textualis are distinct for their height, narrowness, and sharp angularity. The style enjoyed a brief period of popularity in the late 15th century but was crippled by an overabundance of labyrin-
(25) thine derivatives; such as the "littera textualis formata" used for ornamental books and the cursive "littera textualis currens" used for glosses. Although textualis was rarely used in printing after Gutenberg, the revolution-
(30) ary scale of his innovation firmly established blackletter—particularly the Schwabacher and Fraktur varieties—as the preferred script for printed texts throughout Europe.

As the immediate successor of textualis,
(35) the Schwabacher style strove for increased readability with significant reductions to capital embellishment and a smoother, more curvaceous form invocative of handwriting. Though Schwabacher is sometimes associ-
(40) ated with the Italian humanist writings of the early 16th century, it saw substantial use throughout all of Europe and was only

partially deposed by Fraktur in the late 1700s. Schwabacher continued to appear in printed (45) texts as a secondary typeface into the 20th century.

By far the most familiar blackletter style, Fraktur originated at the end of the 15th century through a commission of the Holy (50) Roman Emperor Maximilian I; by the end of the 16th, it was the most widely used typeface in Europe. Though far less calligraphic than textualis, Fraktur is nonetheless more intricate than Schwabacher and combines (55) the soft readability of the latter with the bold regality of the former. By the 18th century, Fraktur had achieved such ubiquity that it became colloquially synonymous with the blackletter style.

(60) Predictably, the cosmopolitan classicists of the 18th century began to prefer the marginalized Antiqua scripts of prior centuries, which, being modeled after ancient Roman letterforms, eschewed medieval ornamen- (65) tation altogether. Antiqua's subversion of blackletter began gradually, appearing primarily in scientific texts (which valued readability over appearance), while literature and newspapers adhered to more aesthetic styles. (70) By the start of the 20th century, the majority of the Western world had accepted Antiqua typefaces as the standard font, but blackletter remained disproportionately common in German-speaking nations.

(75) A lethal blow was dealt to blackletter when, on January 3, 1941, Nazi chancellery Martin Borrmann issued the *Schrifterlass* decree to all of Germany's public offices, which described Schwabacher, Fraktur, and (80) all other forms of blackletter as Judenlettern, or "Jewish letters," and prohibited their use in future printing. It remains to this day unclear what connection the Nazi party saw between the Jewish people and blackletter. (85) Interestingly, however, it is understood that subsequent Nazi biblioclasms sometimes targeted texts based not only on their content but also their typeface. Blackletter made a

brief return following the war but was soon (90) abandoned by a German nation eager to modernize and reinvent its international image.

20. The overall purpose of this passage is

(A) to distinguish between the Old English typeface and the Old English language.
(B) to investigate the origin of blackletter typeface.
(C) to educate readers about the history and evolution of blackletter.
(D) to demonstrate the value of blackletter typefaces.

21. As used in lines 24–25, "labyrinthine" most nearly means

(A) mazelike.
(B) possessing many right angles.
(C) complex.
(D) menacing.

22. Based on the information in the passage, the primary advantage of the Fraktur variety of blackletter was that

(A) it was widespread throughout Europe.
(B) it balanced elegance with functionalism.
(C) it had the support of Maximilian I.
(D) it derived from ancient Roman letterforms.

23. Which choice provides the best evidence for the answer to the previous question?

(A) Lines 28–33 ("Although . . . Europe.")
(B) Lines 47–52 ("By far . . . Europe.")
(C) Lines 52–56 ("Though . . . former.")
(D) Lines 56–59 ("By the . . . style.")

24. Apart from ease of readability, why else might the classicists of the 18th century have preferred using Antiqua typefaces to blackletter?

(A) Using Antiqua typefaces prevented lay people from understanding the classicists' texts.

(B) It distinguished the classicists' texts from those printed in the middle ages.

(C) It was a faster and more efficient way to write in longhand.

(D) It associated the classicist movement with the learning of ancient Rome and the classical period.

25. Which choice provides the best evidence for the answer to the previous question?

(A) Lines 44–46 ("Schwabacher . . . century.")

(B) Lines 56–69 ("By the . . . styles.")

(C) Lines 60–65 ("Predictably . . . altogether.")

(D) Lines 70–74 ("By the start . . . nations.")

26. The main purpose of including the *Schrifterlass* decree in the passage is to

(A) show how typefaces have influenced modern history.

(B) imply that blackletter was never very popular outside of Germany.

(C) illustrate hypocrisy in a Nazi policy.

(D) account for the final demise of blackletter.

27. The passage suggests that the most significant problem with the insular scripts was what?

(A) They lacked consistency in their letterforms.

(B) They were elaborate and time consuming.

(C) They were isolated in England and Ireland.

(D) They were used only in Christian monasteries.

28. As used in line 75, the word "lethal" most nearly means

(A) mortal.

(B) deadly.

(C) final.

(D) venomous.

Questions 29–37 are based on the following passages and chart.

These passages are adapted from the articles written in 2013 about invasive plants.

Passage 1

Today many of the most common and recognizable plants in our arboreal ecosystems
are nonnative to North America. If you take
Line a walk through the woods almost anywhere
(5) in the temperate U.S., you'll probably come
across clusters of honeysuckle, dandelions,
bobbing water lilies, and dense patches of
ivy. Despite their pervasiveness, none of
these plants developed here naturally, but
(10) were introduced by human activity.

Some nonnative plants are introduced to
new territories accidentally via interregional
soil and food trade. Accidental introduction of nonnative organisms can often have
(15) negative and unforeseen consequences. For
example, the Asian chestnut blight fungus
was unexpectedly brought to the United
States through the trade of plants; this fungus
nearly wiped out the entire American chest-
(20) nut population, harming many animals that
depend on chestnuts for food.

Many other species, however, have been
purposefully spread within the U.S. for a
wide range of beneficial uses: stock feed, ero-
(25) sion control, reforestation, and, most commonly of all, ornamental plants in gardens
and parks. Intentional cultivation of nonnative invasive plants is generally far more beneficial than accidental introduction, although
(30) there are exceptions. For example, melaleuca
trees were brought to the Florida Everglades
from Australia; developers thought these
trees would help dry up vast swampy areas,

enabling residential and commercial con-
(35) struction. Unfortunately, the trees spread
widely and covered up large swaths of the
Everglades, displacing native plants. Florida
has had to spend a great deal of money to
remove these invasive trees.

(40)   Although introduced animal species often
become invasive in new ecosystems because
of a lack of natural predation, it is difficult
even for botanists to predict which exotic
plants will flourish in a novel environment.
(45) Some plants require continuous human
intervention and cannot spread independently into the wild. Others—honeysuckle,
dandelions, water lilies, and ivy included—
languish in domestication for a number of
(50) years and then suddenly naturalize, at which
point they often become invasive.

Passage 2

For the past fifty years, it has been the
conventional credence of ecologists and
biologists alike that invasive, nonnative plant
(55) species are, without exception, detrimental
to the host ecosystem. However, recent studies at Penn State University indicate that the
eradication of invasive plants—specifically
fruit-bearing shrubs—can do more harm
(60) than good for the native animal populations.

After conducting studies in urban, rural,
and forested environments, researchers
found that an area's abundance of honeysuckle can function as a direct predictor
(65) of the number and diversity of birds living
within a particular region. Having developed
a mutualist relationship, native species of
birds throughout the Midwest rely on honeysuckle fruit as a staple food source in the
(70) fall. Simultaneously, honeysuckle benefits by
being spread to new regions when its seeds
are eaten and subsequently dispersed by the
birds.

Though common protocol would dictate
(75) that an invasive species like honeysuckle
be removed from areas where it becomes
dominant, these new findings demonstrate

that such action would likely strike a significant blow to native bird populations. What's
(80) more, areas that today are abundant in
honeysuckle typically host 30 to 40 percent
more birds than these same regions did 30
years ago, indicating a long-term change for
the better. Although some invasive species
(85) do cause tremendous and irreparable damage to their ecosystems, environments are
not static. Environments change, develop,
and adapt to transitions, whether they be
natural or humanmade. We must learn to be
(90) more discriminating in our eradication of
invasive plants from those areas where they
have become an integral part of the greater
ecosystem.

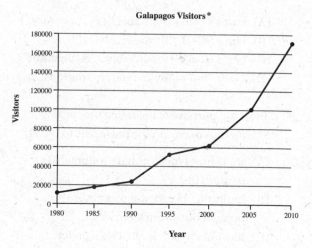

Galapagos Visitors*

The Galapagos Islands have been isolated from
human habitation until relatively recently.
*http://www.galapagos.org/conservation/tourism-growth/

29. The respective approaches to the discussion
     of invasive plants by Passage 1 and Passage 2
     are

     (A) positive and negative.
     (B) pessimistic and optimistic.
     (C) broad and focused.
     (D) argumentative and analytical.

30. Passage 1 and Passage 2 agree that

    (A) intentionally introduced invasive plants have the potential to have a positive impact.
    (B) invasive plants are, without exception, harmful to the natural environment.
    (C) honeysuckle is the most well-known of the invasive plant species.
    (D) the negative consequences of invasive plants can be ameliorated through government intervention.

31. Based on the passages and the chart, what will be the most likely consequence of tourism with respect to invasive plants in the Galapagos in the future?

    (A) Due to an increase in humanity's awareness of the Galapagos, it is more likely that a desire for environmental stewardship of the islands will grow.
    (B) Due to an increase in economic activity as a result of tourism, the inhabitants of the Galapagos will have more money with which to combat unwanted plant species.
    (C) Due to an increase in human contact, it is likely that the number of nonnative organisms introduced by accident will increase.
    (D) Due to an increase in hotel construction as a consequence of tourism, intentional cultivation of invasive species will grow.

32. Which choice in the passages provides the best evidence for the answer to the previous question?

    (A) Lines 8–13 ("Despite . . . trade.")
    (B) Lines 27–30 ("Intentional . . . exceptions.")
    (C) Lines 40–44 ("Although . . . environment.")
    (D) Lines 79–84 ("What's . . . better.")

33. Which of the following, if true, would most undermine the author's argument in lines 27–30 ("Intentional . . . exceptions.")?

    (A) A historical investigation into the origins of invasive plants that demonstrates that the majority were introduced by accident
    (B) A global statistical analysis that demonstrates the net harmful effects from purposefully introduced invasive plant species
    (C) A genetic analysis that establishes that invasive plant species share several fundamental characteristics in their DNA
    (D) Discovery of three instances of invasive plant introduction that had a beneficial impact on the surrounding environments

34. As used in line 42, "predation" most nearly means

    (A) placing events earlier in a sequence.
    (B) habitats suitable for species development.
    (C) plants appropriate for animal consumption.
    (D) preying of one animal on others.

35. What is the primary function of lines 52–56 ("For the . . . ecosystem.") in the first paragraph of Passage 2?

    (A) To establish the narrator's scholarly authority in this field of study
    (B) To state the principal argument of the passage
    (C) To summarize a common understanding that is subsequently refuted
    (D) To contrast the work of ecologists with those of biologists

36. Which of the following situations would be most similar to that discussed in lines 66–73 ("Having . . . birds.")?

    (A) Large whale species consume krill at higher latitudes.

    (B) The male gorilla does not help with infants but does help defend against predators.

    (C) Oxpecker birds eat predatory insects off the backs of zebras.

    (D) Humans consume crabs they fish from the ocean.

37. As used in line 90, "discriminating" most nearly means

    (A) biased.

    (B) intolerant.

    (C) tasteful.

    (D) selective.

Questions 38–47 are based on the following passage and table.

Color Photography

We tend to think of color photography as a profoundly modern innovation, belonging to an era no earlier than the 1950s. Although it
Line
(5) is true that it was not until the mid-twentieth century that compact devices like the Kodak Kodachrome and Polaroid instant camera made color photography widely available to the American public, the first known color photograph was developed about one hun-
(10) dred years prior, in the early 1840s.

Pioneers of color photography such as American intellectual Levi Hill and renowned French physicist A. E. Becquerel were hampered in their efforts by a fidelity to the
(15) then-popular daguerreotype method, which slowly imprints a direct-positive image onto a metal plate treated with light-sensitive iodine and bromine crystals. Colloquially, these photographs were known as "tintypes."
(20) Color variants of this method—such as Hill's toilsome "heliochromy"—often took several days to develop and yielded only dim images

with colors that faded rapidly when exposed to direct light.

(25) A new approach was required before color photography could emerge as a truly viable artistic and documentary medium. Such an approach was theorized just ten years later. While Hill's and Becquerel's labors had
(30) emphasized the search for a novel, chameleonic compound to assume any spectral wavelength shown upon it, Scottish physicist James Clerk Maxwell used as his model the color sensitivity of the human eye.

(35) We are able to perceive colors because of specialized photoreceptor cells lining our retinas called "cones." Generally, humans possess three types of cone cells, each of which produces a distinct, transmembrane
(40) photopsin protein. Depending on the particular chromophore compound associated with the cell's photopsins, the cone will have a peak absorbance of electromagnetic radiation at wavelengths of 420–440 nm, 534–545
(45) nm, or 564–580 nm. On the visible spectrum, these peaks correspond to the colors red, green, and blue, respectively. The brain's integration of photons absorbed by these three types of cones allows us to perceive col-
(50) ored light with wavelengths between roughly 400 and 700 nanometers, which comprises the entire visible spectrum. Because of this mechanism, humans are said to possess "trichromatic vision."

(55) In light of this phenomenon, Maxwell noted that any hue of visible light could be reproduced by a specific combination of three colors. Thus, three black-and-white transparencies of a single scene taken
(60) through red, blue, and green filters will, when projected as a composite image, reproduce with impressive accuracy the original, full-color subject. Problems remained, however, when it came time to develop these nega-
(65) tives onto paper in that the dyes used by photographers were ineffective in expressing certain colors, particularly those comprised of lower wavelengths. By trial and error, it was discovered by Becquerel and German

(70) chemist Hermann Vogel that the addition of dyes made of aniline—an aromatic amine—and chlorophyll to photographic emulsions helped to reflect the reds and yellows that previous dyes had simply absorbed.

(75) Into the early 20th century, color cameras themselves remained somewhat unwieldy; this owed largely to the logistical complexities of exposing three separate, individually filtered plates on the same subject. One

(80) design used a system of prisms and mirrors to split the lens image through three internal filters, which in turn exposed three plates simultaneously. A more compact and less delicate device designed by German

(85) photographer Adolf Miethe simply included a rotating filter disk, which allowed three photographs to be taken in rapid succession. From 1909 to 1915, Miethe's design was used by his Russian protégé, Sergei Prokudin-

(90) Gorsky, in a project appointed to him by Czar Nicholas II to document visually the history, culture, and modernization of the Russian Empire. His extensive and compelling work in the Russian provinces constitutes the

(95) first major series of color photojournalism. However, whenever a moving object was included in the frame—particularly water—the shortcomings of Miethe's design became obvious. The consecutive exposure of plates,

(100) however swift, would always leave some room for visual conflict between the three images.

The issues of both convenience and synchronous exposure were eventually solved

(105) by two professional, classical musicians—Leopold Mannes and Leopold Godowsky, Jr.—working recreationally for the Eastman Kodak Company. Together they designed a film that consisted of three separate emul-

(110) sion layers mounted on a single flexible base, each of which captured and individually filtered the lens image. Their design was marketed by Kodak under the name "Kodachrome" and was the first system to

(115) make the use of color film widely available to lay photographers.

Electromagnetic Waves and Their Wavelengths

Wave Type	Wavelength in Meters
Gamma	1×10^{-11}
X-ray	1×10^{-9}
Ultraviolet	2×10^{-8}
Infrared	1×10^{-6}
Radio	1.0

38. The passage outlines the evolution of the color photography process from being

(A) time consuming and unmanageable to efficient and compact.
(B) an object of widespread interest to a mere curiosity by elites.
(C) the province of artists to the focus of musicians.
(D) a modern innovation to a widespread convenience.

39. The evidence used in the essay is primarily comprised of

(A) esoteric psychological analysis.
(B) chemical and physical description.
(C) scientific and historical anecdotes.
(D) cross-cultural comparative study.

40. The passage suggests that which of the following kept Hill and Becquerel from further innovations in color photographic technology?

(A) A lack of scientific training
(B) Cultural bias toward Euro-American philosophy
(C) A failure to understand past successes
(D) Loyalty to a widespread approach

41. Which choice provides the best evidence for the answer to the previous question?

(A) Lines 11–13 ("Pioneers . . . French")
(B) Lines 14–15 ("hampered . . . method")
(C) Lines 20–24 ("Color . . . light.")
(D) Lines 32–34 ("Scottish . . . eye.")

42. As used in line 61, "composite" most nearly means

(A) crafted.
(B) visual.
(C) combined.
(D) quality.

43. As used in line 76, "unwieldy" most nearly means

(A) unsightly.
(B) cumbersome.
(C) expensive.
(D) precise.

44. The passage suggests that Maxwell was able to make a scientific breakthrough in photographic technology by shifting his focus from

(A) chemistry to biology.
(B) anthropology to astronomy.
(C) physics to mathematics.
(D) artistry to geometry.

45. Based on lines 83–102, it can be logically inferred that a Miethe-designed camera could most successfully photograph a river under what weather conditions?

(A) At high noon on a summer day with a light breeze
(B) On a rainy, blustery day with mild flooding
(C) On a freezing, windless day
(D) It will capture any form of water with equally low quality

46. Based on the information in the passage and in the table, light visible to humans would have wavelengths between which two types of waves?

(A) Gamma and X-rays
(B) X-rays and ultraviolet
(C) Ultraviolet and infrared
(D) Infrared and radio

47. The originators of the Kodachrome film process are best described as

(A) serendipitous tinkerers.
(B) scholarly thinkers.
(C) scientific masterminds.
(D) mathematical prodigies.

35 MINUTES, 44 QUESTIONS

> **Directions:** The passages below are each accompanied by several questions, some of which refer to an underlined portion in the passage and some of which refer to the passage as a whole. For some questions, determine how the expression of ideas can be improved. For other questions, determine the best sentence structure, usage, or punctuation given the context. A passage or question may have an accompanying graphic that you will need to consider as you choose the best answer.
>
> Choose the best answer to each question, considering what will optimize the writing quality and make the writing follow the conventions of standard written English. Some questions have a "NO CHANGE" option that you can pick if you believe the best choice is to leave the underlined portion as is.

Questions 1–11 are based on the following passage.

Matter-Antimatter Asymmetry

It can be described as one of the greatest mysteries of modern physics. In a universe that ❶ tends universally, as it were toward net neutrality, the apparently asymmetrical distribution of the baryon charge is a ❷ singular and tantalizing puzzle. Atoms—and thus, matter, which composes the visible universe—possess a positive baryon charge equivalent to the number of protons and neutrons contained within the nucleus. Following physicist Carl D. Anderson's 1932 gamma ray ❸ experiment which demonstrated the existence of antimatter, scientists anticipated the discovery of negatively charged baryon antimatter throughout the universe in quantities that would precisely counterbalance

1. (A) NO CHANGE
   (B) tends—universally, as it were toward net
   (C) tends—universally as it were, toward net
   (D) tends—universally, as it were—toward net

2. Which choice best expresses the mysterious nature of the asymmetrical distribution of the baryon charge?

   (A) NO CHANGE
   (B) large mystery.
   (C) interesting and fascinating dilemma.
   (D) unparalleled opportunity for knowledge.

3. (A) NO CHANGE
   (B) experiment, which demonstrated the existence of antimatter, scientists
   (C) experiment; which demonstrated the existence of antimatter, scientists
   (D) experiment which demonstrated the existence of antimatter scientists

the positive baryon charge of matter. That discovery, thus far, has not been ❹ <u>unfound.</u>

At odds with the Standard Model of physics, collision and radiation studies of antimatter ❺ <u>has consistently confounded</u> scientists' efforts to reconcile the baryon asymmetry. In fact, the known universe appears to be dominated by up to 0.01 times more matter than antimatter. ❻ <u>Since this is such an influential quantity,</u> such a discrepancy could soon prove to be a silver bullet for both the standard model and general relativity, whose tenets are entrenched in our understanding of everything from the interaction of subatomic particles ❼ <u>to the big bang theory of cosmology.</u>

Physicists at UBC and TRIUMF have proposed scenarios in which the baryon asymmetry is resolved through the antimatter potentially extant in the dark matter regions of space. Dark matter— ❽ <u>unobserved material inferred to exist by its quantifiable gravitational effect on visible galaxies</u>—is estimated to comprise roughly

4. Which choice would conclude the paragraph most consistently with the information in the passage as a whole?

(A) NO CHANGE
(B) surprising.
(C) forthcoming.
(D) acknowledged.

5. (A) NO CHANGE
(B) have consistently confided
(C) had consistently confided
(D) have consistently confounded

6. Which choice would provide the most logical connection between the previous sentence and the current sentence?

(A) NO CHANGE
(B) Though it may initially seem insignificant,
(C) Given the paucity of scientific consensus,
(D) Assuming that scientists are willing to disregard their instrumentation,

7. (A) NO CHANGE
(B) and the big band theory of cosmology.
(C) and the cosmological theoretical foundations of the big bang.
(D) but the big bang theory of cosmology in contrast.

8. Should the underlined portion of the sentence be deleted, with the punctuation adjusted accordingly?

(A) Yes, because it digresses from the primary focus of the paragraph.
(B) Yes, because it is an illogical transition between the beginning and end of the sentence.
(C) No, because without this, the passage would contain no clarification about the amount of dark matter in the universe.
(D) No, because it clarifies a specialized term for nonscientist readers.

23% of the universe by density. Visible atoms, **9** meanwhile, constitute less than 5%. The UBC and TRIUMF theories are hampered, however, by the inherent difficulties of studying the composition of dark matter. Currently, the most promising methods involve searching the sky for the spontaneous decay of protons, which—rarely, it must be acknowledged—may signify an atom's collision with a negative baryon dark matter particle.

Meanwhile, a research team at Fermilab known as the DZero Collaboration recently announced observations of matter-antimatter asymmetries on a scale never seen before. Prior to the DZero study, baryon asymmetry and similar CP violations **10** has been observed in laboratory settings only in much smaller—and thus, less helpful—orders of magnitude. This more substantial muon-antimuon asymmetry constitutes the first opportunity for the physicists to study a recurring anomaly of both charge conjugation and parity inversion in a controlled environment. The findings at Fermilab are at once unsettling in that they will soon necessitate a considerable reforming of our understanding of particle physics **11** but titillating in that they may well lead to a more sophisticated and penetrating understanding not only of particle asymmetry but of the nature and origin of the universe itself.

9. (A) NO CHANGE
   (B) as a result,
   (C) due to this fact,
   (D) precisely,

10. (A) NO CHANGE
    (B) have been observed
    (C) had been observed
    (D) is being observed

11. (A) NO CHANGE
    (B) and
    (C) moreover
    (D) for

Glassmaking

Have **12** you ever noticed something strange about the glass in the windows of old buildings? Look closely, and you'll see that their surfaces, though smooth, have easily discernible inconsistencies in width, especially near the edges. As you look through the glass, you'll see that, like a correctional lens, these imperfections distort the images that pass through them. **13** Well into the 19th century, glass windows were often made using a technique called "glassblowing." Glassblowing is a very ancient craft, the earliest known instances **14** in which date back to more than 5,000 years ago in Egypt and Eastern Mesopotamia.

[1] Though a skilled glassblower can create remarkable (and almost perfectly symmetrical) items like vases, cups, and globes, the process of making a flat pane of glass can be particularly tricky. [2] **15** Traditionally, a bowl-shaped glob of molten glass was flattened into a disk using centrifugal force and then cut to the proper shape and size. [3] However, the viscosity of liquid glass is such that, as spinning progresses, the perimeter of the disk becomes much thicker than the center. [4] In these glass factories, glass is poured slowly into the center of a steel table and allowed to spread under the influence of gravity. [5] Panes created using this technique are usually identifiable for their bulbous centers and wavy surface **16** texture, additionally they are often very fragile, as the edges joining with

12. The author is considering changing the second-person "you" to the third-person "one" throughout the passage. Should the writer make this change?

(A) Yes, because it would make the essay more formal.

(B) Yes, because it would be consistent with general grammatical practices.

(C) No, because the essay would lose the sense of directly addressing the reader.

(D) No, because it would take away the primary focus of the essay on glassblowing.

13. (A) NO CHANGE
(B) Well, into the 19th century glass
(C) Well into the 19th century glass
(D) Well, into the 19th century, glass

14. (A) NO CHANGE
(B) in that
(C) for which
(D) of which

15. What is the best placement of the underlined word in its sentence?

(A) NO CHANGE
(B) before "glob"
(C) before "flattened"
(D) before "proper"

16. (A) NO CHANGE
(B) texture; additionally, they are often very fragile, as
(C) texture. Additionally they are often very fragile as
(D) texture additionally, they are often very fragile, as

the window frame are typically narrower than the pane's body. **⑰**

Today we can produce even very large sheets of glass of nearly uniform thickness using the "float glass" process invented by Sir Alastair Pilkington in the mid-1950s. As the name implies, this technique **⑱** involve floated molten glass on a bath of molten tin. The atmospheric composition within a float furnace must be strictly regulated to prevent the tin from oxidizing. As glass enters the bath, its specific gravity and immiscibility with tin **⑲** causes it to form a continuous ribbon with perfectly smooth surfaces on both sides and an even width throughout. The glass is then gradually cooled until it can be lifted from the tin bath. Typically, its temperature at this time is around 1,100°C. The tin, meanwhile— **⑳** given its relatively high atomic number—remains in a fully molten state. The entire process is inexpensive, reliable, and **㉑** relatively cheap when compared to the laborious task of hand-spinning paned glass. However, a very close look can reveal imperfection even in this modern technique. If the glass is cooled **㉒** to quickly—as is sometimes the case in large-scale industrial production—the ribbon will absorb trace amounts of tin, leaving behind a faint haze on one side of the finished pane.

17. Where is the most logical placement of this sentence in the preceding paragraph?

"A reverse problem emerged in the industrial glassmaking procedures of the early 20th century."

(A) Before sentence [1]
(B) Before sentence [3]
(C) Before sentence [4]
(D) Before sentence [5]

18. (A) NO CHANGE
(B) involve floating molted glass with a bath of molted tin.
(C) involves floated molted glass on a bath of molted tin.
(D) involves floating molten glass on a bath of molten tin.

19. (A) NO CHANGE
(B) causes them to form
(C) cause them to form
(D) cause it to form

20. Which choice would best support the claim made in this sentence, given the information in the paragraph?

(A) NO CHANGE
(B) having a melting point of only 232°C
(C) with its unique molecular structure
(D) provided its atomic mass of approximately 118 units

21. The writer wants to complete this description of the process with a third phrase that will contrast this process with what follows in the sentence. What choice best accomplishes the writer's goal?

(A) NO CHANGE
(B) consistently dependable
(C) remarkably fast
(D) painstakingly challenging

22. (A) NO CHANGE
(B) too quickly
(C) to quick
(D) two quick

Questions 23–33 are based on the following passage and supplementary material.

Electoral College

The United States is the only country in the world to use an Electoral College system to elect its chief executive. Each state has a certain number of electors based on **(23)** their number of senators and representatives. If a candidate wins the majority of the electoral votes, currently 270, **(24)** he or she wins the election. It is high time that America shifts from this undemocratic, elitist system to one in which the president is selected by a simple majority of the popular votes.

(25) Why do Americans allow a system that doesn't permit minority groups in society to have their say? Yet this is something that has happened four times in American history. John Quincy Adams, Rutherford B. Hayes, Benjamin Harrison, and George W. Bush were all elected by a majority of the Electoral College while losing to another candidate in the popular vote. **(26)** The other presidential victors won both a majority of the electoral college and the most popular votes out of any of the candidates. Can you imagine voting for the student council president only to find that the winner did not actually receive the most votes? There would be outrage throughout the school.

23. (A) NO CHANGE
    (B) their numbers
    (C) its number
    (D) our number

24. (A) NO CHANGE
    (B) they win
    (C) they would have won
    (D) he or she won

25. Which choice would best introduce the paragraph?

    (A) NO CHANGE
    (B) Does it make any sense that our country has only elected male presidents with a female not even earning a major party nomination?
    (C) Why should Americans elect presidents who, in retrospect, do not measure up to our country's ideals?
    (D) How can our country call itself a democracy if it can allow someone to become president who did not win the popular vote?

26. The writer is considering deleting the underlined sentence. Should the sentence be kept or deleted?

    (A) Kept, because it specifies the mechanics of the American political process.
    (B) Kept, because it clarifies how the majority of American presidents have been elected.
    (C) Deleted, because it unnecessarily repeats implicit information from earlier in the paragraph.
    (D) Deleted, because it is not factually supported by the general claims made elsewhere in the passage.

The Electoral College should not stay in place simply because it is something that ㉗ has been done for many years.

If the United States were to shift to a majority vote ㉘ system the way, the presidential candidates campaign for office would fundamentally change. Right now, candidates have little reason to bother campaigning in states that typically go strongly for one of the political parties. There is little logic in a Republican trying to win New York or a Democrat trying to win Texas. Instead, candidates focus their energies on ㉙ "swing states" like Florida and Ohio, which are relatively balanced along party lines. A Floridian or Ohioan will currently receive far more candidate visits and attention than a New Yorker or a Texan. ㉚ Ohio has a smaller population relative to Texas, although Ohio does have a greater population density than Texas. This would ensure that all U.S. citizens have an equal voice not just in theory but in reality.

The Electoral College served its purpose in years past when smaller states were concerned that larger states would ㉛ usurp their authority. Now that the union of states is firmly established after the

27. (A) NO CHANGE
(B) had been done
(C) had to be done
(D) have been done

28. (A) NO CHANGE
(B) system the way the presidential candidates campaign, for
(C) system the way the presidential, candidates campaign for
(D) system, the way the presidential candidates campaign for

29. (A) NO CHANGE
(B) "swing states," like Florida and Ohio which
(C) "swing states," like Florida and Ohio, which
(D) "swing states" like Florida, and Ohio which

30. Which sentence would best strengthen the argument of the paragraph by transitioning between the previous and the following sentences?

(A) NO CHANGE
(B) If the Electoral College were abolished in favor of a majority vote system, candidates would have a much stronger incentive to campaign nationwide.
(C) It is inherently unjust that candidates want to spend their time campaigning in places where they will inevitably emerge victorious while ignoring states with undecided voters.
(D) Nationwide polls indicate that the average voters in states from high to low Electoral College representation uniformly agree that the time has come for a seismic shift in the political landscape.

31. (A) NO CHANGE
(B) invade
(C) touch
(D) decline

Civil War and after over two centuries of continuity, it is time to abandon this relic of the past so that everyone in the United States has an equal voice.

33

State*	Estimated 2008 Population	Electoral votes in 2008
Alaska	686,000	3
California	36,757,000	55
Delaware	873,000	3
Ohio	11,486,000	20
Texas	24,327,000	34

*Source: *http://www.fairvote.org/assets/Uploads/npv/2008votersperelector.pdf*

32. Which choice would best reassert the fundamental claim of the passage?

(A) NO CHANGE

(B) our country needs to look with optimism rather than pessimism toward the future.

(C) we must look past our history, acknowledge our mistakes, and move to a more enlightened tomorrow.

(D) the time has come for justice for all peoples of the United States to become not just a dream but a reality.

33. Based on the argument in the passage as a whole and the information in the table, citizens in which state would have the greatest disincentive to abolish the Electoral College?

(A) Alaska

(B) California

(C) Delaware

(D) Ohio

The Lay of Hildebrand

Most English speakers are at least partially familiar with *Beowulf*, one of the oldest known examples of Anglo-Saxon literature. The poem's renown is bolstered **34** <u>not only by its importance to the medieval epic form with also</u> by its contribution to the evolution of the English language. Some controversy surrounds the exact age of the surviving manuscript, but most scholars place it between 900 and 1100 C.E. But for all its fame, it is somewhat surprising that, by comparison, another poem of equal age and perhaps even greater linguistic import is virtually unknown to the English-speaking world. **35**

An alliterative heroic verse like *Beowulf*, "The Lay of Hildebrand" is a genuine puzzle of medieval poetry, and **36** <u>researchers still find the exact meaning of the poem to be quite a mystery.</u> The "Lay" consists of a mere sixty-eight lines, written on two pages of parchment that were preserved in the first and last leaves of a theological codex. Although the manuscript may but slightly predate *Beowulf*, the narrative itself is almost **37** <u>certainly the most ancient,</u> and its form strongly retains and reflects the form of the early Saxonic oral tradition.

34. (A) NO CHANGE
    (B) not only by its importance to the medieval epic form but also
    (C) not only by its importance to the medieval epic form and also
    (D) not only by its importance to the medieval epic form since also

35. Suppose the author is going to write an essay discussing the poem *Beowulf*. Based on the information in this passage, what would most likely be the tone of the *Beowulf* essay?

    (A) Positive and appreciative
    (B) Dismissive and skeptical
    (C) Dogmatic and firm
    (D) Neutral and disinterested

36. Which choice would best support the claim in the first part of this sentence?

    (A) NO CHANGE
    (B) has striking similarities to the poem *Beowulf* because it repeats similar sounds at the beginnings of words.
    (C) scholarship has probably not revealed half of its significance with respect to the Germanic origins of English.
    (D) scholars are on a continual quest to decipher the symbolism of the poem, much like past researchers decoded the Rosetta Stone.

37. (A) NO CHANGE
    (B) certain to be the most ancient of the two,
    (C) certainly the ancient,
    (D) certainly the more ancient,

[1] Penned together in Carolingian minuscule by two separate scribes, it consists of a bizarre blend of Old High German and Old Saxon grammar and vocabulary. [2] (Incidentally, the "Lay" is also the oldest extant Germanic poem.) [3] Theories aimed at resolving this mystery have ranged from **38** <u>its dismissal as a poorly wrought translation</u> to the insinuation that it is a window into a critical point of transition at which English was beginning to emerge from German. **39**

Whatever the case may be, even a superficial study of the text is a truly rewarding experience for any enthusiast of **40** <u>neither English or German</u> literature and language. It tells a story every bit as harrowing as *Beowulf*, and, to some minds, more **41** <u>poetic, Hildebrand, a</u> German long cast out from his kingdom, returns home in the service of an Asian army to overthrow his enemy. Unknowingly, he is **42** <u>welcomed</u> into a duel with the opposing army's champion, his only son. Although he learns of the irony prior to combat, he cannot convince his son of his identity and is forced to fight.

Regrettably, because of the second **43** <u>scribe's large and unwieldy penmanship, the poem's</u> last ten lines or so would not fit on the parchment leaf and are thus lost to history. We are instead left with the compellingly **44** <u>conclusive</u> ending (roughly translated): "The white wood rang / Grimly as they hacked each other's shields / Until the linden slats grew lean and splintered / Broken by blades. . . ."

38. Which choice would provide the most sensible contrast with the latter part of the sentence?

   (A) NO CHANGE
   (B) the realization of its fundamental role in literary history
   (C) its unequivocal demonstration as an outright forgery
   (D) the presence of English and German linguistic roots

39. Where is the most logical placement of this sentence in the previous paragraph?

   "From a linguistic standpoint, the 'Lay' is endlessly fascinating."

   (A) Before sentence [1]
   (B) Before sentence [2]
   (C) Before sentence [3]
   (D) After sentence [3]

40. (A) NO CHANGE
   (B) neither English nor German
   (C) either English nor German
   (D) either English or German

41. (A) NO CHANGE
   (B) poetic; Hildebrand a
   (C) poetic; Hildebrand, a
   (D) poetic Hildebrand, a

42. (A) NO CHANGE
   (B) thrust
   (C) made
   (D) murdered

43. (A) NO CHANGE
   (B) scribe's large and unwieldy penmanship, the poems
   (C) scribes large and unwieldy penmanship the poems
   (D) scribe's large and unwieldy penmanship the poem's

44. Which word best describes the ending of the poem?

   (A) NO CHANGE
   (B) shocking
   (C) ecstatic
   (D) ambiguous

25 MINUTES, 17 QUESTIONS

Directions: For questions 1–13, solve each problem and choose the best answer from the given options. Fill in the corresponding oval on your answer document. For questions 14–17, solve the problem and fill in the answer on the answer sheet grid. Please use scrap paper to work out your answers.

Notes:

- You **CANNOT** use a calculator on this section.
- All variables and expressions represent real numbers unless indicated otherwise.
- All figures are drawn to scale unless indicated otherwise.
- All figures are in a plane unless indicated otherwise.
- Unless indicated otherwise, the domain of a given function is the set of all real numbers x for which the function has real values.

Radius of a circle = r
Area of a circle = πr^2
Circumference of a circle = $2\pi r$

Area of a rectangle = length × width = lw

Area of a triangle = $\dfrac{1}{2}$ × base × height = $\dfrac{1}{2}\,bh$

Pythagorean theorem: $a^2 + b^2 = c^2$

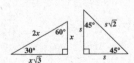

Special right triangles: 30-60-90 and 45-45-90

Volume of a box = length × width × height = lwh

Volume of a cylinder = $\pi r^2 h$

Volume of a sphere = $\dfrac{4}{3}\,\pi r^3$

Volume of a cone = $\dfrac{1}{3}\pi r^2 h$

Volume of a pyramid =
$\dfrac{1}{3}$ × length × width × height = $\dfrac{1}{3}lwh$

KEY FACTS:

- A circle has 360 degrees.
- There are 2π radians in a circle.
- There are 180 degrees in a triangle.

1. $\dfrac{m^{\frac{5}{2}}}{m^{\frac{1}{2}}} = ?$

    (A) m

    (B) m^2

    (C) m^4

    (D) $m^{\frac{1}{5}}$

2. A function never intersects the y-axis. Which of the following could be an equation of the function?

    (A) $y = 2x - 5$

    (B) $y = 4$

    (C) $x = 36$

    (D) $y = x$

3. A pastry chef has a recipe that calls for 3 tablespoons of vanilla extract for a cake. The chef has misplaced his tablespoon and has only a teaspoon available—there are 3 teaspoons for each tablespoon. If the chef is making a total of two cakes, how many teaspoons of vanilla extract should he use?

    (A) 3

    (B) 6

    (C) 12

    (D) 18

4. If $\dfrac{1}{4}a + \dfrac{1}{3}b = 2$, what is the value of $3a + 4b$?

    (A) 4

    (B) 18

    (C) 24

    (D) 36

5. $3a - 3(b - a)$ can also be expressed as:

    (A) $2a - 3b$

    (B) $3a^2 - 3ab$

    (C) $-b + a$

    (D) $3(2a - b)$

6. The following equations could all have the constant k equal zero and have a defined solution EXCEPT:

    (A) $kx = 0$

    (B) $3 = k - x$

    (C) $4k + x = 7$

    (D) $\dfrac{2}{k} = x$

7. A and B are related by this system of equations:

    $$\frac{2}{3}A + \frac{3}{5}B = 4$$

    $$2B = \frac{10}{9}A$$

    What is the value of B?

    (A) $\dfrac{1}{6}$

    (B) $\dfrac{2}{3}$

    (C) $\dfrac{20}{9}$

    (D) $\dfrac{40}{7}$

8. Which of the following equations properly expresses the functional relationship given by this expression?

    "Take an input variable and divide it by 4; then subtract 5 from the result."

    (A) $f(x) = \dfrac{x-5}{4}$

    (B) $f(x) = \dfrac{x}{4} - 5$

    (C) $f(x) = 5 - \dfrac{x}{4}$

    (D) $f(x) = \dfrac{5-x}{4}$

PRACTICE TEST 2

9. Which equation expresses the relationship between x and y shown in the graph below?

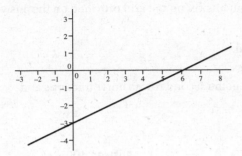

(A) $y = \frac{1}{2}x - 3$

(B) $y = 3x - 3$

(C) $y = 2x + 6$

(D) $y = -\frac{2}{3}x + 6$

10. In the equation below, F stands for gravitational force, m_1 and m_2 stand for the masses of two different objects, G is a constant, and d stands for the distance between the two objects. (Note that mass and distance must have positive values.)

$$F = \frac{G \times m_1 \times m_2}{d^2}$$

What would most minimize the gravitational force between objects 1 and 2?

(A) Minimize d

(B) Maximize m_1 and m_2

(C) Minimize $m_1 \times m_2$ and maximize d

(D) Maximize d, m_1, and m_2

11. How many real solution(s) does this system of equations have?

$$y = 2x - 5$$
$$y = 2x^2 + 4$$

(A) 0

(B) 1

(C) 2

(D) 3

12. The table below gives the values of a sum of the first n numbers, starting with 1:

n	Pattern
1	1
2	$1 + 3$
3	$1 + 3 + 5$
4	$1 + 3 + 5 + 7$
5	$1 + 3 + 5 + 7 + 9$

Which of the following is a correct statement about n?

(A) The product of n and its corresponding sum decreases as n increases.

(B) The difference between each additional value of n and the previous value of n is increasing exponentially.

(C) The sum of the first n odd numbers equals the square of n.

(D) The sum of the first n numbers is comprised solely of prime numbers.

13. If $-16 - 6x + x^2 = x^2 - abx - 8b$, where a and b are constants, what is the value of a?

(A) –6

(B) –2

(C) 3

(D) 5

Grid-in Response Directions

In questions 14–17, first solve the problem, and then enter your answer on the grid provided on the answer sheet. The instructions for entering your answers follow.

- First, write your answer in the boxes at the top of the grid.
- Second, grid your answer in the columns below the boxes.
- Use the fraction bar in the first row or the decimal point in the second row to enter fractions and decimals.

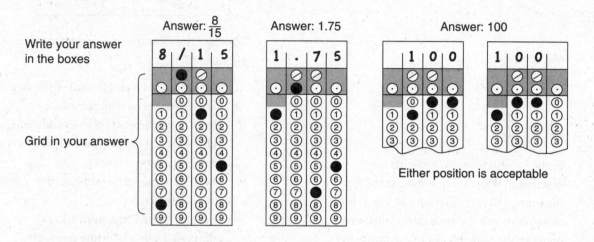

- Grid only one space in each column.
- Entering the answer in the boxes is recommended as an aid in gridding but is not required.
- The machine scoring your exam can read only what you grid, so you **must grid-in your answers correctly to get credit**.
- If a question has more than one correct answer, grid-in only one of them.
- The grid does not have a minus sign; so no answer can be negative.
- A mixed number *must* be converted to an improper fraction or a decimal before it is gridded.

  Enter $1\frac{1}{4}$ as $\frac{5}{4}$ or 1.25; the machine will interpret 11/4 as $\frac{11}{4}$ and mark it wrong.

- **All decimals must be entered as accurately as possible.** Here are three acceptable ways of gridding

$$\frac{3}{11} = 0.272727\ldots$$

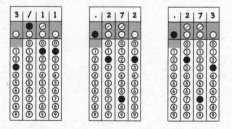

- Note that rounding to .273 is acceptable because you are using the full grid, but you would receive **no credit** for .3 or .27, because they are less accurate.

14. Solve for x in the equation below:

$$4x - y = \frac{1}{2}x - y + 7$$

15. If $f(x) = 7x + 3$ and $g(x) = 2x^2$, what is the value of $f(g(1))$?

16. Consider the following system of equations with variables A and B and constant integers X and Y:

$$A + 2B = 4$$
$$XA + YB = 4X$$

By what number must the sum of X and Y be divisible in order for the two equations to have infinitely many solutions?

17. If a circle has the equation $(x - 4)^2 + (y - 3)^2 = 36$, what is the shortest straight-line distance from the center of the circle to the origin?

Directions: For questions 1–27, solve each problem and choose the best answer from the given options. Fill in the corresponding oval on the answer sheet. For questions 28–31, solve the problem and fill in the answer on the answer sheet grid. Please use any space in the test booklet to work out your answers.

Notes:

- You CAN use a calculator on this section.
- All variables and expressions represent real numbers unless indicated otherwise.
- All figures are drawn to scale unless indicated otherwise.
- All figures are in a plane unless indicated otherwise.
- Unless indicated otherwise, the domain of a given function is the set of all real numbers x for which the function has real values.

Radius of a circle = r
Area of a circle = πr^2
Circumference of a circle = $2\pi r$

Area of a rectangle = length × width = lw

Area of a triangle = $\dfrac{1}{2}$ × base × height = $\dfrac{1}{2} bh$

Pythagorean theorem: $a^2 + b^2 = c^2$

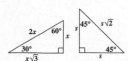

Special right triangles: 30-60-90 and 45-45-90

Volume of a box = length × width × height = lwh

Volume of a cylinder = $\pi r^2 h$

Volume of a sphere = $\dfrac{4}{3}\pi r^3$

Volume of a cone = $\dfrac{1}{3}\pi r^2 h$

Volume of a pyramid =
$\dfrac{1}{3}$ × length × width × height = $\dfrac{1}{3} lwh$

KEY FACTS:

- **A circle has 360 degrees.**
- **There are 2π radians in a circle.**
- **There are 180 degrees in a triangle.**

1. Andrew's sports car has a speedometer that shows a maximum value of 180 miles per hour. Given that there are approximately 1.61 kilometers in one mile, what would be the maximum value of his speedometer (to the nearest whole number) if it were listed in kilometers per hour?

(A) $112 \dfrac{km}{hr}$

(B) $208 \dfrac{km}{hr}$

(C) $290 \dfrac{km}{hr}$

(D) $314 \dfrac{km}{hr}$

2. A recipe that will bake 6 cupcakes calls for 4 eggs, 3 cups of flour, and 6 cups of sugar. If someone wishes to make 15 cupcakes, how many cups of flour should he or she use?

(A) 6
(B) 7.5
(C) 12.5
(D) 13

Questions 3–4 refer to the following information and graph.

The Asian carp has experienced a rapid growth by displacing other fish in the Mississippi River. A researcher gathered three yearly samples from a 500-meter length of the Upper Mississippi River to determine the population trend of the fish over a decade.

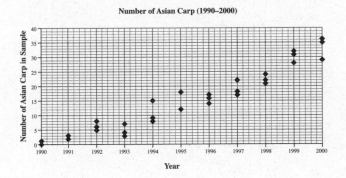

Number of Asian Carp (1990–2000)

3. What is the approximate slope of the best-fit line of the data in the graph, expressed as $\dfrac{\text{change in carp}}{\text{change in year}}$?

(A) 3.3
(B) 4.8
(C) 5.7
(D) 7.6

4. If the number of carp continues to grow at the same rate, what value comes closest to the likely number of carp in the sample in the year 2015?

(A) 52
(B) 83
(C) 129
(D) 172

5. Solve for x in the equation below:

$$7 + 2(x - 3) = -3(x + 1) - 4$$

(A) $-\dfrac{8}{5}$

(B) -1

(C) $\dfrac{3}{8}$

(D) 3

6. $(x^2 + 3x^2)^3 = ?$

(A) $3x^{12x}$

(B) $27x^5$

(C) $28x^6$

(D) $64x^6$

7. $4x^n + x^{4n} =$

(A) $5x^{5n}$

(B) $x^n(4 + x^{3n})$

(C) $5x^{4n^2}$

(D) $4x^n(1 + x^{3n})$

Questions 8–10 refer to the following information and graph.

The following questions refer to the information in the table below. A company has four different stores at 4 different locations throughout a large city. The company gathered data on the initial prices, sale prices, and respective quantities sold of a particular item.

Store	Price Before Sale	Quantity Sold Before Sale	Sale Price	Quantity Sold During Sale
Store A	$12.50	350	$11.00	400
Store B	$13.25	260	$10.00	520
Store C	$11.75	550	$9.50	625
Store D	$14.00	220	$10.25	460

8. Look at how many of the particular item Stores A and B sold at the presale price. What is the arithmetic mean of this set of values to the nearest tenth?

(A) 8.1

(B) 9.7

(C) 10.5

(D) 12.8

9. If a line were graphed using the quantity sold in Store D as the x-value and the price from Store D as the y-value, what would be closest to the y-intercept of the line?

(A) 12.2

(B) 14.4

(C) 17.4

(D) 20.8

10. Which of the following would be the most helpful piece of information to have about the data collected for the table in order to ensure comprehensive and accurate results?

(A) Prices at other retailers, such as restaurants

(B) A calculation of what the prices would be with twice as large a sale

(C) A survey of store managers about employee motivation

(D) If sales tax is included in the prices

_____

11. If n represents m percent of x, how could the value of n be calculated?

(A) $n = \dfrac{mx}{100}$

(B) $n = 0.1mx$

(C) $n = \dfrac{100}{mx}$

(D) $n = 100mx$

12. Bob deposits x dollars into his savings account on January 1, 2015, and the account grows at a constant annual rate of 3%, compounded annually. Assuming that Bob makes no deposits or withdrawals and that there are no account fees or other charges, what will be the amount of dollars in his account on January 1, 2017?

    (A) $0.06x$

    (B) $1.06x$

    (C) $1.0609x$

    (D) $1.092727x$

13. What are the possible values of b in the system of equations below?

$$b = 2a + 1$$
$$b + 2 = a^2$$

    (A) $-3, -7$

    (B) $-1, 7$

    (C) $3, -1$

    (D) $3, 7$

14. $2(a - 4b)(3 + b^3) = ?$

    (A) $2ab^3 - 24b$

    (B) $2ab + 6a - 4b^2 - 12b$

    (C) $2ab^3 + 4a - 6b^4 - 24b$

    (D) $2ab^3 + 6a - 8b^4 - 24b$

15. A librarian works at a constant pace, simultaneously shelving exactly 200 books in an hour and exactly 20 movies in an hour, and shelving only books and movies. If the librarian works for a total of T hours, which expression shows the total number of items (books and movies) that the librarian shelves during that time?

    (A) $220T$

    (B) $20T + 200$

    (C) $220T + 440$

    (D) $200T - 20$

Questions 16–18 refer to the following tables.

The tables below show an investor's percentage allocation in a portfolio. The first table shows the summary of investment types in the portfolio in the year 1995. The second table shows the summary of investment types in the portfolio in the year 2015.

Portfolio Allocation by Percentage of Total Portfolio in 1995

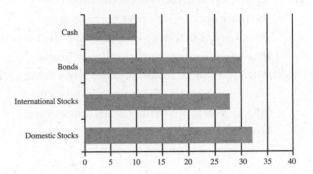

Portfolio Allocation by Percentage of Total Portfolio in 2015

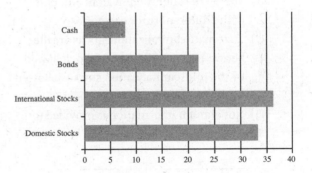

16. If the total value of the investment portfolio in 1995 was $80,000 and the total value of it in 2015 was $200,000, by approximately how much did the amount invested in bonds increase from 1995 to 2015?

    (A) $8,000

    (B) $14,000

    (C) $20,000

    (D) $28,000

17. Use the portfolio valuations from the years given in the preceding question. If the overall portfolio is growing at a linear rate, what should the value of the portfolio be in 2025?

(A) $180,000
(B) $260,000
(C) $340,000
(D) $580,000

18. A portfolio analyst wants to determine the relative impact on the performance of the stock portfolio of large-capitalization stocks, mid-capitalization stocks, and small-capitalization stocks. (Capitalization refers to the overall value of the company.) Based on the information given in the charts, how can you best characterize the impact of these different categories of stocks on the portfolio?

(A) There are more large-capitalization stocks than the other two types combined.
(B) There are roughly equivalent amounts of the different stock categories.
(C) The small-capitalization stocks are the largest percent of the portfolio, followed by the mid-capitalization stocks, followed by the large-capitalization stocks.
(D) Not enough information is provided to come to a conclusion.

---

19. Pam is going to watch a movie on her television at home. She is going to watch the movie as it was shown in movie theaters in its original aspect ratio of 1.85:1 length:height. Her television has an aspect ratio of 4:3 and a length of 48 inches. If the movie takes up the entire length of her television screen, how many inches of screen height, to the nearest whole inch, will NOT be used on her TV screen to show the movie?

(A) 10
(B) 16
(C) 22
(D) 44

20. If an amusement park worker measures 3 riders as being 48 inches, 56 inches, and 40 inches tall and the margin of error of each of the worker's measurements is ±2 inches, what is the possible range of the sum of the riders' actual heights in inches?

(A) $48 \leq$ total height ≤ 144
(B) $42 \leq$ total height ≤ 150
(C) $138 \leq$ total height ≤ 150
(D) $158 \leq$ total height ≤ 180

21. Given that x and n are numbers greater than 1, which of the following expressions would have the greatest overall increase in y values between x values from 2 to 100?

(A) $y = nx + 3$
(B) $y = -nx + 3$
(C) $y = x^n + 3$
(D) $y = x^{-n} + 3$

22. A new spaceship tourism company wishes to design a spacecraft that will allow its passengers to reenter Earth's atmosphere comfortably without losing consciousness. The physicians with whom the company consulted advised the company employees that healthy humans can survive up to $9g$ of force and lose consciousness at $5g$ of force. Which expression gives the range of g-force values, g, that the company's engineers should ensure the spacecraft can provide during reentry?

(A) $g < 5$
(B) $g > 5$
(C) $5 < g < 9$
(D) $g > 9$

23. College football programs are permitted to pay a maximum of 1 head coach, 9 assistant coaches, and 2 graduate assistant coaches. If ABC University wishes to have at least 1 coach for every 4 players, which of the following systems of inequalities expresses the total number of coaches, C, and total number of players, P, possible?

(A) $C = 12$ and $P \le 4C$
(B) $C \le 12$ and $P \le 4C$
(C) $C \le 10$ and $P \le 3C$
(D) $C = 1$ and $P \le 4$

24. The final velocity of a given object is given by the following formula:

$$\text{Final velocity} = \text{Initial velocity} + \text{Acceleration} \times \text{Time}$$

If a ball has an initial velocity of $4\frac{m}{s}$ and a constant acceleration of $6\frac{m}{s^2}$ which inequality shows the range of times, T, that will cause the final velocity to have a value of at least $22\frac{m}{s}$?

(A) $T \ge 3$ seconds
(B) $T \ge 8$ seconds
(C) 3 seconds $\le T \le 5$ seconds
(D) 6 seconds $\le T \le 22$ seconds

25. The approximate relationship between Kelvin (K) and degrees Celsius (C) is given by this equation:

$$K = 273 + C$$

The freezing point of water is 0 degrees Celsius, and the boiling point of water is 100 degrees Celsius. What are the approximate freezing and boiling points of water in Kelvin?

(A) Freezing: 0; boiling: 100
(B) Freezing: –273; boiling: –173
(C) Freezing: 273; boiling: 373
(D) Freezing: 473; boiling: 573

26. A particular black hole has a density of $1.0 \times 10^6 \frac{kg}{m^3}$. A physicist is conducting a thought experiment in which she would like to approximate how much she would weigh if she had the density of a black hole rather than her current weight of 150 pounds, assuming her volume remained the same. Given that her overall body density is approximately $990\frac{kg}{m^3}$ and that there are approximately 2.2 pounds in a kilogram, approximately how many pounds would she weigh in her thought experiment?

(A) 2,178
(B) 151,500
(C) 990,000,000
(D) 2,178,000,000

27. John is taking a rowboat both up and down a 16 km length of a river. A constant current of $1\frac{km}{hr}$ makes his trip downstream faster than his trip upstream since he is moving with the current downstream and fighting against the current when traveling upstream. If a round-trip journey took him a total of 4 hours and if he rowed at a constant pace the whole time, what is the rate in $\frac{km}{hr}$, to the nearest tenth, at which John is rowing independent of the current?

(A) 7.3
(B) 8.1
(C) 8.9
(D) 9.7

Grid-in Response Directions

In questions 28–31, first solve the problem, and then enter your answer on the grid provided on the answer sheet. The instructions for entering your answers follow.

- First, write your answer in the boxes at the top of the grid.
- Second, grid your answer in the columns below the boxes.
- Use the fraction bar in the first row or the decimal point in the second row to enter fractions and decimals.

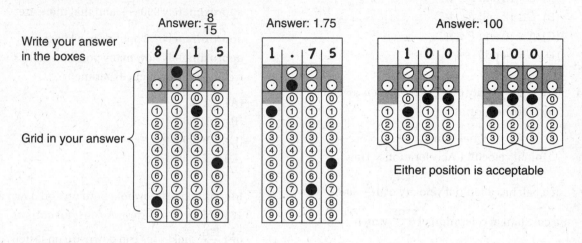

Write your answer in the boxes

Grid in your answer

Answer: $\frac{8}{15}$ Answer: 1.75   Answer: 100

Either position is acceptable

- Grid only one space in each column.
- Entering the answer in the boxes is recommended as an aid in gridding but is not required.
- The machine scoring your exam can read only what you grid, so you **must grid-in your answers correctly to get credit**.
- If a question has more than one correct answer, grid-in only one of them.
- The grid does not have a minus sign; so no answer can be negative.
- A mixed number *must* be converted to an improper fraction or a decimal before it is gridded.

  Enter $1\frac{1}{4}$ as $\frac{5}{4}$ or 1.25; the machine will interpret 11/4 as $\frac{11}{4}$ and mark it wrong.

- **All decimals must be entered as accurately as possible.** Here are three acceptable ways of gridding

$$\frac{3}{11} = 0.272727\ldots$$

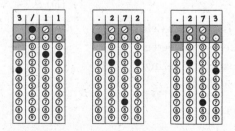

- Note that rounding to .273 is acceptable because you are using the full grid, but you would receive **no credit** for .3 or .27, because they are less accurate.

28. A high school is going to have its prom and is evaluating two different D.J.s—D.J. A and D.J. B. D.J. A has a $300 rental fee and charges $150 per hour. D.J. B has a $200 rental fee and charges $175 per hour. After how many hours of performing will the cost for both D.J.s be the same?

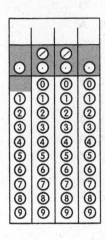

29. Marcus completely filled his truck's 14-gallon gas tank. The computer at the gas pump indicates that Marcus spent $34 in this transaction; the price per gallon was $3. How many gallons of gas did Marcus have in his tank before he started to fill it?

30. A lamp business uses the following equations to express supply and demand as a function of price and quantity for its lamps:

Supply: Price = 30 – Quantity
Demand: Price = 10 + 3 × Quantity

How many lamps does the business need to sell in order for the supply of lamps to equal the demand for lamps exactly, i.e., for the supply and demand to be at equilibrium?

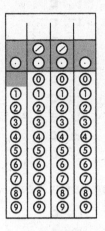

31. What is the value of the smallest side in a right triangle with a hypotenuse of 8 and angles of 30 and 60 degrees?

ANSWER KEY
Practice Test 2

Reading Test

1.	**A**	13.	**D**	25.	**C**	37.	**D**
2.	**C**	14.	**A**	26.	**D**	38.	**A**
3.	**A**	15.	**D**	27.	**A**	39.	**C**
4.	**A**	16.	**C**	28.	**C**	40.	**D**
5.	**D**	17.	**C**	29.	**C**	41.	**B**
6.	**B**	18.	**B**	30.	**A**	42.	**C**
7.	**D**	19.	**C**	31.	**C**	43.	**B**
8.	**B**	20.	**C**	32.	**A**	44.	**A**
9.	**B**	21.	**C**	33.	**B**	45.	**C**
10.	**C**	22.	**B**	34.	**D**	46	**C**
11.	**C**	23.	**C**	35.	**C**	47.	**A**
12.	**A**	24.	**D**	36.	**C**		

Writing and Language Test

1.	**D**	12.	**C**	23.	**C**	34.	**B**
2.	**A**	13.	**A**	24.	**A**	35.	**A**
3.	**B**	14.	**D**	25.	**D**	36.	**C**
4.	**C**	15.	**A**	26.	**C**	37.	**D**
5.	**D**	16.	**B**	27.	**A**	38.	**A**
6.	**B**	17.	**C**	28.	**D**	39.	**A**
7.	**A**	18.	**D**	29.	**C**	40.	**D**
8.	**D**	19.	**D**	30.	**B**	41.	**C**
9.	**A**	20.	**B**	31.	**A**	42.	**B**
10.	**C**	21.	**C**	32.	**A**	43.	**A**
11.	**B**	22.	**B**	33.	**A**	44.	**D**

Math Test (No Calculator)

1.	**B**	6.	**D**	11.	**A**	16.	**3**
2.	**C**	7.	**C**	12.	**C**	17.	**5**
3.	**D**	8.	**B**	13.	**C**		
4.	**C**	9.	**A**	14.	**2**		
5.	**D**	10.	**C**	15.	**17**		

Math Test (With Calculator)

1. **C**	9. **C**	17. **B**	25. **C**
2. **B**	10. **D**	18. **D**	26. **B**
3. **A**	11. **A**	19. **A**	27. **B**
4. **B**	12. **C**	20. **C**	28. **4**
5. **A**	13. **B**	21. **C**	29. **8/3 or 2.66 or 2.67**
6. **D**	14. **D**	22. **A**	30. **5**
7. **B**	15. **A**	23. **B**	31. **4**
8. **D**	16. **C**	24. **A**	

Note: This table represents our *best estimate* of how many questions you will need to answer correctly to achieve a certain score on the PSAT.

PSAT Section Score	PSAT Math (48 Total Questions)	PSAT Evidence-Based Reading and Writing (91 Total Questions)	PSAT Section Score
760	48	91	760
710	45	86	710
660	43	79	660
610	38	71	610
560	34	63	560
510	28	53	510
460	24	43	460
410	18	30	410
360	13	19	360
310	8	12	310
260	4	6	260
210	2	3	210
160	0	0	160

ANSWER EXPLANATIONS

Reading Test

1. **(A)** The passage uses the word "I" throughout, making the point of view first person since the passage is told from the viewpoint of the narrator. A third-person perspective would be from a more neutral, objective viewpoint. The narrator is certainly not objective, given his extreme focus on his own pain and suffering. The narrator is also not omniscient, given his lack of insight into the feelings and thoughts of others.

2. **(C)** The narrator focuses melodramatically on his own sickness and mortality throughout the passage. He is so dramatic that Hollingsworth, his purported friend, grows weary of listening to his many protests—see lines 25–28 in particular for this. The narrator's negativity contradicts being "calmly resolute" or "patiently optimistic," and his negativity is far too mild to be considered "completely morbid."

3. **(A)** Lines 25–28 give direct evidence to support the idea that the narrator is overly dramatic. The other options provide no such evidence.

4. **(A)** The sentence refers to drawing breaths, so "inhale" is the best choice. Breathing is not directly associated with provoking, inferring, or sketching.

5. **(D)** "Irony" means to have something be the opposite of what one would expect. The fact that Coverdale has prepared so much for death yet now finds himself recovering from his illness presents a situational irony. The statement is neither metaphor nor personification, because the situation is clearly expressed. The figure of speech is not an understatement, because if anything, Coverdale has a consistent tendency toward overstatement.

6. **(B)** The introduction to the passage states that Coverdale has moved to a "utopian communal farm." It is this commune to which the word "Community" refers. No evidence is provided in the passage that writers of the 1800s consistently wrote in this manner, as listed in choice (A). Choice (C) is incorrect because nothing indicates that the narrator is interested in larger urban developments. In fact, he has chosen to move to a farming community. Finally, the passage does not mention any other cities (municipalities), making choice (D) incorrect.

7. **(D)** Lines 72–76 indicate that Coverdale believes that Zenobia pursued literature because there was a lack of a "fitter avenue" and that her literary works did not do justice to her intellect. So her intellectual pursuit of literature was primarily a result of a lack of opportunities. Choices (A) and (B) both describe characteristics that would apply to her mindset, but these characteristics would not hold her back. Although Zenobia has passion and zeal for her beliefs, no evidence is provided to indicate that her zeal is religious in nature. Even if it were, religious zeal would not hold her back from her goals.

8. **(B)** Lines 74–76 best illustrate that a scarcity of opportunities led Zenobia to her primary intellectual pursuit of literature. Choice (A) refers to Zenobia's helpfulness toward the narrator. Choice (C) talks about her strength of mind. Choice (D) mentions her passion for reform.

9. **(B)** Rather than being intensely focused on a single intellectual area, Zenobia has a mind "full of weeds" that would cause her to have more diverse thoughts. Choice (A) is a valid

definition of "severe" but does not describe this situation. Choices (C) and (D) are not valid definitions of "severe."

10. **(C)** Zenobia is most interested in the "relation between the sexes" when it comes to social reform. So she is most interested in reforming antiquated gender roles. No evidence is given that her primary reform objective is to change universities that are hostile toward foreigners as listed in choice (A), problems with economic fairness as described in choice (B), or destruction of the environment as shown in choice (D).

11. **(C)** The quote, "I am a citizen of Berlin," most directly demonstrates that Kennedy is expressing that the United States is standing shoulder-to-shoulder with its allies in Germany, making this a clear demonstration of solidarity. The other options fail to capture the primary purpose of the passage.

12. **(A)** Kennedy is recognizing the presence of General Claw with him, making "joined by" the correct option. There is no evidence to support the ideas that Kennedy and Clay were in a business venture, as in Choice (B), or that Clay ordered him to come there, as in Choice (C). Choice (D), "At the request of," is not an acceptable rephrasing of "in the company of."

13. **(D)** The repetition of the sentence, "Let them come to Berlin," shows that Kennedy believes that the common solution to different misconceptions about Berlin is for people to actually come there and see it for themselves. Choice (A) is incorrect because the objections addressed are not primarily historical. Choice (B) is incorrect because the commentary is on the present, not the future. Choice (C) is incorrect because Kennedy is not encouraging such an immigration—just that Berliners observe what is happening.

14. **(A)** Lines 42–45 give direct evidence in support of this when Kennedy states, "I know of no town, no city, that has been besieged for 18 years that still lives with the vitality and the force, and the hope and the determination of the city of West Berlin." He admires them for their exceptionality at being determined and resolute in the face of adversity. The other choices are not supported by evidence in the passage.

15. **(D)** Lines 42–45 best support the idea that Kennedy admires the people of West Berlin for their excellent resolve. The other line selections do not provide direct evidence of this idea.

16. **(C)** Lines 49–54 provide evidence to support this idea, focusing on how families have been divided because of the division of the city and that the people wish to be joined together again. Choice (A) is incorrect because the people of these cities have already had initial interactions since many of them are family. Choice (B) is incorrect because the people want to visit family, not military allies. Choice (D) is incorrect because there is no evidence to support that they wish to be like an ancient empire.

17. **(C)** Lines 49–54 give evidence to support the idea that Berliners wish to be reunited. The other selections do not provide such support.

18. **(B)** Kennedy's speech is coming to an end, so "close" most closely means "finish" in this context. The other options provide alternative meanings of "close" that do not apply in this sentence.

19. **(C)** The second sentence of this paragraph suggests that once all people become free, then there will be peace throughout the world. This assumes that free people will seek to be peaceful—it is possible that free people may want to seek out conflict with one another.

Choice (A) is directly suggested, choice (B) is not mentioned, and choice (C) makes too great a leap as far as what Kennedy thinks the impact of Berliners will be in the future.

20. **(C)** The passage as a whole progresses chronologically. It discusses the origins of blackletter typeface centuries ago. It then elaborates on the evolution of this typeface throughout the centuries until the modern day, giving readers a basic education about blackletter. The other choices are all too narrow in their emphasis.

21. **(C)** In this case, the word "labyrinthine" is used to describe highly ornate works, like ornamental books and glosses. These works would be very complex by nature. Choices (A) and (B) are too literal, and choice (D) is too negative.

22. **(B)** This can be seen in the paragraph from lines 52–59. The author discusses both the intricacy and readability of Fraktur, making this typeface a balance of elegance and functionalism. The other options give accurate descriptions of Fraktur but do not clearly mention advantages of this form of blackletter.

23. **(C)** These lines best support the claim that Fraktur lettering balanced elegance with functionalism. The other choices establish that Fraktur was widespread but do not explain what advantages caused it to have this popularity.

24. **(D)** Lines 60–65 refer to the modeling of the letterforms on ancient Roman scripts. So it is highly plausible that the classicists of the 18th century wished to connect to the culture of ancient Rome. Although the other options may be true aspects of this lettering, they do not relate to its classical origins.

25. **(C)** Lines 60–65 give direct evidence in support of the idea that classicists preferred Antiqua over blackletter because it associated the classicist movement with the learning of ancient Rome and the classical period. The other options are not directly related to the answer to the previous question.

26. **(D)** The last paragraph begins by citing the "lethal blow" that was dealt to blackletter as a result of the *Schrifterlass* decree, meaning that the wide use of blackletter came to an end. Choice (A) is too vague and broad. Choice (B) is not supported by the text since blackletter previously enjoyed widespread popularity. Choice (C) is incorrect because the Nazi approach to this ban is more absurdly nonsensical than hypocritical since what these letters had to do with Judaism is unclear.

27. **(A)** Lines 5–11 refer to the insular scripts as being highly "variable." This means that people handwrote the scripts in a variety of ways, making them difficult to read. Choice (B) is incorrect since only the Carolingian minuscule is mentioned as cumbersome. Choice (C) is incorrect, because the passage does not support the notion that these scripts were limited to England and Ireland. Choice (D) is incorrect because the passage does not support that these scripts were used only in monasteries.

28. **(C)** "Final" makes the most sense here. The historical events described in this paragraph did not completely eliminate blackletter but did make its use much more of a rarity. Since "lethal" is describing the demise of a language and not a living thing, saying that the word means "mortal," "deadly," or "venomous" makes no sense.

29. **(C)** The first passage discusses invasive plants in general, while the second passage focuses much more in depth on how getting rid of invasive plants can do more harm than good to native animal species. Choice (A) is incorrect because neither passage is clearly positive

or negative. Choice (B) is incorrect because Passage 1 is more neutral than pessimistic. Choice (D) is also incorrect because Passage 1 is more analytical than argumentative.

30. **(A)** Both agree that invasive plants can be potentially helpful. This can be seen in lines 22–24 of Passage 1 in which the author states that these plants have been spread for a wide range of "beneficial uses." In lines 79–84 of Passage 2, the author states that the invasive plants have caused a long-term change for the better. Neither author would agree with choice (B). Both agree that honeysuckle is a type of invasive plant, but neither asserts it is the most well-known variety, making choice (C) incorrect. Choice (D) is also incorrect since Passage 2 does not mention any potential benefits from government intervention.

31. **(C)** Lines 11–13 of Passage 1 indicate that some nonnative plants are introduced to new environments through accidental human contact. With an increase in human visitation, the Galapagos Islands will likely experience more accidental introduction of plants. Choice (A) is incorrect because the information does not suggest that an increase in human interaction leads to an overall improvement in conservation efforts. Although Passage 1 mentions using funding to fight the negative consequences of invasive plants, information is not provided to support the notion that an increase in tourism will result in enough money to outweigh the negative consequences of increased human activity. Therefore, choice (B) is incorrect. Choice (D) is not right because the information does not support the notion that humans will consistently seek to introduce invasive species purposefully into new environments.

32. **(A)** Lines 8–13 best support the idea that an increase in human contact will lead to more accidental introduction of plant species. Choice (B) focuses on the benefits of intentionally introducing invasive plants. Choice (C) mentions the difficulty in predicting the consequences of plant introduction. Choice (D) mentions only one type of invasive plant.

33. **(B)** The author argues in these lines that intentional cultivation of nonnative plants is usually a good thing. A global analysis demonstrating that nonnative plants are typically harmful when introduced would therefore undermine—weaken—this argument. Choice (A) is not correct because knowing that most invasive plants were introduced by accident would not give information about their relative benefit. Choice (C) is incorrect because it, too, would not give any facts about how harmful the plants were to their surroundings. Choice (D) is not correct because this would be too small a sample size to make such a sweeping claim.

34. **(D)** A lack of natural predators best accounts for why an introduced animal species becomes invasive. If no other animals eat it, the introduced species will have few obstacles to its spread. Choice (A) draws an incorrect definition based on the word roots. Choice (B) incorrectly labels the environments as inhospitable. Choice (C) is the opposite of what would help animals flourish since the context says "lack of natural predation."

35. **(C)** The author immediately contradicts this statement in the following sentence. The general purpose of placing the sentence from lines 52–56 in the passage is to give a general summary of what many people think about this issue and then to use the entire passage to show why most people are incorrect about this topic. Choice (A) is incorrect since this text only indirectly establishes the author's authority. Choice (B) is not right because the thesis of the passage comes in the sentence that follows. Choice (D) is incorrect because ecologists and biologists are in agreement according to this sentence.

36. **(C)** Lines 66–73 describe a "mutualist" relationship, in which the species help one another. This is most similar to the oxpecker birds eating the predatory insects off the backs of zebras. The oxpeckers are gaining food, and the zebras are being cleaned. Choices (A) and (D) involve relationships beneficial to only one of the species. Choice (B) does not establish a reciprocal relationship with another species.

37. **(D)** "Discriminating" typically has a negative connotation that people associate with prejudice. However, in this context, the author is asserting that we need to be more careful and "selective" when picking which invasive plants to keep and which ones to exterminate. Choices (A) and (B) can apply to discriminating in other contexts. Choice (C) applies only to the quality of art, food, music, and so on.

38. **(A)** The last two paragraphs focus on this evolution. Color photography went from being "unwieldy" and unable to capture moving objects well to having instantaneous Polaroid photos. Choice (B) describes the opposite of the development of photography since over time, color photography became an object of widespread interest. While the creation of Kodachrome was made by musicians, it is too much of a stretch to say that photography in general became the focus of musicians. Therefore, choice (C) is not correct. Choice (D) is incorrect since the primary emphasis of the passage is on the shift in the size and usefulness of camera technology.

39. **(C)** An anecdote is a short and interesting story about something. The author uses scientific and historical anecdotes, sharing stories about the early pioneers of color photography up to modern Kodak researchers. Very little in the passage analyzes the thoughts of people (psychological analysis) as described in choice (A). Choice (B) is incorrect since chemical and physical description is a minor part of the essay. Choice (D) is incorrect since the essay focuses on the development of technology, not on the comparison of cultures.

40. **(D)** Line 14 mentions the scientists' "fidelity" (loyalty) to the then-popular daguerreotype method, which impeded the progress of Hill and Becquerel. Choice (A) is incorrect since the two had solid backgrounds in science. Choice (B) is incorrect since the passage does not mention that cultural bias played any role. Choice (C) is incorrect because the scientists' understanding of past successes likely made them less likely to think for themselves.

41. **(B)** Lines 11–15 provide the best evidence that Hill and Becquerel were hindered in their research by their loyalty to a widespread approach. Choice (A) merely states that the scientists were leaders in their field. Choice (C) refers to inferior methods of the past. Choice (D) refers to Maxwell, who came after Hill and Becquerel.

42. **(C)** Maxwell used black-and-white transparencies taken through red, blue, and green filters to show a combined image that had colors. The image cannot be characterized as "crafted" since it is a photograph, not a humanmade painting or craft. Therefore, choice (A) is incorrect. Although the image is certainly visual and may be of quality, as listed in choices (B) and (D), the primary meaning conveyed is that the image is a combined whole.

43. **(B)** "Unwieldy" most nearly means "cumbersome" (difficult to manipulate) in this context. The color cameras of the time are described as having multiple prisms and mirrors to make an image, which would be far from user friendly. Although the cameras could be "unsightly" or "expensive," as listed in choices (A) and (C), the description that follows focuses on the

complexity of the cameras. Choice (D), "precise," is incorrect because the cameras had not reached a technological level where they could reasonably be labeled as such.

44. **(A)** The third paragraph reports how Hill's and Becquerel's chemistry-based approach toward color photography was ultimately unsuccessful. It also reports that Maxwell was able to make progress by focusing on how the human eye—a biological organ—perceives colors. The other options do not accurately describe this transition.

45. **(C)** Lines 96–99 state that the major shortcoming of Miethe's design was its inability to photograph moving objects properly because it needed a long exposure time. If an object was relatively stable, as objects would likely be on a freezing, windless day, Miethe's design would be more successful. Choices (A) and (B) do not work due to the presence of wind. Choice (D) is incorrect because frozen water could be more clearly photographed than moving water.

46. **(C)** Lines 47–52 state that humans are able to see wavelengths between 400 and 700 nanometers. A nanometer is 1×10^{-9} meters. So the visible wavelengths fall between the ultraviolet and infrared wavelengths.

47. **(A)** The last paragraph describes Mannes and Godowsky as casual tinkerers (as opposed to dedicated researchers) working "recreationally" and who had backgrounds in music rather than science. Thus, their discovery can best be described as "serendipitous," i.e., a fortunate finding by chance. The other options all focus on particular fields of study, which was not the case for Mannes and Godowsky with respect to their photographic research.

Writing and Language Test

1. **(D)** This is the only option that sets off the parenthetical phrase with the same sort of punctuation on either side, i.e., a dash. Commas can also set up parenthetical phrases, but a comma must be placed both before and after the phrase.

2. **(A)** By calling it a "singular" puzzle, the author expresses the remarkable nature of this puzzle. The word "tantalizing" indicates that this puzzle is extremely interesting yet challenging to solve. The other options do not express this same intensity.

3. **(B)** The sentence can still function as a complete sentence without the phrase "which demonstrated the existence of antimatter." So the phrase should be surrounded by commas to set it aside. Choice (A) does not have a necessary pause before the phrase. Choice (C) does not have the necessary completed sentence before the semicolon. Choice (D) has no pauses whatsoever.

4. **(C)** The passage as a whole indicates that a clear answer to this scientific dilemma has not been found nor is an answer expected in the near future. Hence, "forthcoming" makes the most sense. "Unfound" and "surprising" are the opposite of what is needed. "Acknowledged" indicates the solution may have been discovered but not yet recognized.

5. **(D)** The subject of this sentence is "studies," which is plural and requires the word "have." Additionally, this is something that has gone on from the past up to the present day. So using "have confounded" is logical. The word "confounded" means "confused," while the word "confided" means "shared a secret."

6. **(B)** The numerical amount of 0.01 times does not initially seem like a very large number, so choice (B) gives a helpful introductory connection in the current sentence. Choice (A) states that 0.01 is a larger quantity than it actually is. Choice (C) is incorrect because "paucity," which means "a lack of," contradicts the well-founded scientific observations mentioned. Choice (D) involves scientists ignoring their own observations.

7. **(A)** A phrase that starts with "from . . ." can be appropriately joined with "to . . . ." Joining "from . . ." with an "and" or with a "but" does not work in this context.

8. **(D)** Unless someone has studied physics, it is unlikely that he or she will be familiar with the term "dark matter." Thus, providing a scientific definition for the term before proceeding further is helpful. Choice (C) is incorrect because this phrase does not clarify the quantity of dark matter.

9. **(A)** "Meanwhile" provides a logical contrast between the relatively large percentage of dark matter and the relatively small percentage of visible atoms. None of the other options provides a logical contrast.

10. **(C)** This is an event that takes place *prior* to another event in the past, so "had" is needed. Choices (A) and (B) are in the past perfect tense, and choice (D) is in the present progressive tense.

11. **(B)** When using the phrase "at once . . . ," one needs to use "and" to transition to the second item in the list. Why? Since these two things exist "at once," the word "and" is an appropriate way to join them to one another.

12. **(C)** Changing from "you" to "one" would be especially problematic in the first paragraph, where the author focuses on engaging the reader's interest in glassmaking. Choice (D) is incorrect because changing from "you" to "one" would in no way shift the focus away from glassblowing.

13. **(A)** "Well" is used similar to the word "far" in this context, stating that this is for a great duration of time into the 19th century. A comma is needed after "century" to separate the dependent introductory phrase from the independent clause that follows. Choices (B) and (D) break up the phrase "well into." Choice (C) has none of the necessary pauses.

14. **(D)** "Of which" is the correct idiomatic usage of a preposition with "which" in this context. The author is trying to say that "this is the earliest known example *of this.*"

15. **(A)** "Traditionally" should be left where it is since it provides an overall introduction to the way glass used to be made. Choice (B) would change the meaning of "bowl-shaped glob," choice (C) would limit the "tradition" to the flattening process, and choice (D) would limit the "tradition" to the shaping and sizing of the glass.

16. **(B)** The semicolon provides a needed break between the two independent clauses. The comma after "additionally" gives an appropriate pause separating the transition from the complete sentence that follows. Choices (A) and (D) are both run-on sentences. Choice (C) lacks the necessary comma after the introductory word "Additionally."

17. **(C)** Placing the sentence before sentence [4] breaks the paragraph into two halves. The first half focuses on older glassmaking procedures. The second half focuses on later ones.

18. **(D)** "Technique" is a singular subject, so the verb should be "involves." Choice (D) also uses the correct forms of "floating" and "molten" to describe the glass—"molted" does not

PRACTICE TEST 2

work as a word in this context. Choices (A) and (B) have plural verbs, and choice (C) uses "molted" instead of "molten."

19. **(D)** The compound subject of "specific gravity and immiscibility with tin" demands a plural verb, hence "cause" works. In addition, the "it" is correct since the pronoun refers to the singular "glass."

20. **(B)** The sentence is stating that tin remains a liquid in the 1,100°C bath. So a statement about tin's melting point explains why tin reacts this way. Choices (A), (C), and (D) provide irrelevant facts about tin.

21. **(C)** Doing something "remarkably fast" is the best contrast with "laborious" since "laborious" means "involving a great deal of work." Choices (A) and (B) repeat ideas already mentioned in the sentence. Choice (D) does not provide the needed contrast with the second part of the sentence.

22. **(B)** When comparing amounts and sizes of things, "too" is the correct spelling. "Two" is a number, and "to" serves to connect words.

23. **(C)** "Its" refers to each singular state taken on its own, not as part of a group. The other options do not have number agreement with the context already established.

24. **(A)** The candidate would be a singular man or woman, so "he or she" is correct. "Won" is used when there is a plural subject and the phrase is in the past tense.

25. **(D)** The paragraph goes on to explain that a candidate winning the electoral college vote but not the popular vote does NOT occur frequently but, in the eyes of the author, is still a problematic occurrence. Choice (D) therefore best introduces the paragraph. Choices (A), (B), and (C) focus on political concerns but not on the ones discussed in this essay.

26. **(C)** Earlier in the paragraph, the author mentions that the winning candidate did not win the popular vote four times in U.S. history. It is reasonable to infer that the other times, the winning candidate *did* win the popular vote. Leaving this sentence in the paragraph is just wordy. Choice (D) is not correct because there is nothing in the passage that contradicts this information.

27. **(A)** The passage indicates that the Electoral College is still in place up to the present day. So "has been" is appropriate because it uses the singular past perfect tense, unlike the other options.

28. **(D)** Placing just one comma after "system" provides a break between the dependent introductory clause and the independent clause that follows. Moreover, it maintains the logic of keeping the phrase "the way the presidential candidates campaign" together as a unified whole, unlike choice (A).

29. **(C)** This choice uses commas to set off the examples of swing states. The sentence would still function as a complete sentence without this phrase, so the phrase can be set aside.

30. **(B)** The previous sentence explains that voters in swing states receive far more attention than voters in states that are more uniformly one party. Choice (B) would therefore connect to the concluding sentence that points out that a majority vote system would ensure that voters everywhere would have an equal say. Choice (A) focuses on irrelevant population density. Choice (C) describes the opposite of what occurs. Choice (D) does not provide a logical transition from the previous sentence.

31. **(A)** "Usurp" means to "seize power," usually inappropriately. This is the best word to convey the fears that the smaller states had. The larger states are not literally going to "invade." To "touch" or "decline" authority would pose no threat to the power of smaller states.

32. **(A)** The passage focuses on the need to abandon the Electoral College, which would be the "relic" mentioned in this choice, in favor of a majority vote system. Choices (B), (C), and (D) are too vague.

33. **(A)** According to the data in the table, citizens of Alaska have a greater per capita voice in the Electoral College than do citizens of the other states listed. Since Alaskan citizens have more say under the current system, they would not have a very strong incentive to abolish it.

34. **(B)** In this context, the phrase "not only . . ." should be followed by the transition "but also." No comma needs to come between these two phrases unless the phrases being compared are also complete sentences. "With," "and," and "since" are not accepted connections to "not only."

35. **(A)** The author would like "Lay" to achieve the same recognition that *Beowulf* does. The argument is not that *Beowulf* should receive less recognition than "Lay" but that "Lay" is worthy of the same sort of recognition as *Beowulf*. Thus, the author's tone would most likely be positive and appreciative. Choices (B) and (C) are too negative, and choice D is too dispassionate.

36. **(C)** This choice gives the most specific justification as to why scholars do not yet fully understand this poem. The other choices are rather vague.

37. **(D)** This option does not have unnecessary wording and also provides a needed pause before the second part of the sentence. It also provides an appropriate comparison between the two things by using the word "more." The word "most" is incorrect because it is used to compare three or more things. Choice (C) does not provide a comparison since it lacks any comparative words.

38. **(A)** This choice provides a contrast that appropriately focuses on the linguistic elements, with the possibilities ranging from something of poor quality to something of monumental significance. The other choices do not provide theories that would help explain the mystery of the origins of the "Lay."

39. **(A)** Placing this sentence at the beginning of the paragraph introduces the overall topic of the paragraph, namely what is interesting linguistically about the poem. If the sentence is not placed in this position, the paragraph would begin without a clarification of its subject.

40. **(D)** The author is arguing that a study of the text *would* be interesting to certain people. So saying "either" and its counterpart "or" makes sense.

41. **(C)** The semicolon is a softer linkage between two complete ideas than is a period. The idea after the semicolon clarifies why the "Lay" is potentially as interesting as and more poetic than *Beowulf*. The comma sets off a clarifying phrase. Choices (A) and (D) lead to run-on sentences, and choice (B) lacks a comma.

42. **(B)** "Thrust" indicates that Hildebrand was forced into the duel against his will, which was most certainly the case given that he was unwillingly fighting his son. Choices (A) and (C) are too mild in representing what happened. Choice (D) is incorrect because Hildebrand was likely not murdered *prior* to the duel.

43. **(A)** An apostrophe before the "s" is needed to show that the singular "scribe" possesses the penmanship and also to show that the "poem" possesses the "lines." A comma is also needed after "penmanship" to indicate the end of the parenthetical phrase.

44. **(D)** The transliterated passage presented in the text shows that there is not a clear ending to the story, making "ambiguous" the best option. The other choices indicate much more decisive outcomes.

Math Test (No Calculator)

1. **(B)**

$$\frac{m^{\frac{5}{2}}}{m^{\frac{1}{2}}} \rightarrow \text{Factor out an } m^{\frac{1}{2}} \text{ on the top} \rightarrow \frac{m^{\frac{1}{2}}m^2}{m^{\frac{1}{2}}} \rightarrow$$

Cancel the $m^{\frac{1}{2}}$ from the top and bottom $\rightarrow m^2$

2. **(C)** $x = 36$ does not have a y-intercept since it runs parallel to the y-axis. Therefore, this equation never intersects the y-axis. Here is a graph of $x = 36$:

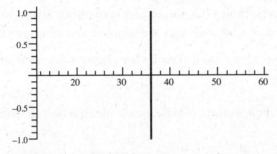

All of the other choices intersect the y-axis one time since they have a y-value when $x = 0$.

3. **(D)** There are 3 teaspoons in each tablespoon. So multiply $3 \times 3 \times 2$ to get the 18 total teaspoons needed for the 2 cakes.

4. **(C)** To format the equation like $3a + 4b$, multiply the entire equation by 12:

$$\frac{1}{4}a + \frac{1}{3}b = 2 \rightarrow \text{multiply by } 12 \rightarrow 3a + 4b = 24$$

Since there are two variables with just one equation, you need to do some sort of manipulation like this because a and b cannot be solved for individually without having another intersecting equation.

5. **(D)** Expand the expression and factor:

$$3a - 3(b - a) \rightarrow 3a - 3b + 3a \rightarrow 6a - 3b \rightarrow \text{factor} \rightarrow 3(2a - b)$$

6. **(D)** $\frac{2}{k} = x$ is undefined if $k = 0$. Dividing by 0 results in an undefined solution. All of the other equations have a solution for x when $k = 0$.

7. **(C)** Use substitution to solve for B.

$$2B = \frac{10}{9}A \rightarrow A = \frac{9}{5}B$$

Plug this into the other equation:

$$\frac{2}{3}A+\frac{3}{5}B=4\rightarrow\frac{2}{3}\left(\frac{9}{5}B\right)+\frac{3}{5}B=\frac{18}{15}B+\frac{9}{15}B=\frac{27}{15}B=4$$

$$B=\frac{60}{27}=\frac{20}{9}$$

8. **(B)** When you are told, "Take an input variable," that refers to x. Then divide the x by 4 and subtract 5 from this, which gives the function $f(x)=\frac{x}{4}-5$.

9. **(A)** This line has a y-intercept of –3 since that is where the line intersects the y-axis. You can calculate the slope using points on the line, (0, –3) and (6, 0):

$$\text{Slope} = \frac{\text{Rise}}{\text{Run}} = \frac{y_2 - y_1}{x_2 - x_1} = \frac{-3-0}{0-6} = \frac{1}{2}$$

Putting this in slope-intercept form ($y = mx + b$) results in the equation of the line:

$$y = \frac{1}{2}x - 3$$

10. **(C)** To minimize the overall gravitational force, the value of the numerator should be as small as possible and the value of the denominator should be as large as possible. Out of the possible answers, choice (C), would best accomplish this. It would make the value of $m_1 \times m_2$ as small as possible and make the denominator d^2 as large as possible.

11. **(A)** Set the two equations equal to each other. Express the result as a quadratic equation:

$$2x - 5 = 2x^2 + 4 \rightarrow 2x^2 - 2x + 9$$

Plug these values for a, b, and c into the quadratic equation. The only solutions are imaginary:

$$\frac{-b\pm\sqrt{b^2-4ac}}{2a} = \frac{2\pm\sqrt{4-4\times18}}{2\times2} = \frac{2\pm i\sqrt{68}}{4}$$

12. **(C)** Rewrite the table by calculating the actual sums:

n	Pattern	Sum
1	1	1
2	1 + 3	4
3	1 + 3 + 5	9
4	1 + 3 + 5 + 7	16
5	1 + 3 + 5 + 7 + 9	25

Each value in the "Sum" column is the corresponding value of n squared:

$$1 = 1^2 \,; 4 = 2^2 \,; 9 = 3^2 \,; 16 = 4^2 \,; 25 = 5^2$$

13. **(C)** The different terms on the two sides of the equation equal each other. So $-16 = -8b$, $-6x = -abx$, and $x^2 = x^2$. Why? This occurs because the constants must equal each other, the terms with an x must equal each other, and the terms with an x^2 must equal one another. Since $-16 = -8b$, $b = 2$. Plug in 2 for b in the second equation and cancel out the $-x$ to solve for a:

$$-6x = -abx \rightarrow 6 = a \cdot 2 \rightarrow a = 3$$

14.

2 Cancel out the y-terms on each side, and solve for x:

$$4x - y = \frac{1}{2}x - y + 7 \rightarrow 4x = \frac{1}{2}x + 7 \rightarrow 3.5x = 7 \rightarrow x = 2$$

15.

17 Work inside out by first solving for $g(1)$:

$$g(x) = 2x^2 \rightarrow g(1) = 2(1)^2 = 2.$$

Then put 2 in for x in the $f(x)$:

$$f(x) = 7x + 3 \rightarrow f(2) = 7(2) + 3 = 17$$

16.

3 There will be infinitely many solutions if the two equations are multiples of the same equation. The coefficients of the A and B terms in $A + 2B = 4$ add up to 3 since they are 1 and 2. Since $XA + YB = 4X$ is divisible by 4 on the right-hand side as is the other equation, the sum of X and Y must also be divisible by 3 in order for the two equations to be multiples of one another. To replicate the structure of the first equation, Y must equal $2X$ so that the two equations will be multiples of one another. To see this with greater clarity, consider this example:

$$A + 2B = 4$$
$$XA + YB = 4X$$

If the second equation had $X = 2$ and $Y = 4$, the equation would be twice the first equation: $2A + 4B = 8$. This equation is simply a multiple of the first one, making them essentially identical. As a result, there are infinitely many solutions since the equations overlap each other when graphed.

17.

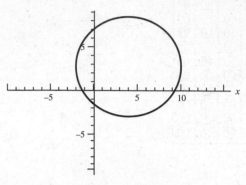

5 Based on the general equation of a circle, $(x - h)^2 + (y - k)^2 = r^2$, the center point is (h, k). For this circle, the center point is $(4, 3)$. This point is a distance of 5 from the origin, which has the coordinates $(0, 0)$. The graph of the circle is as follows:

You can calculate the shortest straight-line distance by using the distance formula or, even easier, recognizing that these numbers form a Pythagorean triple: 3-4-5. Recognizing that this is a Pythagorean triple will save you the time and trouble of calculating the distance using the distance formula.

Math Test (With Calculator)

1. **(C)** Multiply 180 by 1.61 to get the maximum value of the speedometer in kilometers per hour:

$$180\frac{\text{miles}}{\text{hr}} \times 1.61\frac{\text{km}}{\text{mile}} \rightarrow \text{the miles cancel} \rightarrow (180 \times 1.61)\frac{\text{km}}{\text{hr}} \approx 290\frac{\text{km}}{\text{hr}}$$

2. **(B)** Set up a proportion to solve for the unknown number of cups of flour.

    Use the ratio 6 cupcakes to 3 cups of flour $\rightarrow \frac{6}{3} = \frac{15}{x} \rightarrow x = 7.5$

3. **(A)** Some approximate points that would be on the best-fit line are (1990, 0) and (1996, 18).

    Calculate the approximate slope: $\frac{18-0}{1996-1990} = 3$, which comes closest to choice (A).

    You can also visualize this by drawing the approximate best-fit line on the graph:

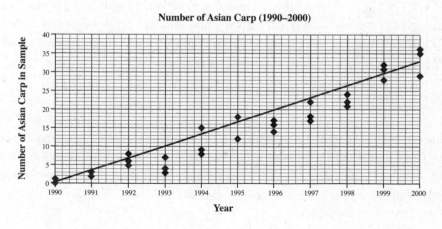

Number of Asian Carp (1990–2000)

4. **(B)** In the 10-year period shown in the graph, the number of carp has increased by approximately 35. After 15 more years of growth, there will be approximately 1.5 times the amount

of growth that occurred during the 10-year period. To find the approximate total number of carp in 2015, calculate $35 + (1.5 \times 35) = 87.5$. This value is closest to choice (B). Since the calculation is an approximation, having a little variance in the answer is acceptable.

5. **(A)** Start by distributing the 2 through the parentheses on the left and the 3 through the parentheses on the right:

$$7 + 2(x - 3) = -3(x + 1) - 4$$
$$7 + 2x - 6 = -3x - 3 - 4$$

Simplify and solve for x:

$$1 + 2x = -3x - 7 \rightarrow$$
$$5x = -8 \rightarrow$$
$$x = -\frac{8}{5}$$

6. **(D)** Simplify by combining the like terms within the parentheses:

$$(x^2 + 3x^2)^3 = (4x^2)^3$$

Next cube both the 4 and the x^2:

$$(4x^2)^3 \rightarrow (4^3)(x^2)^3 \rightarrow 64x^6$$

7. **(B)** Factor an x^n out of the expression to get the answer:

$$4x^n + x^{4n} = x^n(4 + x^{3n})$$

You cannot combine x^n and x^{4n} into one term because they are not raised to the same power.

8. **(D)** The arithmetic mean is the average. Solve this problem using a weighted average. In other words, calculate the average by factoring in the relative amounts sold of the item by each store.

Store	Price Before Sale	Quantity Sold Before Sale	Sale Price	Quantity Sold After Sale
Store A	$12.50	350	$11.00	400
Store B	$13.25	260	$10.00	520
Store C	$11.75	550	$9.50	625
Store D	$14.00	220	$10.25	460

Store A sold 350 items for $12.50 each, and Store B sold 260 items for $13.25 each. The total number of items sold is $350 + 260$. You can compute the average as follows:

$$\frac{\text{Total income}}{\text{Total number of items sold}} = \frac{(12.50 \times 350) + (13.25 \times 260)}{(350 + 260)} \approx 12.8$$

9. **(C)** Calculate the slope of the line:

$$\text{Slope} = \frac{\text{Rise}}{\text{Run}} = \frac{y_2 - y_1}{x_2 - x_1} = \frac{14 - 10.25}{220 - 460} = -0.015625$$

Then create an equation for the line in slope-intercept form ($y = mx + b$) and solve for the y-intercept:

$$y = -0.015625x + b$$

Substitute a set of values from Store D to solve for b:

$$14 = (-0.015625 \times 220) + b \rightarrow b \approx 17.4$$

10. **(D)** The table does not specify whether or not sales tax is included in the given prices. If it is, the impact on the sales may be less pronounced than if sales tax is not included since consumers will still have to pay money in tax even if the item is on sale. The other choices would give irrelevant information. Choice (A) is incorrect because the prices at other retailers would not help determine the impact of sales at these stores. Choice (B) is incorrect because conducting a calculation will not give concrete information that will help you make a better prediction. Choice (C) is incorrect because no clear connection exists between employee motivation and the impact that these specific discounts would have on sales.

11. **(A)** The formula for calculating a percentage is $\frac{\text{Part}}{\text{Whole}} \times 100 = \text{Percentage}$.

So m represents the overall percentage, n represents the part, and x represents the whole. Plugging these values into the original equation gives:

$$\frac{\text{Part}}{\text{Whole}} \times 100 = \text{Percentage} \rightarrow$$

$$\frac{n}{x} \times 100 = m \rightarrow$$

$$n = \frac{mx}{100}$$

Alternatively, you can rephrase the question using concrete numbers:

"*If 10 represents 50 percent of 20, how can we calculate the value of 10?*" The only solution that gives the correct answer is choice (A):

$$\frac{\text{Part}}{\text{Whole}} \times 100 = \text{Percentage} \rightarrow$$

$$\frac{10}{20} \times 100 = 50 \rightarrow$$

$$10 = \frac{50 \times 20}{100}$$

This equation is in the same format as the equation shown in choice (A):

$$n = \frac{mx}{100}$$

12. **(C)** To determine a 3% increase on an original amount of x, add 3% to the original amount:

$$x + 0.03x = 1.03x$$

You can save time if you recognize that you can simply multiply x by 1.03 to determine the total of x plus 3% interest. The amount in the account is compounded twice. So multiply x by 1.03 twice:

$$x \cdot 1.03 \cdot 1.03 = 1.0609x$$

13. **(B)** Use substitution to solve for a:

$$b = 2a + 1 \text{ and } b + 2 = a^2 \rightarrow (2a + 1) + 2 = a^2$$
$$2a + 3 = a^2 \rightarrow$$
$$a^2 - 2a - 3 = 0 \rightarrow (a - 3)(a + 1) = 0$$

When $a = 3$, $b = 7$, and when $a = -1$, $b = -1$.

14. **(D)** Use FOIL to calculate the product of the terms in parentheses:

$$2(a - 4b)(3 + b^3) = 2(3a + ab^3 - 12b - 4b^4) = 6a + 2ab^3 - 24b - 8b^4$$

Rearrange the values to put them in the order shown in the choices:

$$2ab^3 + 6a - 8b^4 - 24b$$

15. **(A)** For each hour the librarian works, he or she shelves a total of 220 items. Therefore, the total number of items shelved during T hours is $220 \times T$. The other answer choices have constants either added or subtracted to the term multiplied by T. These answer choices would illogically mean that the librarian could shelve or remove items without spending any time at all doing so.

16. **(C)** Bonds represented 30% of the 1995 portfolio and 22% of the 2015 portfolio. You can find the increase in bonds by subtracting the 1995 bond amount from the 2015 bond amount:

$$(0.22 \times 200,000) - (0.3 \times 80,000) = 20,000$$

17. **(B)** Based on the numbers in the previous question, the portfolio is increasing by $60,000 every 10 years. You add $60,000 to the 2015 value of $200,000 to get $260,000. Alternatively, you could calculate the slope of increase. However, noticing this simple pattern will save you time.

18. **(D)** The tables give information only about the allocation of international and domestic stocks. They do not contain any information about the allocation of large-capitalization stocks, mid-capitalization stocks, and small-capitalization stocks. So not enough information is provided to reach a conclusion.

19. **(A)** The height of Pam's television is 36 inches since 48:36 reduces to her screen ratio of 4:3. You can determine how many inches of height the movie image will take up on Pam's TV by setting up a ratio: $\frac{1}{1.85} = \frac{x}{48} \rightarrow x \approx 26$. Now subtract the height of the movie from the height of the TV screen to determine how many inches of screen height will NOT be used: $36 - 26 = 10$.

20. **(C)** Since there are three separate measurements that are each off by up to 2 units, you can determine the range of possible values by adding all the individual measurements together and then including a range of plus or minus 6:

$$48 + 56 + 40 = 144$$
$$144 + 6 = 150$$
$$144 - 6 = 138$$

Choice (C) shows the correct range.

21. **(C)** Try plugging in some sample values, like 2 and 100, for x and assume n is a constant like 3 to see how the equations behave:

Equation	Substitute $x = 2$ and $n = 3$	Value when $x = 2$ and $n = 3$	Substitute $x = 100$ and $n = 3$	Value when $x = 100$ and $n = 3$
A. $y = nx + 3$	$y = 3 \times 2 + 3$	9	$y = 3 \times 100 + 3$	303
B. $y = -nx + 3$	$y = -3 \times 2 + 3$	-3	$y = -3 \times 100 + 3$	-297
C. $y = x^n + 3$	$y = 2^3 + 3$	11	$y = 100^3 + 3$	1,000,003
D. $y = x^{-n} + 3$	$y = 2^{-3} + 3$	$3\frac{1}{8}$	$y = 100^{-3} + 3$	3.000001

Choice (C) clearly has the greatest overall increase, going from 11 to 1,000,003.

Alternatively, you can simply realize that a number greater than 1 to a power more than 1 will be greater than the other possibilities.

22. **(A)** Since the company does not want the passengers to lose consciousness, the passengers must not experience g forces equal to or greater than 5. The only possible range of g-values is $g < 5$, in which all the g-values are less than 5.

23. **(B)** The programs are permitted a maximum of 12 coaches. So C must be equal to or less than 12. Choice (B) is the only option with this statement. All of the other options do not allow for the full range of possible values for the number of coaches. Moreover, the number of players will be limited by the number of coaches if the university is to maintain a ratio of a maximum of 4 players per coach. By making the number of players less than or equal to 4 times the number of coaches, $P \leq 4C$, the university will ensure that it has at least 1 coach for every 4 players.

24. **(A)** Plug the given values into the equation:

$$\text{Final velocity} = \text{Initial velocity} + \text{Acceleration} \times \text{Time}$$

$$\text{Initial velocity} = 4\frac{\text{m}}{\text{s}}$$

$$\text{Acceleration} = 6\frac{\text{m}}{\text{s}^2}$$

$$\text{Final velocity} = 22\frac{\text{m}}{\text{s}}$$

The final velocity must be *at least* $22\frac{\text{m}}{\text{s}}$. Set up the inequality so that the result for the final velocity could exceed $22\frac{\text{m}}{\text{s}}$:

$$22 \leq 4 + 6T$$
$$18 \leq 6T$$
$$3 \leq T$$

25. **(C)** Plug the freezing point of water in degrees C into the equation:

$$K = 273 + C$$
$$K = 273 + 0 = 273$$

Choice (C) is the only option that has 273 for the freezing point. You can also plug in 100 for the boiling point in degrees C. You will get 373 as the result.

26. **(B)** Divide $1.0 \times 10^6 \dfrac{\text{kg}}{\text{m}^3}$ by $990 \dfrac{\text{kg}}{\text{m}^3}$ to determine by what multiple her weight will increase. Her weight will be 1,010 times greater. Then multiply 1,010 by 150 pounds to get 151,500 pounds.

27. **(B)** Use the formula Distance = Rate × Time to make your calculations. The distance is 16 km for the journey in either direction. The rates, however, are different. The rate going upstream is $1\dfrac{\text{km}}{\text{hr}}$ less than the rate at which John is actually rowing because he is going against the current. The rate going downstream is $1\dfrac{\text{km}}{\text{hr}}$ more than the rate at which he is actually rowing because he is going with the current. If x is the rate at which John is rowing, the time, u, to go upstream is:

$$d = ru \rightarrow 16 = (x-1)u \rightarrow u = \frac{16}{x-1}$$

The time going downstream, t, can be calculated in a similar way:

$$d = rt \rightarrow 16 = (x+1)t \rightarrow t = \frac{16}{x+1}$$

Since the total time of the journey is 4 hours, combine these two expressions together into one equation:

$$\frac{16}{x-1} + \frac{16}{x+1} = 4$$

Then solve for x:

$$\frac{16}{x-1} + \frac{16}{x+1} = 4 \rightarrow \frac{16(x+1)}{(x-1)(x+1)} + \frac{16(x-1)}{(x+1)(x-1)} = 4 \rightarrow$$

$$\frac{16(x+1)+16(x-1)}{x^2-1} = 4 \rightarrow \frac{16x+16+16x-16}{x^2-1} = 4 \rightarrow$$

$$\frac{32x}{x^2-1} = 4 \rightarrow 32x = 4x^2 - 4 \rightarrow 4x^2 - 32x - 4 = 0 \rightarrow x^2 - 8x - 1 = 0$$

Use the quadratic formula to solve:

$$\frac{-b \pm \sqrt{b^2-4ac}}{2a} \rightarrow \frac{8 \pm \sqrt{(-8)^2 - 4 \cdot 1 \cdot (-1)}}{2 \cdot 1} = \frac{8 \pm \sqrt{68}}{2} = \frac{8 \pm 2\sqrt{17}}{2} = 4 \pm \sqrt{17}$$

You get two solutions. However, you can use only $4 + \sqrt{17}$ since velocity cannot be negative.

The value of $4 + \sqrt{17}$ is approximately 8.1.

28.

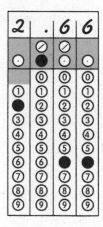

4 Set up equations expressing the total costs for each D.J., where T represents time:

$$\text{D.J. A's cost: } 300 + 150T$$
$$\text{D.J. B's cost: } 200 + 175T$$

Set the equations equal to one another, and solve for time:

$$300 + 150T = 200 + 175T \rightarrow 100 = 25T \rightarrow T = 4$$

29.

2.66 or 2.67 Marcus purchased $34 of gas at $3 a gallon. You can determine how many gallons of gas he purchased:

$$\frac{34}{3} = 11.33\overline{3}$$

Then subtract 11.333 from the total capacity of the tank:

$$14 - 11.333 \approx 2.67$$

You can answer 2.66 or 2.67—the PSAT will be fine if you round up or round down. Just be sure to fill out all the spots in the grid.

30.

5 Since the supply and demand are at equilibrium, set the two expressions equal to one another and solve for the number of lamps:

$$30 - \text{Quantity} = 10 + 3 \times \text{Quantity}$$
$$20 = 4 \times \text{Quantity}$$
$$5 = \text{Quantity}$$

31.

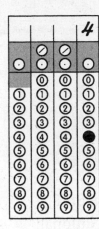

4 You can see what the side lengths are of this particular triangle in the drawing below:

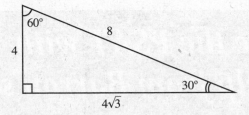

You can easily calculate these side lengths because this is a 30-60-90 triangle. So the side lengths can be expressed as x, $\sqrt{3}x$, and $2x$. (This formula is provided at the beginning of the math section.) The hypotenuse of 8 equals $2x$, and the shortest side equals x. Do the calculations to find the length of the shortest side:

$$8 = 2x$$
$$x = 4$$

Alternatively, you can just recognize that ratio of the smallest side to the hypotenuse in a 30-60-90 triangle is 1:2. So the value of the smallest side in a right triangle with a hypotenuse of 8 is 4.

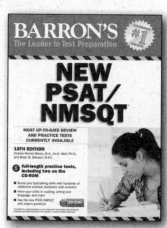